The Law of Evidence

The Law of Evidence

By

Dr. Ibrahim Imam

NCE, (COED ORO) LL.B, (UDU, SOKOTO) BL, (NLS ABUJA), LLM, (O.A.U, ILE-IFE) PhD (UNILORIN)

m a l t h o u s e

Malthouse Press Limited

Lagos, Benin, Ibadan, Jos, Port-Harcourt, Zaria

© Ibrahim Imam 2017
First Published 2017
ISBN 978-978-959-721-5

Published and manufactured in Nigeria by
Malthouse Press Limited
43 Onitana Street, Off Stadium Hotel Road,
Off Western Avenue, Lagos Mainland
E-mail: malthouse_press@yahoo.com
malthouselagos@gmail.com
Tel: +234 802 600 3203

Dedication

This book on the the Law of Evidence in Nigeria is dedicated to Almighty Allah, my parents, Late Shykh Abubakar Imam Agbarigidoma and Late Khadijat Ayoka Imam, my wife and children and to all renown authors on the subjects, whose work are highly acknowledged.

Preface and Acknowledgements

The impetus for writing this book was developed from my experience over many years of teaching the Law of Evidence. Firstly, as a lecturer in the Department of Common Law, School of Law, Kwara State College of Arabic and Islamic Legal Studies, Ilorin between the years of 2001 to 2008 and secondly, as a lecturer in the Department of Public Law, Faculty of Law, University of Ilorin, Ilorin, Nigeria since 2010 till date.

I discovered that although, there exists admirable textbooks on the subject, however, most of the textbooks were written on the strength of the old Evidence Act cap 112 and later cap E14 2004 Laws of the Federal Republic of Nigeria. The main aim of writing this book thus, is to produce a book in view of the innovations introduced into and in line with amended Evidence Act Cap E14, Laws of the Federal Republic of Nigeria 2011 with sufficient details to meet the yearning of students taking law degrees and practitioners in the field of law. The book contains detailed exposition of the new innovations introduced into the amended Act by the National Assembly.

The book's title, *The Nigeria Law of Evidence*, is unique because it has taken a step to explicate the new development introduced into the Act partly due to advancement in technology and in compliance with international best practices. Example of such new innovations in the amended Act is section 3 which repeal the admissibility of certain evidence which are not covered in the act but made admissible by virtue of section 5 of the Old Act and thus, in the amended Act, admissibility of evidence is acceptable subject only to the fact that the evidence is contained in a legislation validly in force in Nigeria. Similarly the position of the law under section 14(2) of the old Act which requires a custom to be severally acted upon before it can be judicially noticed has been repealed by section 17 of the amended Act to the extent that once a custom is acted upon by a superior court of record, judicial notice shall be taken of such custom without need for further proof in subsequent case(s). Another unique innovation is the sections on hearsay evidence that is sections 37 and 38 as well as section 14 which makes courts the discretion to allow or exclude illegally obtained evidence relevant and admissible. The most unique innovation introduced into the Act is the sections which take into account the advancement in technology and the global shift into electronic or digital transactions. There are several sections of the Act dealing with Computer/Electronically generated document/evidence include sections 84-86 on admissibility of statement produced by computer, section 93(2)-(3) that deals with electronic/digital signature and 153(2) on presumption of telegraph and electronic messages etc.

I have tried to give sufficient explanations on these innovations incorporated into the 2011 amended Act with application of relevant important case law in order to assist students towards understanding how the amended law of evidence works. I have chosen to provide a firm grounding in the case law and experiences from other jurisdictions rather than expose or develop any individual theory of the Law of Evidence.

This is the first edition of the book as such I acknowledge the fact that only Allah is perfect, therefore, welcome and shall appreciate any constructive comments and observations on the book. It is my belief that the comments and observations shall further enhance the quality of the book in future edition.

In writing this book I have been assisted by some people, thus I must in particular appreciate my friend Dr. H. A. Hammed of Al-Hikma University, Ilorin for reading the draft. In addition I equally appreciate the duo of Professor Wahab Olasupo Egbewole and Professor Muhammed Mustapha Akanbi for their consistent and persistent advice, encouragement and sincere mentoring, more particularly the undiluted belief in my productivity and ability.

Finally I appreciate my parents (deceased) wife Mrs. Habibat Imam and my children Ibrahim Ibrahim Imam, Aishat Bukola Imam, Khadijat Olohutoyin Imam, Abubakar Imam and Maryam Akanke Imam for their patient and understanding and always supporting my initiatives.

Dr. Ibrahim Imam (Agbarigidoma)

Table of Cases

List of Statutes

Table of Contents

Chapter 1

Introduction

The function of courts of justice are three-fold, first is to ascertain the existence or non-existence of certain facts and the second is to apply the substantive law to the ascertained facts and third is to declare the rights and liabilities of the parties. Against these functions, court has to receive, scrutinize, peruse, analyse and shift evidential materials presented before it and put it in an imaginary scale to determine which side the scale tilt. The means through which court informs itself of the existence (probability) or nonexistence (improbability) of these facts is called "Evidence." Thus, the significance of evidence in court proceedings are to:

i. convince a court, tribunal, a fact finder or an arbiter as to the existence or non existence of facts in dispute;

ii. removes the unreliability in the testimony of person asserting or denying of facts in disputed;

iii. assists an arbiter or fact finder to ascertain facts as stated by the parties;

iv. remedy the weakness in a party against a stronger party in presenting his/her case;

v. supports, establishes or verifies facts as contain in pleadings charge/information sheet which are mere statement of facts;

vi. ensures the independence of a judge or an arbiter in deciding solely on evidence available before the court;

vii. assists the court in exercising discretion, forming opinion and judgment;

viii. reinforces, support, establish the facts in disputes as asserted or denied by parties;

ix. prevents parties from making frivolous unwarranted or unsupported assertion or denial in dispute;

x. increases the amount and quality of information gain from parties and witness;

xi.   it is the material reflection of things, the amalgam of thought, deed and action, it is what we see, touch, feel, conjecture, and images. See section 286 Evidence Act;

xii.   it is derived from deductive reasoning, logical inference and supposition.

Essentially, the law of evidence is the study of fact, which is allow in law to establish the existence or non-existence of facts in issue brought before a competent court for determination. A lawyer will lose his case if he is not conversant with the facts of his case and good in Evidence. Everything a lawyer needs to establish his case creditably well in court are based on the law of evidence because courts do not act on speculations or hypothesis. Evidence Law, is the law's substantive and procedural instructions for the use of evidence. Consequently, all facts upon which a party is relying to establish his case must be adequately supported by evidence. Judges saddled with judicial powers are human being as such they cannot penetrate human's conscience but will only decide matters based on probative value of evidence adduced before them as a third party interventionist.

Arguably, courts are constitutionally saddle with the duty of doing justice in all matters and between all manners of men who are in the matter. In doing justice to a case, courts must consider and evaluate the totality of evidence before arriving at a decision. It is after such duty that the court then comes to a conclusion as to whether or not the case has been established.[1] This makes the law of evidence paramount in all proceedings before a court of justice either in criminal or civil matters.

Definition of Evidence

Though like any legal concept under consideration there can be no single and encompassing definition of evidence. The difficulty associated with definitions generally attracted a court remark in the case of *Federal Republic of Nigeria* v. *Mike*[2] where the court observed that:

> ...Definitions are definition because they reflect the idiosyncrasies, inclinations, prejudice, slants and emotions of the person offering them. While a definer of a word pretend to be impartial and unbiased, the final product of his definition, will in a number of situations, be a victim of bias.

---

[1] *Amaechi* v. *INEC* (2008) 1 MJSC 1, *Ogidi* v. *State* (2005) 21 NSCQR 302 at 318
[2] *Federal Republic of Nigeria* v. *Mike* (2004) 1 SC (pt i) 27 at 55

However, attempt can always be made to give some definitions, such as proffer by scholars, academicians or legal practitioner and so on. Against the above background and in a literary sense, Evidence is construe as a means of proving or disproving an unknown or disputed fact. While in the legal parlance, evidence has been given diverse definitions, for instance in BBC English Dictionary[3] the term "Evidence" means, *the thing you see, experience or told, which makes you believe that something is true*. In *Black's Law Dictionary,* [4] Evidence is given multifarious definitions as:

> In a broader perspective, evidence is defined as the means from which an inference may logically be drawn as to the existence of a fact, or that which makes facts clear, explicit or plain. In another perspective evidence may be considered as the demonstration of facts, or signifies that which demonstrates, makes clear, or ascertains the truth of every fact or point in issue, either on the one side or on the other.

In legal acceptation, the term "evidence" includes all the means which any alleged matter of fact the truth of which is submitted to investigation is established or disproved. Or any species of proof legally presented at the trial of an issue, by the act of the parties and through the medium of witnesses, records, documents, concrete objects and the like.[5]

Phipson [6] views evidence as the testimony, whether oral or documentary, which may be legally received in other to prove or disprove some facts in dispute.

Cross Wilkinson[7] Opined that Evidence determines how fact may or may not be proved. He looks at evidence as all facts which must be proved before a court to enable the court pronounce on the legal right, duties and liability of the parties. He describes such Evidence as judicial Evidence; which consist of testimony; hearsay, statement, documentary, things and fact which the court will accept as facts in issue.

From the generality of the definitions above given, it could be summed up as follows; In a case or matter of judicial proceedings, evidence is a condition precedent in coming to a final conclusion by the

---

[3] *BBC English Dictionary* page 390
[4] Bryan A. G., *Black's Law Dictionary*, (8th ed. Thomson West Publishing Co. London, 1999), 595
[5] Ibid.
[6] Phipson, *Law of Evidence*, (11th ed., Sweet & Maxwell London, 2000)
[7] Cross & Tapper, *Cross & Tapper on Evidence*, (8th ed., Butterworth London, 1994) P. 11

court or a tribunal when convinced as to the existence or non – existence of facts, issues or matters adjudicated before it.

The above establish the accusatorial/adversarial nature of the Nigeria judicial system as opposed to inquisitorial.[8]

Objects of Evidence

The objectives of evidence were developed over several centuries and are based upon the rules from Anglo-American common law brought to the New World by early settlers. The rationale behind this development is to ensure fairness, justice and equity between disputing parties thereby disallowing a party from raising allegations without a basis in provable fact. Instructively, these procedures are sometimes criticized as legal technicality, but notwithstanding, are important parts of the administration of justice for achieving a just and unbiased result. Consequently the rule of evidence has been formulated to assist the court in the addressing four basic principles, namely: (a) the party who bears the burden of proof? This is usually clear. In civil cases the burden lies on the party who assert the affirmative, be the plaintiff or the defendant.[9] Pertinently, the standard of proof required of the party asserting the affirmative in civil cases are based on preponderance of evidence.[10] In realm of criminal cases, the burden of proof lies on the prosecution[11] but, with exception, for instance where the accused raised a defence for his action, inaction or omission, here the burden of establishing the facts, shifts on him.[12] For example; if X is accused of murder and he pleaded the defence of insanity. This is a case in which burden of proof of X's insanity may be on X. Note that the standard of proof in criminal matters is a proof beyond reasonable doubt;[13]

(b) The facts that may be proved by the parties

The general principle of law is that, a party must establish every material fact upon which he intends to rely by sufficient evidence. This does not

---

[8] *Ainuse* v. *Odili* (2005) 6 NWLR (pt 952) ,416 at 496

[9] Usually the person instituting an action (plaintiff or claimant) is the party asserting the affirmative and bears the burden of proofing his case by preponderance of evidence. However, the defendant may equally be asserting affirmatively when he counter claim, thus, the burden of proof shifts on him to establish his case against the original plaintiff/claimant.

[10] *Adaka* v. *Akun* (2003) 7 MJSC 26 and *Iyanru* v. *Mandilas* (2007) 7 MJSC 163 at 181, see sections 132 and 133 Evidence Act 2011, Cap. E14 Laws of the Federal Republic of Nigeria, (to subsequently refers to as Evidence Act (Nigeria)

[11] *Shehu* v. *the State* (2010) 3 MJSC (pt ii) 74, see Ibid.; section 135 Evidence Act (Nigeria)

[12] See sections 137 and 138 Evidence Act (Nigeria)

[13] *Jau* v. *The State* (2010) 2 MJSC 152

mean that there are no exceptions to this rule. Such exceptions may be in respect of fact which the court must take judicial notice of or in civil proceedings where there had been admission in pleadings, which may not require any further proof.

In the perspective of above explained, the purpose of evidence is to demonstrate to the court the truth or probability of the facts upon which the success or failure of a party's case depends in law. Evidence therefore must be confined to the proof of facts which are required and necessary for that purpose. The proof of supernumerary un-related facts will not assist the court and may prejudice the mind of the court against a party, whereas, the facts may have no probative value on the issues actually before it;[14]

(c) The facts that must be excluded from court's cognizance

Not all facts related to a matter must be presented to the court. Generally, proof of fact in issue and facts relevant to the fact in issue are allowed.[15] An example can be given thus, the fact that Adoku was seen dipping his hand in Bujuwoye's Pocket is relevant to the fact in issue which is the stolen of Bojuwoye's money. This proposition was explained by the Supreme Court in the case of *Ebhota v. PIPDC LTD*,[16] where Ejiwunmi JSC said:

> While there is no doubt that parties are bound by their pleadings it is not expected that all the facts germane to the case of a party must be pleaded. However, where facts are pleaded which raise a reasonable inference of law, the inference cannot be excluded from the consideration of the court.

(d). The modes or means of proof acceptable in law

Under the Nigerian legal jurisprudence certain kinds of proofs are recognized to wit; proof by real/direct evidence, documentary evidence, including electronically generated evidence, oral evidence, circumstantial evidence, visiting a place for inspection (visit to *locus inquo*) and proof by electronic device. All these are modes acceptable by the Nigerian Courts to establish or disprove facts in issues placed before them for adjudication as

---

[14] Peter Murph: *A Practical Approach to Evidence*, (2nd ed. Blackstone Press Ltd,. London, 1985)

[15] Section 1 Evidence Act (Nigeria), which provides that; evidence may be given in any suit or proceeding of the existence or non-existence of facts in issue and of such facts as are hereinafter declared to be relevant and of no other.

[16] *Ebhota v. PIPDC LTD* (2005) 23 NSCQR 317 at 333-334

shown in the case of *Navy* v. *Lambert*,[17] where Tabai Mohammed JSC rightly observed:

> The guilt of an accused person may be proved by confessional statement, circumstantial evidence or direct evidence from eye witnesses to the commission of the offence.

The Scope of Evidence

The Law of Evidence falls within the precinct of adjectival law. It sets out the legal mechanisms for implementing and enforcing substantive legal rights, duties and liabilities. The function of the law of evidence therefore is to regulate the process of proof of conflict or dispute between two or more contending parties in any legal proceedings.[18] Thus, within the Nigerian legal jurisprudence, there are two broad divisions of law namely;

i. **Substantive law:** this concerns the determination of right, duties and liabilities. Subjects like, Contract, Torts, and Criminal law fall within this purview; and

ii. **Adjectival or procedural law**: deals with the procedure, practice or machinery on which substantive law is applied. Subjects like civil procedure, criminal procedure and law of evidence fall within this purview. They regulate the conduct of litigation and concern with establishing the facts on which rights, duties and liabilities are founded.

What fact is in issue may not really be the concern of the law of evidence, but may be derived from the substantive law applicable to the cause of action, charge, or defence in each case. In procedural terms, they are to be found in the pleadings, indictment or charge as the case may be.[19]

In civil matter for instance, facts are in issue if, having regard to the pleadings and the substantive law, is a fact necessary for the success of any claim or defence disclosed on the pleadings. In respect of the facts that a party must prove in order to establish his claim or defence, the party is said to bear the legal burden of proof. Pleading in a civil action are of

---

[17] *Navy* v. *Lambert* (2007) 11 MJSC 1 at page 10, and *Emeka* v. *State* (2001) 14 NWLR (pt 734) 660

[18] Dennis, I. H., *The Law of Evidence*, (2nd ed. Sweet & Maxwell, London, 2002), 2

[19] Ibid. page 8

cardinal important in determining the facts in issue. Their object is precisely that the court should be informed what the issues are[20]

In the spectrum of criminal case, the substantive law specifies the elements of the offence charged, the indictment or information provide brief particulars of the allegations of facts which constitute the offence. It is normally the case that the defendant had no obligation at any stage to state which, if any of the prosecution's allegations he admits and which he denies. But in certain circumstance the defendant has statutory obligation to provide a defence; statement setting out the nature of his defence; Lord Goddard[21] CJ said:

> Whenever there is a plea of not guilty everything is in issue, and the prosecution has to prove the whole of their case, including the identity of the accused, the nature of the act and the existence of any necessary knowledge or intent.

Application of Evidence Act in Judicial Proceedings

The Evidence Act applies to all judicial proceedings in or before any court or tribunal established to act in judicial capacity in the Federation of Nigeria. The Act[22] defines court as including all Judges, Magistrate and except Arbitrators, all people legally authorized to take evidence. Instructive, the Constitution of the Federal Republic of Nigeria states the courts vested with judicial powers as thus:

> The Judicial Powers of the Federation shall be vested in the courts in which this section relates, being Courts established for the Federation;[23]

> This Section relates to: The Supreme Court of Nigeria; The Court of Appeal; The Federal High Court; The High Court of the Federal Capital Territory, Abuja, A High Court of a State; The Sharia'ah Court of Appeal of the Federal Capital Territory, Abuja; A Sharia'ah Court of Appeal of a State; The Customary Court of Appeal of the Federal Capital Territory, Abuja; A Customary Court of Appeal of a State; Such other Courts as may be authorized by law to exercise jurisdiction on matters with respect to which the National Assembly make laws.[24]

---

[20] Ibid., 8

[21] Sin; (1946) KB 539 at 539, culled from Dennis; the *Law of Evidence*, 7

[22] Section 256 Evidence Act (Nigeria)

[23] Section 6(1) Constitution of the Federal Republic of Nigeria 1999 (as altered in 2010)

[24] Ibid., Section 6(1)

The definition of court in the above section encapsulates the fact that anybody or persons performing judicial or quasi judicial functions are empowered to take evidence and pursuant to the enabling statute would fall within the ambit of the definition of a "court". Notwithstanding the above constitutional provision, the Evidence Act in section 256 determines with finality the Courts in which Evidence Act applies.[25]

Against the above background, it is pertinent to examine the Evidence Act dealing with the application of the Evidence Act from a historical perspective.[26] The section dealing with the application of the Evidence Act before the 2011 amendment provides that the Act shall apply to all judicial proceedings in or before any court established in the Federal Republic of Nigeria, but it shall not apply:

(a) to proceedings before an Arbitrator or

(b) to a field general court martial.[27]

The inference that can be drawn from the above section of the old Evidence Act is that it applies to any proceedings before all courts established in the Federal Republic of Nigeria as defined by the Constitution. This was the position of old Evidence Law before its amendment.[28] However the new Act incorporated new innovation and the relevant provision of the Act as amended[29] provides that; This Act shall apply to all judicial proceedings in or before any court established in the Federal Republic of Nigeria, but it shall not apply:

(a) to proceeding before an Arbitrator, or

(b) to a Field General Court Martial, or

(c) to judicial proceedings in any civil cause or matter, in or before any Shariah Court of Appeal, Customary Court of Appeal, Area Court or Customary Court unless the President, Commander-in-Chief of the Armed Forces or the Military Governor or Military Administrator of a State, by order published in the Gazette, confers upon any or all Shariah Courts of Appeal, Customary Courts of Appeal, Area Courts or Customary Courts in

---

[25] Section 256 Evidence Act 2011

[26] The Evidence Act (CAP 112 and E14, Laws of the Federation of Nigeria, 1990 and 2004 respectively)

[27] Section 1(2) cap 112 Evidence Act 1990 (Nigeria) (Repealed)

[28] by degree No 61 of 1991 now an Act deemed duly enacted by the National Assembly by virtue of the provisions of Section 316 (of the Constitution of the Federal Republic of Nigeria, 1999, See also Evidence Act Cap E14 LFRN 2004).

[29] The Evidence cap 112, 2004 was amended in 2003 that is section 1(2) Evidence Act cap E14 and now section 256 Evidence Act (Nigeria)

the Federal Capital Territory, Abuja, or a State as he case may be, power to enforce any or all the provisions of this Act;

(3) In judicial proceedings in any criminal cause or matter in or before an Area Court, the Court shall be guided by the provisions of this Act and in accordance with the provisions of the Criminal Procedure Code Law;

(4) Notwithstanding anything in this section, an Area Court shall , in judicial proceeding in any criminal cause or matter be bound by the provisions of Sections 138, 139, 140, 141, 142 and 143 of this Evidence Act Cap E14 LFRN 2004 now sections 134-139 Evidence Act cap E14 LFRN 2011.[30]

A passionate reading of the above section reveal that the position of the law as per the applicability of the Evidence Act is now different from the position before the amendment of 2004 Act cap 112. Thus, the position of the provisions in the new Act which is clear and unambiguous is that the Act shall be applicable to all judicial proceedings in or before any court established in the Federal Republic of Nigeria with limited sense and therefore:

1. The Act is not applicable in proceeding before arbitrator or Court Marshal
2. The Act is not applicable in civil cause or matter before any Shariah Court of Appeal, Customary Court of Appeal, Area Court or Customary Court either of the Federal Capital Territory or States
3. The Act may be applicable to all Shariah Courts of Appeal, Customary Courts of Appeal, Area Courts or Customary Courts in the Federal Capital Territory, Abuja, or a Stat, subject to order by the President or Governor or Military Administrator of a State, published in the Gazette.
4. The Area Court shall be guided by the provision of the Evidence act in criminal proceedings
5. The Area Court shall be bound by the provisions of the act in matters stated in sections 134-139 Evidence Act cap E14 LFRN 2011.

An inference deducible from the old section shows the only exception, that is; the Act would not apply in proceedings before an arbitrator and field general court martial. It is therefore unequivocal that in the old law of Evidence in Nigeria, the Evidence Act was applicable to all courts in Nigeria, subject to the exceptions provided by the Act itself.

---

[30] Section 256 Evidence Act (Nigeria)

What, therefore, are novel and the legal implication of the amendment in the new Act? The amendment incorporated an additional paragraph to Section 1(2) of the Act, which is now 256(1), (2) & (3) Cap E14 LFRN 2011 and which is to the extent that Evidence Act may apply to the Customary Court of Appeal, Shariah Courts of Appeal or Area Courts, when the Governor or President as the case may be, confers power on the courts to enforce any or all the provisions of the Evidence Act.

It is instructive to note that the position of the amended Evidence Act as can be clearly gleaned from the foregoing is that the Evidence Act is not absolutely inapplicable to Customary Courts though they are established and recognized pursuant to the Nigeria Constitution, but the Act is only applicable in civil cause or matter before Customary Court, Shariah Court or Area Court in Nigeria, subject to the conferment of its applicability by the Governor or President as the case may be, by an order published in the Gazette.

It is also submitted that the clear provisions of the Evidence Act, invokes the entire provisions of the Evidence Act to guide and guard judicial proceedings in all criminal causes or matters before Area or Customary Courts. Notwithstanding, this does not make the provisions of the Act applicable absolutely to such matters, rather, it is designed to guide or assist the court toward achieving fairness and justice in criminal proceedings.

However the Area or Customary Courts is bound to apply Evidence Act in criminal cause or matters relating to the provision of the following Sections of the Evidence Act 2011, that is 135(1)-(3), 136(1) & (2), 138(1) & (2) and 139(1) & (2) Evidence Act 2011 which deal with burden of proof.

Sources of the Nigerian Law of Evidence

i) Evidence Act

The principal and primary source of the Law of Evidence in Nigeria is the Evidence Act.[31] Nigeria law of Evidence owned its origin to the English judicial system introduced during the colonial Era. The history of the modern law of Evidence can be traced to 1914 when the Provincial Courts Ordinance of that year was enacted as the first regulation on evidence. Section 10 of the Ordinance made the common law of evidence applicable to the colony and protectorate of Nigeria. Therefore it thus, existed before

---

[31] Cap 112 of the Laws of Federal Republic of Nigeria (now cap E 14 Laws of Federal Republic 2004) any further reference to the Act shall simply be refer to as Evidence Act.

1945, (1943) a duality of Evidence law, while the common law rules of Evidence was made applicable in English Courts, Customary Rules of Evidence remain enforceable in Native Courts[32].

In 1943, the Evidence Ordinance of that year was passed based on Stevens *"Digest of the law of Evidence"* 12th Edition, this ordinance came into force in 1945 and was incorporated into the Laws of the Federation of Nigeria and Lagos 1948 as Evidence Act cap 62.[33]

However, the Constitution [34] of the Federal Republic of Nigeria brought Evidence Act under the Exclusive Legislative List. This means that it is only the Federal Government through the National Assembly that can pass laws with respect to the Law of Evidence.[35]

ii) English Common Law

The English Common Law is another source of the law of Evidence or any relevant local Statute. These are resorted to, to supplement the provisions of the Evidence Act where there is lacuna (necessity)[36]. It is worthy to note that, the Act [37] provides and allows evidence that is not otherwise admissible to remain so admissible; it provides"

> Noting in this Act shall prejudice the admissibility of any Evidence, which would apart from the provisions of this Act, be admissible.

The importance of this provision was illustrated in *John Agagariga Itule*.[38] The evidence sought to be tendered was the confessional statement of an accused person, which was in the accused person's favour. The Supreme Court held that for evidence to be inadmissible, as the matter was not dealt with expressly in sections 27-32 of the Evidence Act, the Common Law rules would apply by virtue of section 5 (a) of the Evidence Act.

Incidentally, Section 5 of the old Act 2004 which allowed certain English common law applicable in the Nigerian court is not specifically

---

[32] Aguda T.A: The Law of Evidence (3rd ed. Spectrum Books Limited Ibadan, 1998), 1-2

[33] Ibid.

[34] Constitution of the Federal Republic of Nigeria 1979 and the subsequent constitutions that follow, 1989, 1993, 1995 and the 1999

[35] Exclusive Legislative List; Second Schedule Part 1 item 23 of the Nigeria Constitution 1999

[36] Osinbajo Yemi: *Cases & Materials on Nigeria Law of Evidence*, (Macmillan, 1992), 1 - 4

[37] Section 5(a) of the Evidence Act (Cap E14, 2004,amended in Cap E14 2011 LFRN)

[38] John Agagariga Itule (1961) 1 All NLR 463

provided for in the new Evidence Act, 2011 and by implication repealed.[39] To better appreciate the position of the new Act the said section provides thus:

> Nothing in this Act shall prejudice the admissibility of any evidence that is made admissible by any other legislation validly in force in Nigeria.[40]

In view of the above provision, it is doubtful whether English common law principles or doctrines which have not been specifically provided for under the 2011 Act or any other Nigerian legislation can still be applicable to cases in our Courts today. It is posited that such evidence is only receivable or admissible where it has been made admissible by either the Evidence Act 2011 or by any other Nigerian legislation. This has foreclosed the possibility of having recourse to common law principles on evidence, unless such principles have been statutorily recognized by a Nigerian legislation.

iii) Fundamental Human Rights Provisions

The concept of Fundamental Human Rights is most cherished heritage of a humane and civilized world. Fundamental Human Rights are internationally and regionally[41] recognized norms in all democratic and civilized communities and has become common features in their Constitution.

The Fundamental Human Rights listed in Chapter IV [42] of the Constitution, is another important sources of the Law of Evidence. This is because it has a great respect, link and influence on evidence in practice in our courts. Fundamentally, they specify how facts in issue shall be established and for another, the provisions have universal application in all courts.[43]

The first point of reference under the Nigeria Constitutional provisions, which relates to or has a linkage with the law of evidence, is that relating to the right of disputing parties to a fair hearing/trial in any

---

[39] Dada, J.A., the *Law of Evidence in Nigeria*; (Calabar, University of Calabar Press, 2004), 71; See also the case of *Suberu* v. *State* (2010) All FWLR (Pt 520) 1263

[40] Section 3 Evidence Act (Nigeria)

[41] United Nations Convention on Human Right, European Convention of Human Rights, Convention of the Rights of Persons with Disabilities, African Charter on Human and Peoples' Rights etc

[42] Constitution of the Federal Republic of Nigeria 1999 (any further reference to this constitution 1999 shall be simply refers to as the constitution) except otherwise

[43] *Fawehinmi* v. *Abacha* (2000) 4 SC (pt ii) 1

court or tribunal in Nigeria as a party to a suit, civil or criminal, and which they shall be entitled to and within a reasonable time.[44] The Constitution of the Federal Republic of Nigeria[45] provides:

> In the determination of his civil rights and obligations, including any question or determination by or against any government or authority, a person shall be entitled to a fair hearing within a reasonable time by a court or other tribunal established by law and constituted in such manner as to secure its independence and impartiality.

This Chapter on Human Rights is so significant to the extent that any provisions/rules of evidence (or procedure) that is contrary to this principle of fair hearing shall be void and of no effect. The provisions of the Constitution having a significant bearing on the law of evidence are discussed hereunder:

a) Rights to Fair hearing[46]

The Nigerian Constitution provides that in the determination by any government or authority, a person shall be entitled to fair hearing within a reasonable time by any court or other tribunal established by law and the constitution in such manner as to secure its independent and impartiality. This right is explained in two legal maxim *Audi altram partem* (hear the other party) see *Buhari* v. *Yusuf*[47] and *Nemo judex incausa sua* (no man is a judge in his own case). See *Bamayi* v. *The State*[48]

b) Rights to an Interpreter[49]

It significant to note that the language of the courts is English, however it is an undisputable fact that not all parties and witnesses appearing before a court understand the language of the courts, hence the imperative of an interpreter. The Constitution of Nigerian in safeguarding this right provides that every person who is charge with a criminal offence shall be entitled without payment to the assistance of an interpreter. It is only relevant when the person charged with criminal offence does not understand the language used at the trail. This principle was affirmed in

---

[44] Section 36 (1) and (2) Nigerian Constitution, see Okeke v. State (2003) 2 SC 63

[45] Ibid.

[46] Ibid.

[47] *Buhari* v. *Yusuf* (2003) 6 SC (pt 11)

[48] *Bamaiyi* v. *The State*(2001) 4 SC (Pt i) 18

[49] Section 36 (6) (c) Nigerian Constitution, 1999 (as amended), (to subsequently refer to as "Constitution (Nigeria)"

the case of *Effiong* v. *State*,[50] where it was held that, when the accused person does not understand the language of the court, it is the interpreter that will inform him in details of the charge against him, even where he understand, the charge must be read and explain to him.

Notwithstanding, it is an obligation on the defendant or his counsels to inform the court that he needs an interpreter.[51] In *Madu* v. *The State*,[52] the Supreme Court said:

> The fact that the accused person does not understand the language, which the trial is being conducted, is a fact well known to the accused. It is for the accused or his counsel to take the initiative of bringing the notice to the court at the earliest opportunity or as soon as the situation has arisen. If he does not claim the right at the proper time... he may not be able to have a valid complaint afterwards for example on appeal.

It is trite and settled law that when an interpreter has been employed in recording of statement in civil or criminal proceedings before a court, the statement is inadmissible unless the person who interpreted it is called as a witness as well as the person who wrote it down.[53]

c) Right of an accused person to time and facility to prepare for a case
The Constitution [54] provides that the accused person must be given adequate time and facility to prepare for his case. Therefore, if an accused person asks for an adjournment the court shall grant his request especially if it is to enable him brief his counsel or to call a material witness.[55] This right affords an accused person opportunity, to consult his counsel, prepare adequately to defend the allegation of crime against him and call witness or witnesses in proof of innocence, etc.

d) *Right to cross-examine witness*
The Constitution[56] provides for the right of an accused to cross-examine the prosecution witness(es). The trial court must accord the accused person the right to cross-examine each of the prosecution witnesses as

---

[50] *Effiong* v. *State* (1995) I NWLR

[51] *Nwachukwu* v. *State* (2007) 11 MJSC 39 at 55-56)

[52] *Madu* v. *The State* (1997) 1 SCNJ 44 at 54

[53] *Olalekan* v. *State* (2001) * NSCQR 207 at 232 and *Anyanwu* v. *State* (2006) 6 SC (pt ii) 173 at 179-180

[54] Section 36(6) (f), Constitution (Nigeria)

[55] *Udofia* v. *The State* (1988) 7 SC (pt i) 59 at 68

[56] Section 36(6) (d) Constitution (Nigeria)

they give evidence. However, if the accused is denied or refused this right, but court merely ask the witness(es) several questions the Supreme Court held that, that will amount to a breach of section 36 (6) (d).[57]

e) The Constitution[58] provides that an accused person shall not be compelled to give evidence and it shall not be a subject of comment by the prosecution. The accused may choose not to say or give evidence, though he must be worn of the implication to remain silent.

f) The Constitution[59] provides that an accused person shall not be tried twice for the same offence. This enable the accused to raise the defence of *autrefois acquit (formerly acquitted) and autrefois convict (formerly convicted)* so as to avoid double jeopardy.[60] In *Chief of Air Staff* v. *The State[61]*, the Supreme Court said:

> The constitutional guarantee provides for the common law rule against double jeopardy in criminal cases. The Common Law rule, which is generally *autrefois acquit or autrefois* convict is also, provided for in section 181 CPA and section 223 of the CPC. By the provision of the common law rule, the State is barred from instituting criminal proceedings against its subject *ad-infinitum.*

g) Similarly the Constitution[62] provides that if an accused is shown to have been pardon for the commission of an offence such person cannot be tried for the same offence again. Example of such exercise of power is the pardon granted Alameseigha, former governor of Abia State, General Ojukwu, etc.

h) The accused person can only be convicted of an offence defined within the law,[63] where the conviction of an accused was set aside on the ground that the offence (adultery) for which he was found guilty was not an offence under the Criminal Code which was applicable in the Southern

---

[57] *State* v. *Aibangbe* (1988) 7 SC (pt ii) 96 at 132

[58] Section 36(9) Nigeria Constitution (Nigeria); see Sections 160 -166 of Criminal Procedure Code Cap 30 LFRN 1990

[59] Ibid.

[60] *Nafiu Rabiu* v. *State* (1980) 2 NLR 112

[61] *Chief of Air Staff* v. *The State* (2005) 21 NSCQR 645 at 689

[62] Section 36(10) Constitution (Nigeria)

[63] Ibid. Section 36(12), Aoko v. Fagbemi (1963) 1 ALL NLR 400

part of Nigeria. *In Federal Republic of Nigeria* v. *Ifegwu*[64] the Supreme Court said:

> Immunity from trial and conviction of a person with respect to an act or omission, which at the time of the commission or omission did not constitute any offence under the law, no person can be so tried and convicted on it.

All the above explain the rationale and significance fundamental rights as part sources of evidence in any court proceedings in Nigeria and denying the a party of any of the rights may render the proceedings defective in law.

iv) Customary Law as Sources of Evidence

According to A. E. W. Park, *Customary* Law in Nigeria is a question of fact to be proved in evidence.[65] This, he explain is firstly due to the fact that Nigerian judges have had no formal training in customary law, the rules which are not generally assessable in a written form and secondly because customary law is part of the Nigerian legal system.[66] It is pertinent to note though that the new Evidence Act introduce an innovation to the extent that it sufficient for courts to take judicial notice of a custom when it has been proved once to be a rule accepted by a particular community as a law/rule regulating their affairs. Thus, in any subsequent proceeding such custom need not to be proved again in a dispute relating to the same custom.[67]

vi) Islamic Law

This is also a source of the Evidence in Nigeria particularly in matters involving Muslims. Muslims customary practices such as marriage, divorce, guardianship, inheritance and *waqf* and matters which are purely determined upon Islamic principles as recognized legal system in the Nigerian Constitution.[68]

---

[64] Federal Republic of Nigeria V Ifegwu (2003) 5 SC 252 at 263

[65] Sections 18-19 Evidence Act (Nigeria)

[66] Park A. W., Sources of Nigeria Law, see also sections 15-19 and 70-73 Evidence Act (Nigeria) and the case of *Adedibu* v. *Adewoyin* (1951) 3 WACA 91

[67] Section 18 Evidence Act (Nigeria)

[68] *Abdulsalam* v. *Salawu* (2002) 6 SCNJ 193 and *Saidu Usman* v. *Saliu Kareem* (1995) 2 NWLR (pt 379) 537. See Sections 262 (2) & 275 (2) of the Constitution (Nigeria)

It should be noted that Islamic law has gotten three sources (1) The Holy Quran, Hadith and *Ijma'a* which consist of *Qiyas, Ijitihad, Istihsan, Istidlal,*[69] etc.

Application of Evidence in Civil and Criminal Cases

Evidence as previously explained applies to all proceedings before any competent court of justice or tribunal in Nigeria. Thus:

In criminal cases standard of proof required is a proof beyond reasonable doubt while in civil cases the standard is determined by preponderance of evidence. However, where in a civil matter there is an allegation of crime, the allegation must be proof beyond reasonable doubt.[70]

i.   In civil and criminal cases, un-sworn evidence may be admissible on affirmation or oath.

ii. In criminal cases only voluntary admission is admissible all admissions are admissible in civil cases.[71]

iii. Dying declarations are admissible in murder and manslaughter, but not generally admissible in civil cases.[72]

iv. Evidence of accused person's good character is usually admissible in criminal cases, while evidence of good character of either party in civil matter is not admissible.[73]

v.   Spouse of the accused may not be a compellable witness in criminal cases,[74] but in civil case the parties' spouses are competent and compellable witness.

---

[69] Ambali M.A (1998) *The Practice of Muslim Family Law in Nigeria*; (Tamaza Publishing Ltd Zaria, 1998), 4-13. And Rasid S. K., *Islamic Law in Nigeria, Application and Teaching Islamic*, (Publication Bureau, Kaduna, 1986), 43

[70] *Koiki* v. *Magnusson* (1999) 5 SC (pt ii) 30

[71] *Sunday Akpan* v. *State* (1992) 6 NWLR (pt 248) 439

[72] Section 45 Evidence Act (Nigeria)

[73] Ibid.; Sections 77 and 81; Section 81 of the Evidence Act (Nigeria); provides; "In criminal proceedings, evidence of the fact that a defendant is of good character is admissible"

[74] *Okoro* v. *State* (1998) 12 SC 134 at 145

Chapter 2

Means of Proof

There are three crucial aspect of any dispute (civil or criminal); first is the evidence, second is the relevant law applicable to facts, thirdly the tactics of the case. Evidence is usually very important key to proof a dispute in court and in fact, very few cases are won without strong evidence to support the successful party's argument. There is plethora of court judgment stating the recognized methods by which a dispute either criminal or civil could be proved in court. Prominent among these means are explained in the preceding sections.

Oral Evidence

Oral evidence is a verbal assertion on oath or affirmation of a witness offered in court to prove or disprove the truth of what is being asserted. Oral evidence includes testimony and hearsay evidence. By virtue of the Evidence Act,[1] all facts except the content of documents may be proved by oral evidence. The value of oral evidence was clearly set out in *Butera* v. *DPP*,[2] the High Court of Australia in a concise statement said, thus:

> A witness who gives evidence orally demonstrates, for good or ill, more about his or her credibility than a witness whose evidence is given in documentary form. Oral evidence is public, written evidence may not be. Oral evidence gives to the trial the atmosphere which, though in tangible, is often critical to the jury's estimate of the witness. By generally restricting the jury to consideration of testimonial evidence in its oral form, it is thought that the jury's discussion of the case in the jury room will be more open, the exchange of views among jurors will more easily occur than if the evidence were given in writing or the juror were each armed with a written transcript of the evidence.

---

[1] Sections 125 and 126 Evidence (Nigeria)

[2] *Butera* v. *DPP* (1987) 164 CLR 180 at 189, culled from Dennis op cit 402

According to the Evidence Act,[3] oral evidence must in all cases be direct. Meaning that in all proceedings before a court where oral evidence is required, such oral evidence should be the direct testimony of a person who can give direct account of incident in dispute.[4] Thus, if oral evidence refers to that which can be seen, heard, perceived it must be the evidence of a witness who says he saw, heard or perceived the fact. If it refers to an opinion or grounds on which opinion is held, it must be the evidence of the person who holds that opinion on those grounds.[5]

It is exceptionally rare in Nigeria for a case to be heard and decided without at least some testimonial evidence given by a witness or more orally. This appears to be in line with the provision of the Act which provides: 125 "All facts, except the contents of documents, may be proved by oral evidence."[6] The preference for oral testimony is reflected in and enforced against hearsay rule, the effect of which is that a statement (oral or written) made otherwise than in the course of proceedings is not admissible to prove existence or non-existence of facts asserted in the statement.

Real Evidence

Real evidence is anything, other than testimony, admissible hearsay or a document, the contents of which is offered as testimonial evidence, which may be examined by the court as a means of proof. The material thing in question may be movable or immovable. If movable e.g., guns or dresses or matches, they are tendered in court as exhibits. If immovable e.g. land or property attached to land or the scene of an accident or murder, and the court has to take the view of the thing, then an inspection is cogent and material to the determination of the questions in dispute.[7] The procedure lay down in the provision of the Evidence Act[8] must be followed, this procedure is known as visit to *locus inquo*:

---

[3] ibid, Section 126 Evidence Act (Nigeria)

[4] See *Ubani* v. *State* (2003) 12 SC (pt ii) 1

[5] *Esangbedo* v. *State* (1989) 7 SC (pt ii) 36 at 42 - 44

[6] Section 125 Evidence Act (Nigeria)

[7] Ibid; Section 127

[8] Ibid; Section 127(1) (a) – (d)

i. The power of the presiding judge to conduct a visit to *locus inquo* is provided for in section 127(d) of the Evidence Act.[9] The basic requirements for the conduct of a visit to *locus inquo* are:[10]

ii. The court shall either be adjourned to the place where the subject matter of the said inspection is and proceedings shall continued at that place until the court further adjourns back to its original place of sitting, or to some other place of sitting.[11]

iii. The court shall either attend and make an inspection of the subject matter only, evidence if any of what transpired there are to be given in court afterwards. In criminal case the accused person shall be present at the scene.[12]

iv. In case of conflicting evidence as to physical facts, the judge may use his own discretions and observations at the *locus inquo*, taking into consideration the totally of the evidence, to resolve the conflict.[13]

v.   In all criminal cases, the presence of the accused at the *locus inquo* while the court is carrying out the inspection is no excuse for not complying with this requirement.

vi. It is usual to carry out inspection before the close of the case for both side as and it is permissible to carry out the inspection after the judgment has been reserved.

vii. Whenever the inspection is done, the parties should be given a right to cross-examine each other and counsel a right to further address the court if necessary.

viii. It is important to record the purpose of inspection and to record in the book that the inspection was carried out. If observations made thereon are to be used in arriving at any decision the judge ought to make notes of such observations in the record of proceedings. An inspection of locus inquo is as much a part of the entire proceedings in any suit and rules of evidence apply equally to such inspection as to any other portion of the proceedings.[14]

---

[9] Section 127 (d) (11) of the Evidence Act (Nigeria)

[10] *Azuokwu* v. *Nwokanma* (2005) 5 SC (pt11) 23 at 30

[11] *Olusanmi* v. *Osasoma* (1992) 6 SCNJ (pt 2) 282 at 291

[12] *Aboyeji* v. *Momoh* (1994) 4 SCNJ (pt 2) 302 at 313

[13] *Olubode* v. *Salami* (1984) 2 NWLR (pt 7) 282

[14] *Oguntolu* v. *State* (1987) 1 NWLR (pt 50) 464 C.A

Consequence of non-compliance with the rules of procedure

This depends on the effect, which the refusal to comply will have on the judgment as a whole whether or not it will occasion a miscarriage of justice or not.

Hearsay Evidence

When a third party relates a story to another as proof of content of a statement, such story is hearsay. Hearsay evidence is all evidence, which does not derives its value solely from the credit given to the witness himself, but which rests also, in part, on the veracity and competence of some other person. A piece of evidence is hearsay if it is evidence of the contents of a statement made by a witness who himself is not called to testify.[15] In of *Ijiofor* v. *State*,[16] the Supreme Court observed that:

> The hearsay rule is a salutary rule. Indeed. It is a rule, which is grounded upon commonsense, as the focus of it, is to prevent a person from being accused or found guilty of an offence, which he did not commit. It is a self-evidence fact. Malevolent people could manufacture such evidence as they would, to falsely accused persons of offence, which they did not commit.
>
> By reason of this rule, courts are enjoyed and indeed under a duty not to accept and / or convict an accused person upon testimony of witnesses who did not see, hear, or had perceived by any other sense or in any other manner, the facts given in their testimony at a criminal trial of an accused person, as in the instance case, or even in a civil case...

a). Meaning of hearsay

In *Ojo* v. *Gharoro*[17] the Supreme Court define hearsay evidence as "...whatever a person is heard to say or whatever a person declares on information.... In most cases, hearsay evidence is as to the following or like effect;" I was told by XYZ that, or XYZ told me that, or I heard that XYZ told ABC that, or I made inquiries and I was told that.'

Hearsay evidence is indirect evidence or second hand evidence and a testimony of facts not actually perceived by the witness with one of his senses. It is tendered as a proof by him of a statement narrated to him by another who himself or herself is not called as a witness to testify in court. By virtue of the provision of the Evidence Act Hearsay evidence is not

---

[15] *Utteh* v. *State* (1992) 2 NWLR (pt 223) 257 at 273

[16] *Ijiofor* v. *State* (2001) 4 SC (pt 11) 1 at 78

[17] *Ojo* v. *Gharoro* (2006) 2-3 SC 105 at 113

admissible except as provided in the Act or under any other provision of the Act or any other Act.[18]

In view of the above, evidence may be hearsay if the purpose is to establish the truth of the statement and it is inadmissible. However, it may not be hearsay and admissible if its aim is to establish that the statement was in fact made.[19]

b). Rule against hearsay evidence

The Evidence Act[20] provides among others that oral evidence must in all cases be direct. This provision therefore makes hearsay evidence inadmissible.[21] The section[22] provide that oral must be direct and that if it refers to a fact, which:

i.   Could be seen, it must be the evidence of a person who says he saw that fact; or

ii.   Could be heard, it must be the evidence of a person who says he heard that fact; or

iii. Could be perceived by any senses or any other manner, it must be the evidence of a witness who says he perceived that fact in that sense or manner; or

iv.   Refers to an opinion or grounds on which the opinion is held, it must be the evidence of the person who holds that opinion or ground.

c). Rationale for the rules against hearsay evidence

Inadmissibility of hearsay evidence stems from the followings reasons:

i.   The unreliability of the original maker of the statement who is not in court and not cross-examined;

ii.   The depreciation of the truth of the statement arising from repetition;

iii. The likely opportunities for fraud;

iv.   The tendency for such evidence to lead to prolonged inquires and proceedings; and

v.   The possibility of encouraging substitution of weaker evidence for strong evidence.[23]

---

[18] Section 38 Evidence Act (Nigeria)

[19] *Beauty Achora* v. *Attorney General Bendel State* (1990) 7 NWLR 92

[20] Section 126 (a) – (e) Evidence Act (Nigeria)

[21] See *Ejioffor* v. *State* (2001) 4 SC (pt ii) 1 pages 6-7 or (2001) 6 NSCQR (pt i) 209 at 220,221 & 236 and *Subramania* v. *D.P.P.* (1956) 1 WNLR 969

[22] Section 126 Evidence Act (Nigeria)

[23] J.D Heydon (1991) 3rd ed., *Evidence Case & Materials,* Butter worth London. Pages 321-341

d) Exception to inadmissibility of hearsay evidence rule

There are exceptions to the inadmissibility of hearsay evidence and consequently the following evidences are admissible, though, are not direct testimony of the maker or in a situation where the maker is not available in court as a witness, but generally admissible as exceptions to the inadmissibility of hearsay evidence.

1) Dying declarations. Cases in which evidence of a statement made by a dying person may be given are (a) under res gestae rules; (b) in statement by testator; (c) in depositions taken in accordance with the Magistrates' Court Act and admitted under the Criminal Law. [24] According to J.D Heydon[25] dying declaration can be described as;

    Declaration against interest oral or written statement made by a deceased person of a fact which he knew to be against his pecuniary or proprietary interest at the time he made it. It is admissible as evidence of fact and all collateral facts mentioned provided the declarant had personal knowledge. The basis of its admissibility is that, truth is guaranteed by the unlikelihood of a man lying against his own interest. This exception arose in civil case involving contract property or status much more than in criminal case because the declarations had to tend to impose pecuniary or proprietary, but not criminal liabilities. The result of the rule is that, the accused cannot tender a confession by a third party that he was guilty."

2) Statement of an accused person at preliminary investigation or coroner inquest.[26]

3) Entries in the book of account regularly kept in the course of business are relevant.[27]

4) Entries in public record made in performance of duty.[28]

5) Relevancy of statement in maps; charts and plans.[29]

6) Statement as to facts of public nature contain in certain Acts, notifications.[30]

7) Certificate of Central Bank officers.[31]

---

[24] See Sections 39 and 40 Evidence Act (Nigeria), see also *Hausa* v. *State* (1997) 7-8 SCNJ 164

[25] Heydon, *The Law of Evidence*, 339-341, see also *Ali* v. *Alesinloye* (2000) SC (pt 1) 111

[26] Section 48 Evidence Act (Nigeria)

[27] Ibid; Section 51

[28] Ibid; Section 52

[29] Ibid; Section 53

[30] Section 54 Evidence Act (Nigeria)

[31] Ibid; Sections 55 and 56

8)   Admission and Confession.

9)   Affidavit evidence.[32]

10)   Statement made in *res gestae*. It may however be argued that the doctrine of *res gestae* is no longer relevant and admissible by the Nigerian Court. This position is justified by the provision of the new Evidence Act which expressly stated that all relevant evidence that: "Nothing in this Act shall prejudice the admissibility of any evidence that is made admissible by any other legislation validly in force in Nigeria."[33]

It is submitted that such common law principles or doctrines which have not been specifically provided for under the 2011 Act or any other Nigerian law be cannot relevant and admissible in the Nigerian Courts.

11)   Expert opinion. [34] It is instructive to note here that it is not mandatory for expert who gives his/her expert opinion to (i.e. Medical officer) to be present in court in order to give evidence during trial. If being a public officer gives sufficient reason for nonattendance his/her evidence may be admissible by invoking section 39 of the Evidence Act to the extent that such evidence is admissible as fact made by dead person that cannot be found or incapacitated to give evidence or procurement of such a person will amount to delay or expenses.[35]

12)   Admission of written statement of Investigating Police Officer (IPO).[36]

13)   Where a narration of event or conversation took place between two or more persons in the presence of the accused person, reference to such narration or conversation at the trial of the accused by one or all such persons is admissible.[37]

Documentary/Electronic Evidence

This is the evidence derived by court from inspection of some documents produced before the court. Document may be used as testimonial, circumstantial or real evidence and when used as testimonial evidence

---

[32] Ibid; Sections 108-120

[33] Ibid; Section 3 Evidence Act 2011 Cap E14, the section repeal section 5 of old Evidence Act Cap E14 2004

[34] Section 57 ibid,

[35] *Edoho* v. *State* (2010) 4 MJSC (pt i) 1 at 14, see section 249(3) 0f the Criminal Procedure Code

[36] Section 49 Evidence Act (Nigeria)

[37] Ibid; Sections 8 ibid see *Utteh* v. *State* (1992) 2 NWLR (pt 223) 257 at 270

their content may be direct evidence or hearsay evidence[38]. Hearsay evidence applies to documentary evidence where direct oral evidence of a fact or fact in issue is admissible.[39]

The use of documentary evidence is but one aspect of the law of evidence, and many of the rules that govern the admissibility of evidence generally are relevant to the use of documentary evidence. Thus, a document can be defined as: any record of information, anything in which there is marks, figures, symbols, perforations having a meaning to a person qualified to interpret them or anything from which sounds, images or writing can be reproduced with or without the aid of everything else or a map, plan, drawing or photographs. A document can be put into an electronic form and stored in a computer as one or more files.[40]

Therefore, any statement made by a party in a document, electronic or otherwise, tending to establish fact or facts in issue, the statement shall be admissible in evidence by the production of the original document to establish such fact or fact in issue. The maker of the statement must either:

i). had personal knowledge of the matters dealt with in the document; or

ii). called as a witness in the proceedings; or

iii). he has no the knowledge, but the statement was made to him by a person who had or might reasonably presumed to have personal knowledge of the matter, provided that the document form part of a record purporting to be a continuous record made in the performance of a duty.[41]

It is settled principle of law that a maker of a document is expected to tender it in evidence. There are two exceptions to this principle of law. The law[42] provides to the effect that this principle will not operate if;

1. the maker is dead;

2. the maker can only be procured by involving the party in so much expense that could be outrageous in the circumstance of the case.[43]

---

[38] Ibid; Section 125

[39] Ibid; Section 83 (1) & (2)

[40] Ibid; Section 84

[41] Section 83(1) (a), Evidence Act (Nigeria)

[42] Ibid; Section 83(1) (b)

[43] *Omega Bank Nig Ltd* v. *O. B. C.* (2005) 1 SC (pt 1) 49 at 73

A document may be tender as admissible hearsay evidence of its content in any civil proceedings in as much as the court is satisfy in all circumstances of the case that undue delay or expenses will be caused.[44] The rationale behind this principle of law is that, while the maker of a document is in position to answer questions on it, the non-maker of it may not be in such position.[45]

Circumstantial Evidence

Circumstantial evidence relates to a series of facts other than the particular fact sought to be proved. The party offering circumstantial evidence argues that this series of facts, by reason and experience, is so closely associated with the fact to be proved that the fact to be proved may be inferred simply from the existence of the circumstantial evidence. Circumstantial Evidence is also known as indirect evidence. It is distinguished from direct evidence, which, if believed, proves the existence of a particular fact without any inference or presumption required.

It is a device which assists the court to resolve a dispute in the absence of direct evidence based on logical inferences a court can make from the surrounding circumstances of the particular case. Circumstantial evidence has been defined as the testimony of a witness as to other relevant fact(s) from which fact in issue may be inferred. *In Igabele* v. *State*[46] the Supreme Court said that:

> The law is not only that the circumstantial evidence required to grant a conviction must be cogent, complete, unequivocal, positive, overwhelming but must equally be compelling and lead to the irresistible conclusion that the accused and no one else is the murderer. The evidence must leave no ground for reasonable doubt particularly as any doubt must, by law, be resolved in favour of the accused.[47] The following examples illustrate circumstantial evidence:

> For example: If Olooto testifies that he saw Alagidi rise a gun and fire it at Surulere and that Surulere then fell to the ground, Olooto's testimony is direct evidence that Alagidi shot Surulere. If court believes Olooto's testimony, then it must conclude that Alagidi did in fact shoot Surulere.

> If, however, Olooto testifies that he saw Alagidi and Surulere go into another room and that he heard Alagidi say to Surulere he was going to shoot him, heard a shot, and saw Alagidi leave the room with a smoking

---

[44] Section 91 (2) Evidence Act (Nigeria)

[45] *Omega Bank Ltd* v. *O. B. C.*

[46] (2006) 25 NSCQR 321 at 349

[47] See *Ganiyu Nasiru* v. *State* (1999) 9 SC (pt1) 14

gun. Here, Olooto's testimony is circumstantial evidence from which it can be inferred that Alagidi shot Olooto. The court must determine whether Olooto's testimony is credible or not.

Another example: For instance if Jide is suing his wife, Elizabeth, for a divorce, claiming she is having an affair with Karimu. Thus, where Karimu's fingerprints are found on a book in Jide and Elizabeth's bedroom, a judge may infer that Karimu was in the bedroom. The fingerprints are circumstantial evidence of Karimu's presence in the bedroom.

Circumstantial evidence is usually not as good as direct evidence (i.e. if it is an eyewitness that saw Karimu in the bedroom) because it is easy to make the wrong inference.

Circumstantial evidence may be the best evidence, particularly where it is overwhelming and leads to no other conclusion than the guilt of a defendant. However, circumstantial evidence to ground a conviction must be strong and unequivocal. A court is only permitted to draw the inference that is irresistibly warranted. It must be cogent and compelling.[48] The law is trite, that circumstantial evidence is the best evidence, once it meets the requirement of the law to qualify as such, namely:

1) it must be positive;
2) it must be direct;
3) it must be unequivocal; and
4) it must irresistibly and conclusively link the accused person with the commission of the offence.[49]

In *Nweke* v. *State*,[50] the accused was convicted for the murder of his wife on the suspicion that his wife was carrying pregnancy for another man. The evidence of PW 3 and PW 4 upon which the accused was convicted were that the accused and his pregnant wife passed by them heading for their farm, they heard some noise coming from the direction of the accused farm. The accused on his way back from the farm alone stopped over at the witnesses to ask for and was given water to drink. The witnesses were curious and peeped into the load the accused was carrying and found embedded therein, same cloths and slippers the accused wife wore on their way to the farm. On the witnesses' curiosity they proceeded to the place where the noise earlier emanated, only to discover to their horror the deceased's corpse lying naked with her throat slashed. From all

---

[48] See the cases of *Uluebeka* v. *State* (2000) 7 NWLR (Pt. 665) 404

[49] *Akinmoju* v. *State* (2000) 6 NWLR (Pt. 662) 608 and *Aigbadion* v. *State* (2000) 7 NWLR (Pt. 666) 705

[50] (2001) 5 NSCQR 360 at 372

these circumstantial evidences, the court held that the guilt of the accused was established with accuracy of mathematics.

Note that circumstantial evidence must leave no ground for reasonable doubt particularly as such doubt must by law, be resolved in favour of the accused person.[51] Where a circumstantial evidence is capable of being given two interpretations the prosecution has not prove his case beyond reasonable doubt. Oguntade JSC in *Ogidi* v. *The State*[52] quoting the court decision in The *State* v. *Muhtari Kura*[53] said:

> ...When circumstantial evidence is capable of two possible interpretations, one against and the other in favour of the accused, then in those circumstances, there has been no proof beyond reasonable doubt.

The justification for this is that offences or crimes are not things which are usually carried out in the open and since it will be practically abdicating its duty for a court to always wait for direct evidence or the confession of an accused before it can convict on a charge, reliance must be placed on evidence of circumstances as can be inferred from the facts of a case. This becomes even more imperative in the case of an offence of conspiracy which has secrecy as one its main ingredients.

Circumstantial evidence is most often employed in criminal trials. Many circumstances can create inferences about an accused person's guilt in a criminal matter, including the accused person's resistance to arrest; the presence of a motive or opportunity to commit the crime; the accused person's presence at the time and place of the crime; any denials, evasions, or contradictions on the part of the accused; and the general conduct of the accused. In addition, much Scientific Evidence is circumstantial, because it requires a court to make a connection between the circumstance and the fact in issue. For example, with fingerprint evidence, a court must make a connection between this evidence that the accused handled some object tied to the crime and the commission of the crime itself.

It is instructive to note that lawyers sometimes encounter situations where a client approach them thinking that he has a clear-cut case, for instance where there is a written agreement and the client believes the other party had clearly breached the agreement. However, things are not usually straightforward and very often there will be a dispute about the

---

[51] See *Igabele* v. *The State*

[52] (2005) 21 NSCQR 302 at 345

[53] (1975) 2 SC 53 at 89

facts of a particular situation. Even where a clear breach of agreement can be established, the opponent may claim that you did something to occasion the breach of agreement first. There are very few cases where the evidence is so overwhelming and unchallenged that the court can decide with evidence in support.

Chapter 3

Fact

The term "fact" is applied broadly to whatever is subject to perception or consciousness. The term fact when use in the law of evidence must be clearly distinguished from its meaning in the ordinary and common usage. The Act[1] defines fact as:

a. Anything state of thing or relation of things, capable of being perceived by the senses; or

b. Any mental condition of which any person is conscious.

Therefore, when a witness testifies in court as to the existence of a state of affairs, the facts therein stated are those he is presumed to have personal knowledge of as above defined and as envisage in the Act[2] unless where exceptions are allowed.

ii) Fact in Issue

The term "fact in issue" is defined in the Act[3] to include any fact from which either by itself or in connection with other facts the existence or non-existence, nature or extent of any right, liability or disability asserted or denied in any suit or proceedings necessary follows.[4] Thus, a fact in issue seems to mean, fact which in any suit or proceeding is;

a) A party must prove to establish his case.

b) Affects the credibility of any witness or admissibility of any piece of evidence.[5]

The fact in issue in a case, sometimes called ultimate facts, are the facts which a party to litigation (including prosecution in criminal case)

---

[1] Section 258 Evidence Act (Nigeria)

[2] Ibid; Section 126

[3] Ibid; Section 2

[4] Ibid; Section 258

[5] *Olufosoye* v. *Olorunfemi* (1989) I NWLR (pt 59) 26

must prove in order to succeed in his claim or defence and to show his entitlement to relief (or to obtain a conviction).[6] Thus, fact in issue are all facts that a plaintiff in a civil case must prove in other to establish his claims if they are not admitted by the defendant, and which the defendant must prove in other to establish his defence. While in criminal case fact are those, which the prosecution must prove in order to establish the guilt of an accused person.

Generally, facts in issue are determined by substantive law, in civil cases, by pleadings while in criminal cases, the charges take the place of pleadings and the fact in issue are those ingredients of the offence that must be established or proved by prosecution to sustain the charge and those to be proved by the accused person to sustain any defence.

It is apposite to submit that facts and facts in issue are the basis of the topic, *"Relevancy and Admissibility"*. This is so because of the fact that the entire law of evidence is dependent on the rules governing admissibility and inadmissibility of evidence.

iii) Relevancy and Admissibility

Relevancy and admissibility are fundamental conditions to admissibility of evidence and evidence that is irrelevant is inadmissible. Relevant evidence thus, means having any tendency to make the existence of any fact that is of consequence to the determination of the action more probably or less probable than it would be without the evidence.

Relevant evidence is *prima facie* admissible, on the basis that its admission will tend to promote the aim of the law of evidence. It may however be made inadmissible by virtue of an exclusionary rule. Exclusionary rules now operate mainly in criminal cases. In modern law, there are fewer exclusionary rules in civil cases and those that still exist, such as the rule against evidence of character and other misconduct, tend to be less strict[7] Consequently, when the relevancy of evidence depends upon the fulfillment of a condition of fact, the court shall admit it upon, or subject to, the introduction of evidence sufficient to support a finding of the fulfillment of the condition. And when the relevance of evidence depends on the existence of a separate fact, the evidence is considered to be "conditionally relevant.

---

[6] Pete Murphy, *A practical Approach to Evidence* (2nd ed. Blackstone Press Ltd. London, 1989), 7

[7] Dennis; *Law of Evidence*, 50

As a general rule, it is only fact which are relevant to the fact in issue or some other facts relevant to fact in issue that can serve as foundation for admissibility of a piece of evidence. Therefore evidence will be admitted only in proof of facts in issue, fact relevant to fact in issue and facts relevant to some other facts, which are relevant to the fact in issue. In *Elegusi v. Oseni*, [8] the Supreme Court, on the rule of relevancy and admissibility in court, said:

> It is elementary rule of evidence that before considering admissibility of any evidence or document in support of a party's case, it must be shown that the evidence sought to be led is relevant. Relevancy is therefore the main purpose for admissibility of any evidence or document under the law of evidence, whether it is civil or criminal matters.

Arguably, the question of whether facts are relevant and legally admissible cannot be determined unless and until another question "which facts are relevant to the facts in issue" is first of all asked and determined. Thus, section 6 of the old Act, made a fact admissible in evidence if it is relevant to the facts in issue. Incidentally this principle is still sustained under the new Evidence Act 2011 and the provisions of the old Act on relevance and admissibility are retained. Notwithstanding, the new 2011 Act has introduced dimensions which have, in a way retained the judicially affirmed principles on the law of evidence as it relates to relevance and admissibility. The section provides:

> For the avoidance of doubt, all evidence given in accordance with section 1 relating to facts in issue and relevant facts shall, unless excluded in accordance with this or any other Act or any other legislation validly in force in Nigeria be admissible in judicial proceedings to which this Act applies.

> Provided that admissibility of such evidence shall be subject to all such conditions as may be specified in each case by or under this Act. [9]

The entire law of Evidence is dependent upon facts governing relevancy and admissibility and whether evidence is admissible or not, is dependent on fact in issue in every particular case.

---

[8] *Elegusi* v. *Oseni*

[9] Section 2 Evidence Act (Nigeria)

Relevancy and admissibility are closely related term but with certain distinctions. While relevancy is based on logic, admissibility is dependent on law. Admissible evidence must be a relevant fact and must not be prohibited from being proof by any rule of law. This is as provided under the Evidence Act[10], that evidence may be given in any suit or proceeding of the existence or non existence of every facts as are herein after declared to be relevant and of no others provided that:

> The court may exclude evidence of fact which though relevant or deemed to be relevant to the fact in issue, appears to it to be too remote to be material in all the circumstances of the case, and

> This section shall not enable any person to give evidence of a fact, which he is disentitled to prove by any provision of the law for the time being in force.

From the foregoing, the court may reject evidence of a fact, even though it is relevant, if in the opinion of the court, it is too remote to be material.

iv. Relevancy and Admissibility of illegally obtained evidence

One of the novel innovations in the new evidence Act 211 in the realm of relevancy and admissibility of evidence is the codification of the rule of evidence which allows evidence illegally obtained relevant and admissible. The sections provide thus:

> Evidence obtained-improperly or in contravention of a law; or in consequence of an impropriety or of a contravention of a law, shall be admissible unless the court is of the opinion that the desirability of admitting the evidence is outweighed by the undesirability of admitting evidence that has been obtained in the manner in which the evidence was obtained.[11]

> For the purposes of section 14, the matters that the Court shall take into account include- the probative value of the evidence; the importance of the evidence in the proceeding; the nature of the relevant offence, cause of action or defence and the nature of the subject-matter of the proceeding; the gravity of the impropriety or contravention; whether the impropriety or contravention was deliberate or reckless; whether any other proceeding (whether or not in a court) has been or is likely to be taken in

---

[10] Section 1(a) & (b) Evidence Act (Nigeria)

[11] Section 14 Evidence Act (Nigeria)

relation to the impropriety or contravention; and the difficulty, if any, of obtaining the evidence without impropriety or contravention of law.[12]

The inference that can be drawn from the provision of the above section is that it accepts the tendering of improperly or illegally obtained and urges the Court to admit same evidence. This new provision of the Act is a reaffirmation of judicial position[13] as concisely put in the case *Karuma* v.. *R*[14] by the Privy Council where it was held:

The test to be applied in considering whether evidence is admissible is whether it is relevant to the matter in issues. If it is, it is admissible, and the court is not concerned with how the evidence was obtained.

The principle of admissibility of illegally obtained evidence applies to civil and criminal proceedings in all Nigerian Courts. Note that evidence that is obtained involuntary or oppressively such as confessional statement, is an exception to the rule under consideration.[15]

iv) Similar Facts which are Relevant

Sir James Fitzjames Stephen's seminal Indian Evidence Act of 1872[16] has had an enduring legacy. Many Common Law jurisdictions which had modelled their evidence statute after this seminal work in the late 1800s continue to retain the legislation. Nigeria which originally enacted its Evidence Act in 1893, is one of jurisdictions. In an attempt to modernise the Act the statute was amended in 2011. Amongst the amendments were changes made to the provisions on hearsay and expert opinion evidence.[17] Specifically, the scope for the admissibility of such evidence was broadened to take into account the practices and realities of modern litigation,[18] but the concept of judicial exclusionary discretion was also expressly introduced to curtail admissibility if needed. The relevant section of the Act provides:

---

[12] Ibid; Section 15

[13] *Musa Sadau & ors* v. *The State* (1968) N.M.L.R. 208 and *Igbinovia* v. *The State* (1981) 2 S.C.5,

[14] (1955) 1 All E. R. 236 at 239

[15] See Section 29(2)(a) Evidence Act (Nigeria)

[16] Stephen Digest of the Law of Evidence 12 ed, culled from Peter Murphy, 7 - 8

[17] Section 14(1) Evidence Act 2011 as amended

[18] The legislature created exceptions to hearsay rules in sections 39 to 58 of the Evidence Act 2011

> The court may exclude evidence of facts which though relevant or deemed to be relevant to the issue, appears to it to be too remote to be material in all circumstance of the case..."[19] and that;

> Evidence obtained improperly or in contravention of a law or in consequence of an impropriety or of a contravention of a law, shall be admissible unless the court is of the opinion that the desirability of admitting the evidence is outweigh by the undesirability of admitting evidence that has been obtained in the manner in which the evidence was obtained.[20]

In other words, the courts can exclude certain types of hearsay and expert opinion evidence even if they are found relevant under the EA. Strangely however; the provisions on similar fact evidence are left completely intact. The understanding of this legislative position is premised on the proposition that Evidence Act provisions on similar facts evidence, like those on hearsay and expert opinion evidence also represent codified exceptions to the so-called exclusionary rules. Thus, to statutorily limit the judicial discretion to exclude relevant fact evidence, hearsay or expert opinion evidence creates an immediate incongruity and it consideration by court will be based on weight to be attach to such evidence. This perspective can be underscored for example in the Act which provides:

> In estimating the weight if any to be attached to a statement rendered admissible as evidence by this Act, regard shall be had to all the circumstances from which any inference can reasonably be drawn as to the accuracy or otherwise of the statement...[21]

Instructively, the admissibility of an item of similar fact evidence is a question of law for the trial judge. Its ultimate weight is a question of fact for the trial of fact.[22] When faced with the prosecution's offer of similar fact evidence the trial judge has three distinct questions to resolve:
1. First relates to whether a basis exists for admitting the evidence at all. Here it requires the judge to ascertain the probative strength of the

---

[19] Section 4 Evidence Act (Nigeria)
[20] Ibid; Section 14 Ibid.
[21] Section 34 Evidence Act (Nigeria)
[22] Hoffmann, *Similar Facts After Boardman* (1975) 91 L.Q.R. 193

evidence and then to balance that strength against the prejudice, confusion and delay which admitting the evidence would produce.

2. Second, whether the evidence, if admissible, is admissible at the point in the trial it was offered. This the determination of whether the issue on which the evidence has been found to have sufficient probative force actually is in the case at the time the evidence is offered or, if it is not, can fairly be considered available to the defence.

3. Third, what instructions to give the jury (or himself if he is the trier of fact) concerning the evidence received. This question further depends on whether the ground upon which the evidence was received is, at the end of the case, still a real one.

Properly considered, the admissibility of a piece of similar fact evidence depends upon its *probative strength, i.e.,* the degree to which it tends to prove the proposition for which it is being offered.

In many common law jurisdictions Nigeria inclusive, similar fact rule is traditionally part of a broader subject known as circumstantial evidence or character evidence. In the criminal law context, the rule essentially does not limits the admissibility of evidence that goes not towards proving directly that an accused has committed the crime he has been charged with but towards other circumstances which are so connected with the crime such as his past conduct, cogent and compelling and that may form a basis for inferring that the accused has committed the said crime.

Though under exclusionary rule such evidence may not be admissible because the first thing to be considered is that generally in most exclusionary rules, only the most relevant evidence should be admitted to prevent or reduce:

1. The introduction of collateral and tangentially relevant issues;
2. Unnecessary protraction of the length and cost of the trial;
3. Distraction or confusion of the fact-finder; and
4. Implicit judicial endorsement of sloppy criminal investigation.[23]

The second main consideration is perhaps more specific to similar fact evidence and relates to the concept of prejudice, in that while circumstantial evidence such as an accused person's past conduct may seem intuitively and logically relevant and therefore aid in the court's

---

[23] Ho Hock Lai, *An Introduction to Similar Fact Evidence*, 19 Singapore Law Review, (1998) 167

search for the truth, such evidence may be more prejudicial than probative[24] because thus:

1. It may generally be unconnected to the offence but may unduly influence the judge by painting the accused as a criminal from the outset;
2. It may catch an accused by surprise in court when he is confronted with evidence from his past;
3. It may constitute a risk of cognitive error *vis-à-vis* the inference of recidivism; and
4. It may ultimately be given undue weight as to its relevance. [25]
5. It may create undue tendency to suggest decision on an improper basis, commonly, though not necessarily, an emotional one.

Be that as it may, similar fact is fondly referred to as i.e. comparison of other facts with the facts in issue in a given case whether civil or criminal. In *DPP* v. *Kilboure*,[26] Lord Simion of Glaisdate said; *evidence is relevant if it is logically probative or disapprobative of some matter which requires proof.* It is sufficient to say, even at the risk of etymological tautology, that relevant (i.e., logically probative or disapprobative) evidence is evidence which makes the matter which requires proof more or less probate". A more comprehensive definition was given in Digest of the Law of Evidence 12 by Stephen:[27]

> Any two facts to which it is applied are so related to each other that according to the common course of events one either takes by itself or on connection with other facts proves or renders probable the past, present or future existence or non-existence of the other.

The general rule is that, similar facts, which are relevant only, because of their similarity to the fact in issue, are not admissible to prove existence of fact in issue. This is because, apart from their similarity, they may not necessary bear any logical link to the fact in issue and are therefore irrelevant. However, there are exceptions to this general rule. The reasons for admitting evidence of similar facts (facts which are relevant) in exceptional cases are:

---

[24] Robert Margolis, The Concept of Relevance: In the Evidence Act and the Modern View, 11 Singapore Law Review (1990), 24–27

[25] Ibid.

[26] *DPP* v. *Kilboure* (HL) (1973) AC 729 at 756

[27] Stephen Digest of the Law of Evidence, 7 - 8

1. To prove systematic conduct;
2. To prove the defence of accident;
3. To show origin of locality;
4. To show intention (*mens rea*); and
5. To show knowledge

The Nigerian Evidence Act 2011[28] reinforces the admissibility of similar fact evidence when it provides that; similar facts or facts which are relevant, though not otherwise relevant may be relevant if,

a) they are inconsistent with any fact in issue or relevant fact.

b) by themselves or in connection with other facts they make the existence or non-existence of any fact in issue or relevant fact probable or improbable.

Consequently, by the provision section 9 of the Act,[29] similar facts evidence are relevant and admissible if they are so connected with the fact in issue to the extent that, a court or tribunal come to the conclusion that the state of affairs in disputed is proved or disproved.

The followings are facts which are relevant and admissible statutorily though they are not direct evidence:

i). Facts forming part of the same transaction are relevant whether they occur at same times and places or different times and places;[30]

ii). Facts which are the occasion, cause or effect, immediate or otherwise of relevant facts or facts in issue or which constitute state of things under which they happened are relevant facts;[31]

iii). Similarly, facts that afforded opportunity for the occurrence or transaction of relevant facts or facts in issue are relevant facts[32]. However, this section cannot be relied upon to admit what, under English common is termed hearsay evidence;

iv). Any facts, which shows or constitutes a motive or preparation for any relevant fact or fact in issue is also relevant fact;[33]

---

[28] Section 9 Evidence Act (Nigeria)

[29] Ibid.

[30] Section 4

[31] Ibid; Section 5

[32] Ibid; Section 11; however, this section cannot be relied upon to admit what, under English common is termed hearsay evidence.

[33] Ibid; Section 6(1);

v).   The conduct of any party or any agent to any party, to any proceedings, in reference to such suit or in reference to any such relevant fact or fact in issue in proceeding is a relevant fact;[34]

vi).   Any conduct of any person, an offence against whom is subject of any proceeding is relevant.[35] For instance the fact that it is Auchi who assault Bauchi, the declaration by Bauchi in the presence of Auchi that it was Auchi who assaulted him is relevant;

vii).   Fact necessary to explain or introduce a fact in issue or a relevant fact, or which support or rebut an inference suggested by a fact in issue or relevant fact, or which establish the identity of any thing or person whose identity is relevant, or fix the time or place at which any fact in issue or relevant fact happened or, which show the relation of parties by whom any such fact was transacted, are relevant in so far as they are necessary for that purposes;[36]

viii). Where there is reasonable ground to believe that two or more persons have conspired together to commit an offence or an actionable wrong, anything said, done or written by any one of such persons (conspirators) in execution or furtherance of their common intention after the time when such intention was first entertained by any one of them, is relevant facts as against each of persons believe to be so conspiring, as well for the purpose of proving the existence of the conspiracy.[37]

Note however, that statement made by individual conspirators as to measure taken in the execution or furtherance of any such common intension are deem not relevant as such as against any conspirators, except those by whom or in whose presence such statements are made.[38]

v) Facts relevant on some special circumstances or grounds
It is instructive to note that there are certain evidence which though not relevant but because of their peculiar circumstance made relevant. These may include the following:

---

[34] Ibid; Section 6(2); Evidence Act (Nigeria)

[35] Ibid.

[36] Ibid, Section 7

[37] Ibid; Section 8

[38] Ibid.

1. *Title or interest on land*
In section 66 of the Evidence Act[39], where title to or interest on communal or family land is in dispute, any evidence of family or communal tradition concerning such title or interest is relevant.[40]

2. *Titled to land may also be proved by act of possession.*
Act of possession and enjoyment of land may be evidence of ownership or of right of occupation.[41] Act of possession itself is, nevertheless, a good title against the whole world except the true owner.[42] Similarly a person can certainly be in possession through a third party such as servant, agent or tenant. Also possession of a predecessor in-title is in law deemed to be continued by his successor.[43]

3. *Receiving stolen property*
By virtue of the provision of the Evidence Act[44] where a charge of stolen property is made against a person or being in possession of stolen property is in issue, evidence that;

   i.   Other property stolen within twelve months precede the date of offence charged was found or had been in possession of the accused or

   ii.   That within five years proceeding the date of the offence involving fraud or dishonesty is relevant.[45]

This contradicts the general principle that, evidence that an accused person has committed other offence other than the one charged is admissible to prove that he committed the present offence.[46] The second point cannot be proved unless:

   a.   Seven (7) days notice in writing is given to the offender that proof of such previous conviction is intended to be given in court

   b.   Evidence has been given that the property in respect of which the offender is being tried was found or had been in his possession.

---

[39] Section 66 Evidence Act (Nigeria)

[40] *Balogun* v. *Akanji* (2005) 22 NSCQR 104 at 117

[41] Section 143 Evidence Act (Nigeria)

[42] *Akibu* v. *Azeez* (2003) 1 SC (pt i) &1 at 88-89

[43] *Adewole* v. *Bada* (2003) 1 SC (pt ii) 66 at 71 - 72

[44] Section 36(a); Constitution (Nigeria); see also section 167; Evidence Act (Nigeria)

[45] Ibid.

[46] Ibid; Sections 36 and 167 sub section (2) Evidence Act op cit

c.   However, it is trite that the offence presently charged must be proved independently before evidence under Section 36 of the Evidence Act can be given to prove guilty knowledge or intent. [47]

4) *Facts which affect the credibility of a witness*

These facts are relevant by virtue of the provision of the Evidence Act[48] as:

(a) To test the accuracy or veracity or credibility of a witness

(b) To discover who he is and his position in life

(c) To shake his credit by injuring his character

A party other than the party calling a witness can impeach the credit of the witness or with the consent of the court by the party calling him:

a. That they, from their knowledge of him, believe him to be unworthy of credit;

b. That the witness has been bribed or receives enough inducement to give evidence;

c. That his former statement is inconsistent with any part of his evidence, which is liable to be contradicted.[49]

5) *Tendering secondary evidence*

By virtue of the provisions of the Evidence Act,[50] tendering of secondary evidence becomes relevant on special ground where primary evidence could not be tendered in court.

6) *Relevancy of previous proceedings in trying a later case*

Evidence of previous proceedings in trying a later case is not relevant except on special circumstance as envisaged by the Act.[51] This can be proved by production of certificate of conviction duly signed by registrar or other officer of the court either it is Nigeria or outside Nigeria.[52]The evidence in an earlier case by a person who also testify in the later case may be used for the purpose of cross examination, as to credit, but is of no higher value than that. The Supreme Court in the case of *Dada* v. *Bankole*[53] per Tabai JSC, observes as follows:

---

[47] See section 427 Criminal Code and 317 Penal Code

[48] Sections 223 and 224 Evidence Act (Nigeria)

[49] Ibid; Section 233 Ibid.

[50] Ibid; Sections 88, 89, 90 Ibid.

[51] Ibid; Section 229 Evidence Act 2011

[52] Ibid; Section 248 and 249 Ibid.

[53] *Dada* v. *Bankole* (2008) 3 MJSC 1 at 33 per Tabai JSC,

It is settled law that evidence given in previous case cannot be accepted as evidence in subsequent proceedings except on conditions where the provision of section 34 (1) of the Evidence Act applies. Even where a witness who testifies in a previous proceeding testifies again in a subsequent proceeding, the previous evidence has no greater value than its use in cross-examination of witness as to his credit.

In *Elegusi* v. *Oseni*,[54] the plaintiff tendered exhibit, C and B. Exhibit C was the certified true copy (CTC) of the proceedings on a previous suit in which parties therein (namely Suit No 1/302/55) were *Oba Onibeji (for himself and members of his Ibeju family* v. *Salimanu Oyabode*[55] who were not, per chance the same parties in this suit. And exhibit BB a proceeding in suit No LD/117/72 between *City Property Ltd* v. *Attorney General and others* who were not shown to be the same parties in the present case. The defendant objected to the admissibility of the exhibits. The Supreme Court held that, the exhibits are inadmissible and not useful either as evidence of the truth of the facts they contained, or for the purpose of impeaching the credit of the witness through which they are tendered. That since the DW 4 in that suit (exhibit C) was not the same witness in exhibit BB, whether the evidence is tendered under sections 34 (1), 93, 109, 111, or 112 of the Evidence Act they are still inadmissible.[56]

The Supreme Court in *Onu* v. *Idu*[57] held that under section 34 (1) of the Act, evidence in previous proceedings will be relevant in a later case on satisfaction of the following conditions:

a.   The proceeding was between the same parties or their privies or their representatives in interest.

b.   That the adverse party in the first proceeding had the right and opportunity to cross-examine the parties and their witnesses in the case, and

c.   That the questions in issue are substantially the same in the first suit as in the second proceeding.

In *Elegusi* v. *Oseni*[58] the Supreme Court held further that, the three conditions stipulated in section 34(1) (a), (b) and (c) of the Evidence Act

---

[54] *Elegusi* v. *Oseni* (2005) 23 NSCQR 193

[55] *Ibeju family* v. *Salimanu Oyabode*

[56] *Owoyemi* v. *Adekoya* (2003) 12 SC (pt i) 1

[57] *Onu* v. *Idu* (2006) 9 MJSC 199 at 214

[58] *Elegusi* v. *Oseni, op. cit.*

must co-exist, subject however to the fact that the relevancy and admissibility of previous proceeding in a later case is based on any of the following circumstances;

i)   When the witness is dead or

ii)   When the witness cannot be found or

iii) When the witness is incapable of giving evidence or

iv) When the witness is kept out of the way of the adverse party or

v)   When his presence cannot be obtained without an amount of delay or expense, which is the circumstance of the case, the court considers unreasonable[59]

It is wrong and improper to treat the evidence given by a witness in a previous proceeding as one of truth in a subsequent or later proceeding, in which he has not given evidence.[60]

g). Similar facts evidence are also relevant on special circumstances as provided in the provisions of the Act.[61]

The doctrine of *Res gestae*

The common law doctrine of *Res gestae* is used in the English law of evidence in connection with facts in issue. *Res gestae* simply refer to as; *"Things done; event that occurred"*.

These are facts, which become relevant to a fact in issue because it explains, by reason of its proximity in point of time place or circumstances to the fact in issue. *Res gestae* can also be described as inadmissible evidence which becomes admissible because it accompanies and clarifies a fact in issue. Conditions for the application of *Res gestae* are that:

1) The fact to be admitted must be contemporaneous with the fact in issue.

2) The fact must explain and clarify the fact in issue and not merely an unconnected statement.

3) The statement must emanate or made by the principal actor or participant.[62]

In *R* v. *Bangweyeku*,[63] where the accused was charged for murder and the only important evidence against him was the statement of the

---

[59] See Section 39 Evidence Act 2011

[60] *Obawole & Air* v. *Coker* (1994) 5 NWLR (pt 345) 416

[61] Sections 4, 5, 6, 7, 8, 9, 10, 11, 12 and 13; Evidence Act 2011

[62] Dennis, *op. cit.*, page 115

deceased, shortly after he was stabbed to the effect that *"Bang has shot me"*. The statement was held inadmissible as it was made some appreciable time after the actual wound was inflicted.

Res gestae under the Nigerian Law

The Evidence Act does not mention the term *res gestea*, however the popular view is that was that the provision of the old Evidence Act[64] contains provision similar to the common law doctrine of *res gestae*. The section provides that; Fact which though not in issue are so connected with the fact in issue as to form part of the same transaction are relevant, whether they occur at the same time and place or at different time and place.[65]

The applicability and admissibility of the doctrine under the Nigerian law of evidence was justified by virtue of a provision of the old Evidence Act 2004[66] that provides thus; *"Nothing shall prejudice the admissibility of any evidence which would apart from the provision of this Act be admissible.* However, the position seems to have changed following the amended of the Act in 2011. The position of law presently is that such evidence is only admissible pursuance to provision of the Act or any other legislation validly in force in Nigeria.[67]

Though the scope of the old section 4 (before section 7 of the old Act) appears to be wider than the principle of *res gestae*, and admissible by virtue of section 5 of same old act cannot be applicable in Nigeria by virtue of the amended section 4 of the new Act 2011.

Thus, the position of the court in *Sunday Akpan v. State*,[68] that was convicted for the murder of a 12 years old boy based on the only prosecution witness who stated that, he was on bed the night of the incidence and later heard his mother shout *"Sunday has killed me"* and that when he ran out he saw the appellant cutting his mother with a matched can no longer represent the position of the law.

---

[63] *R* v. *Bangweyeku*

[64] Section 7 of the Evidence Act cap E14, 2004 (now section 4 of the Evidence Act 2011 cap E14)

[65] Ibid.

[66] Section 5 (a) of the old Evidence Act Cap E14 2004 op cit

[67] Section 4 Evidence Act (Nigeria)

[68] *Sunday Akpan v. State* (1967) NMLR 185

Common Evidence Found "Unfairly Prejudicial"

Probability evidence

Using statistical evidence to imply that it would be highly unlikely that another person committed the crime (*ex. at* trial, defence claims mistaken identity, while pros. brings in statistician who claims a one in a million chance someone else did it), that is because Auta's father is a notorious thief, thus his son Kutugi could be a thief.

Evidence of excessive violence

It is improper to offer evidence of a horrific act of violence when it is sure to so blind a judge to the facts as to push them to an emotional decision; evidence cannot be so violent in appearance that a reasonable judge will "lose its lunch" as a result of viewing it.

Scientific evidence

If evidence is not "substantially similar" to the even it is trying to create, it can be highly prejudicial and thus be excluded; (falls usually to experts opinion)

Similar occurrences, happenings, and events

When there is a lack of evidence, use of similar occurrences is attempted to corroborate their theory; some time allowed in:

a) to show causation;

b) to show a dangerous condition existed;

c) to show the mental state of a party when it is at issue;

d) to rebut a party's claim of impossibility;

e) to show the sales of other real property (to prove value);

f) to show the meaning of a contract, contract provision or document; and

g) to show the meaning of a contract, contract provision or document (custom)

Chapter 4

Proof of Facts

Proof in the law of Evidence consists of the aggregation of facts and circumstances that convince a court or tribunal of the truth of some allegations. It can equally be described as those methods by which the existence or non existence of facts are established to the satisfaction of the court. It is however trite that all facts in issue and other relevant facts to a dispute must be established or proved in court by evidence, which could be oral, documentary or real. That is why the courts are duty bound to examine all evidence placed before it in its judgment. The Supreme Court in *Onoh* v. *State*[1] said:

> The High court and all courts of law are duty bound to give critical examination to evidence adduced before them and ensure that the innocent are not punished or the guilty set free. They should act on evidence and not on hunches rumours or suspicion so as to ensure that justice in its purest form is administered in court to all and sundry.

The above represent the basic rule of evidence, but under the Evidence Act there are provisions for list of matters, which need not be proved by evidence they are as explained hereunder.

Facts, which need not be prove

Similar facts in a given case may be taken as proved by court(s) either because such fact is deemed to be within the court own knowledge or because such facts are presumed to exist. In other word the existence of such facts is taken for granted by the court and do not need to be proved. This no doubt is an exception to the fact that facts on which court(s) can base its decision in any litigation must be proved to exist by evidence. The followings are the exceptions.

---

[1] *Onoh* v. *State* (1985) 3 NWLR (pt. 12) 236 at 244

1) Facts judicially noticed

Facts are judicially noticed when court(s) accept the existence of such facts without any further proof. This based on the ground that they are facts within the court(s) own knowledge. They are:

Judicial notice which may be mandatory or discretionary

Mandatory refer to facts which court must take judicial notice such as those specifically mentioned in section 122 (2) (a)-(m). [2] While discretionary refer to those facts or state of affairs the court may take judicial notice of its existence. An example is customary law which form a group of facts court may take judicial notice of, without proof, once it has been acted upon by a superior or competent court as in section 16(1) & (2) of the Evidence Act.[3]

Notorious fact

That is the discretionary notice the court may take in the light of the facts, which are so notorious that they are assumed to be within the knowledge of the courts. For example; a court will take judicial notice that two weeks is too short a period for human gestation or that dogs cats, goats etc are domestic animals.

Vulgar abuses

In *Yinusa Bakare* v. *Rassaki Ishola Jibowu CJ*[4] took judicial notice of the fact that people commonly abused themselves as a prelude to a fight and call each other as *ole, elewon* which no one take seriously as they are words of anger and abuses. In *Williams* v. *West African Pilots*[5] the court took judicial notice of the fact that the West African Pilot was a national daily in Nigeria and the reader are within and outside the country, or that cat, goat, dogs, camel are domestic animal and that young person are naturally playful.

2) Facts Admitted

An admission as defined in Black's Law Dictionary[6] "is a statement made by one of the parties to an action which amounts to a prior acknowledgement by him that one of the material facts relevant to the

---

[2] *Lakanmi* v. *Adene* (2003) 4 SC (pt ii) 92 and *Amusa* v. *State* (2003)1 SC (pt iii) 14

[3] *Ogolo* v. *Ogolo* (2003) 12 SC (pt i) 56

[4] *Yinusa Bakare* v. *Rassaki Ishola*, Ibewu CJ

[5] *Williams* v. *West African Pilots*

[6] *Black's Law Dictionary*, 47

issues is not as he now claims." The position of the law is that facts admitted require no further evidential proof.[7] The Evidence Act define admission as oral, written or documentary statement which suggest any inference as to any fact in issue or relevant fact and which is made by any of the person as in the circumstance hereinafter mentioned in the Act.[8]

> An admission is a statement, oral or documentary, which suggests any inference as to any fact in issue or relevant fact, and which is made by any of the person, and in the circumstances, hereinafter mentioned.

An admission is either formal or informal. Formal admissions are usually contained in the pleadings in a pending case and are treated as conclusive being a concession by one or both of the parties of the truth of alleged facts. Where the truth of a fact is so admitted proved of it in the course of litigation is dispensed with.[9] Thus the Evidence Act[10] provides that:

> No fact need be proved in any civil proceedings which the parties thereto or their agents agreed to admit at the hearing, or which, before the hearing, they agreed to admit by any writing under their hands, or which by any rule or pleading in force at the time they are deemed to have admitted by their pleadings; provided that the court may, in its discretion, require the facts admitted to be proved otherwise than by such admission.

Similarly, in *NASL* v. *UBA*[11] the Supreme Court held; the law is elementary that a party has no legal duty to prove what is admitted. The courts take admitted fact as a fact and use it in the judgment."

An informal admission applies to both criminal and civil cases. A formal admission may be made under the following situations:

(a) Pleading

An admission of fact or facts could be made in pleadings, and such admission need not be proved[12] similarly any fact(s) in pleadings not

---

[7] *Nigeria Advertising Service Limited* v. *UBA Plc* (2005) 23 NSCQR 127 at 139

[8] Section 20 and see generally sections 20-27; Evidence Act (Nigeria)

[9] *Niamco* v. *Niamco* (1995) 5 SCNJ 442 at 462

[10] Section 123 Evidence Act (Nigeria)

[11] *NASL* v. *UBA* (2005) 223 NSCQR 127 at 139, see also the cases of *Oladiti* v. *Raimi* (1999) 10-12 SC 109, *CAPPA* v. *Akintilo* (2003) 4 SC (pt 11), *Faguwa* v. *Adibi* (2004) 19 NSCQR 415, *Egesimba* v. *Onuzuruke* (2002) 9-10 S C at 59, *Bajoden* v. *Irowanimu* (1995) 7 NWLR (pt 410) 655

supported by evidence will be deemed to have been abandoned because pleading do not constitute evidence[13]. Pleadings is a written statements which set forth in summary form the material facts on which parties to a case intends to relies in support of claims or defence, [14] in criminal proceeding they the essential ingredients of the offence as defined by the law creating the offence and which the prosecution must proffers evidence to prove his case.

(b) In answer to an interrogations

Interrogatories are never at large; they must have a nexus with the matter or matters in issue. This does not mean that the interrogatories are strictly confined to the facts directly in issue, but extend to the existence or non-existence of the facts directly in issue. The answers to the interrogatories need not to be conclusive on the issues provided that they have some bearing on them. The main aim of interrogatories is to uphold the case of the party interrogating and destroy that of his opponent. Interrogatories elicit admissions from the opponent and admissions are most valuable evidence for determining liability. Interrogatories should be directed at obtaining admissions of facts or other pieces of information which are materially important for proving the case of the party administering them. A party may not interrogate to elicit information that has bearing exclusively on the case of his opponent for in such a case, the interrogatories will not assist him in establishing his own case[15]. The Supreme Court in *Abubakar* v. *Yar' Adua* [16] per Tobi JSC define interrogatories as:

> Interrogatories are a set of written questions drawn up for the purpose of being propounded to a party, witness or other person having information or interest in the case. They are a pre-trial discovery device consisting of written questions about the case submitted by one party to the other party or witness. The answers to the interrogatories are usually given under oath i.e. the person answering the question signs a sworn statement that the answers are true. Interrogatories are legal questionnaires submitted to an opposing party as part of pre-trial discovery. The plural noun "interrogatories" derive from the common place or market place expression

---

[12] *Faguwa* v. *Adibi, op. cit.*

[13] *OGH* v. *S. M. Nig Limited* (2007) 9 MJSC 90 at106

[14] E. Ojukwu & C. N. Ojukwu (2002) *Introduction to Civil Procedure*; Helen Robert Nig. page 134

[15] *Abubakar* v. *Yar'adua* (2008) 2 MJSC 1 at page 24

[16] Ibid.

of interrogation which means the act or process of questioning in depth or question as a form of discourse.

(c) Admission by counsel.[17]
Admission by agreement in writing under their hands.
Admission arising from an answer to notice to admit.

In *Temile* v. *Awani*,[18] the Supreme Court on admitted fact said; In respect of facts in a statement of claims which are admitted or not disputed by the defendant and accordingly issued was joined between the parties, no evidence is necessary or admissible in further prove of such admitted fact(s).

(f) Uncontroverted Affidavit.
In *Honda Plac (Nig) Ltd* v. *Glob Motors (Nig) Ltd*,[19] the Supreme Court said; The position of the law is that when in a situation in which facts are provable by affidavit, one of the parties deposed to facts, his adversary has a duty to swear to an affidavit to the contrary if he dispute the facts. Where such a party fails to swear to an affidavit to controvert such facts, they are regarded as duly established.

3) Proof of Customary Law
Customary Law is a question of fact to be proved by evidence. The onus is usually on the party alleging the existence of the particular custom in question. He must call credible evidence to establish its existence. Although where a custom has been adjudicated upon once by a superior court judicial notice of the same shall be taken and court will not require further proof of the same custom.[20] The general rule under the Nigerian legal jurisprudence is that, where there is a rule of customary law (Native law and custom and Islamic law) applicable to a matter in dispute between two Nigerians, the matter must be decided according to such rule. Notwithstanding, the rule of customary law will not apply if it is repugnant to the rule of natural justice, equity and good conscience or contrary to public policy or it was established that the parties to the dispute intended

---

[17] *Adewunmi* v. *Plastic Nig Ltd* (1986) 3 NWLR (pt 32) 767

[18] *Temile* v. *Awani* (2001) 6 NSCQR pt ii 1081 at 1099

[19] *Honda Place (Nig) Ltd* v. *Globe Motors (Nig) Ltd* (2005) 23 NSCQR 74 at 92

[20] Section 17 Evidence Act (Nigeria) and the cases of *Sokwo* v. *Kpongbo* (2008) 4 MJSC 130 at 156 and *Agbai* v. *Okagbue* (1999) 9-10 SCNJ 49

that the rule of the received English Common Law regulate the transaction.[21]

A custom does not become repugnant to the rule of natural justice equity and good conscience or contrary to public policy simply because it does not conform to the English law. In *Mojekwe* v. *Iwuchukwu*,[22] the Court of Appeal declared a native law and custom of "Oli Ekpe", which qualified a male child to inherit property if no male child, and make the brother of the deceased (owner of property) to inherit, even where the deceased was survived by female children, repugnant to natural justice equity and good conscience. The decision was reversed by the Supreme Court, which held that:

> It must be remembered that a custom cannot be said to be repugnant to natural justice equity and good conscience just because it is inconsistent with English Law concept or some principles of individual right as understood in any legal system. The court must hear the parties and act with solemn deliberation over all the circumstances, before deciding or pronouncing a custom repugnant.

In any case, a custom under the Nigerian legal system remain a question of fact, which must be proved by evidence as to its existence and non-existence.[23] Arguably, this does not include a custom, which has been judicially noticed.[24] Therefore, a party who asserts and or denied the existence or non-existence of a customary law is bound to prove its existence or non-existence by credible evidence so also is, when a custom is not judicially noticed.[25] The Evidence Act provides:

> Where a custom cannot be established as one judicially noticed, it shall be proved as a fact[26] and where the existence or the nature of a custom applicable to a given case in issue, there may be given in evidence the opinions of persons who would likely to know of its existence in accord with section 73.[27]

---

[21] *Labinjo* v. *Abake* (1924) 5 NLR 33

[22] *Mojekwe* v. *Iwuchukwu* (2004) 4 SC (pt1) 1 at 13

[23] *Ogolo* v. *Ogolo* (2003) 12 SC (pt i) 56

[24] See section 14 Evidence Act 2011

[25] *Oyene* v. *Ebere* (2001) 6-7 SC 52 at 60, see Section (14) (3)

[26] Section 18(1) of the Evidence Act 2011

[27] Section 18(2) ibid

By the provision of section 70 of the Evidence Act, opinion evidence of an expert is relevant and admissible, to prove the existence or non-existence of a customary law. The Evidence Act provides:

> In deciding question of native law and custom, the opinion of traditional rulers, chiefs or other persons having special knowledge of the customary law and custom and any book or manuscript recognized as legal authority by people indigenous to the locality in such law or custom applies, are admissible.[28]

> When a court has to form an opinion as to the existence of any general custom or right the opinions, as to the existence of such custom or right, of persons who would be likely to know of its existence if it existed are admissible.[29]

Commenting on proof of customary law as directed by law and the standard of proof require thereof, the Supreme Court in *Isiobafor* v. *Isiobafor*[30] per Niki. Tobi JSC observed, proof of customary law is not one of the areas in our adjectival law that needs corroboration. While it could be desirable that a person other than the person asserting the customary law should testify in support of the customary law, it is not desperation. This is because; the Evidence Act does not so provide the anchor. The sub-section merely provides that a custom "can be proved to exist by evidence" and a single witness or more witnesses can lead evidence on the existence of the custom:

> It is not my understanding of the law that a village or community of witnesses must be called to satisfy the provision of section 14. In the evidential scene in the context of probative value, it is not the number of witnesses that mater but the quality of the evidence given. So a situation may arise where single witness gives credible evidences which, a number of witnesses may not, because they are bundle of contradiction. Therefore, emphasis should be on the guilty of evidence given rather than the quantity.[31]

Judicial notice of a customary law
Accepting that a custom is a question of fact to be established by evidence, the question must have been repeatedly proved in court by evidence. The

---

[28] Section 70; Evidence Act (Nigeria)

[29] Ibid; Section 73

[30] *Isiobafor* v. *Isiobafor* (2005) 21 NSCQR 746 at 759

[31] Ibid.

answer to this poser can be fathomed from the provision of section 14 of the Evidence Act, which says; a custom may be adopted as part of the law governing a particular set of circumstances, if the custom has been judicially noticed.[32] The Evidence Act provides:

> A custom may be adopted as part of the law governing a particular set of circumstances, if it can be noticed judicially or can be proved to exist by evidence, the burden of proving a custom shall lie upon the party alleging its existence.
>
> A custom may be judicially noticed when it has been adjudicated upon once by a superior of record. [33]

It is instructive to note that under the old Evidence Act, 2004 custom was one of those matters that need no proof by evidence when such custom had been judicially noticed.[34] The question on when a custom can be taken as judicially noticed had however been a subject of controversial pronouncement by Supreme Court. The controversy was on the number of times a superior court must pronounce on a custom for it qualify to be take notice of judicially. For instance in the case of *Cole & Anor* v. *Akinyemi & Ors*[35] the Supreme court held that a single previous judicial pronouncement on a custom would be sufficient authority to enable lower Courts or equal Courts to take judicial notice of a custom. However in several other later cases[36] the Supreme Court had held that a custom can only be judicially noticed after it has been considered; accepted and applied in many decisions. Adekeye JSC said:

> Native Law and Custom are matters of evidence to be decided on facts presented before the court, unless it is of such notoriety and has been so frequently followed by the court that judicial notice would be taken of it without proof.[37]

---

[32] *Nsirim* v. *Nsirim* (2002) 19 NSCQR 193 at 210

[33] Section 16(1) & (2) Evidence Act (Nigeria)

[34] See Section 14(2) of the old Evidence Act, Cap E14, 2004 LFRN

[35] (1960) 5 F.S. C.84

[36] *Onyejekwe* v. *Onyejekwe* (1999) 3 NWLR (pt 596) 482, *Ibrahim Olabanki & Anor* v. *Salami Adeoti Omokewu* (1992) 6 NWLR (pt 68); (1992) 7 SCNJ (pt 11) 266 at 280, *Alli* v. *Alesinloye* (1990) 2 NWLR (pt 135) 178, *Ogunleye* v. *Oni* (1990) 2 NWLR (pt 135) 745, *Mogaji* v. *Cadbury Nig. Ltd* (1985) 2 NWLR (pt &)

[37] *Orlu* v. *Gogo-Abite* (2010) 1 MJSC (pt ii) 186 at 221See also *Romaine* v. *Romaine* (1992) 5 S. C.N.J 1; (1992) 4 NWLR (pt 238) 650 at 669 and *Oko* v. *Ntukidem* (1993) 2 SCNJ

The cases of *Orlu* v. *Gogo-Abite*, [38] *Onyejekwe* v. *Onyejekwe*, [39] *Ibrahim Olabanki & Anor* v. *Salami Adeoti Omokewu*,[40] *Alli* v. *Alesinloye*, *Ogunleye* v. *Oni*[41] and *Mogaji* v. *Cadbury Nig. Limited* [42] nullified the Supreme Court position in *Cole & Anor* v. *Akinyemi & Ors* thus before amendment and coming into force of the 2011 Evidence Act, the Supreme Court had settled with firm finality the issue of notoriety of custom to the effect that a custom must have been severally acted or pronounced upon by the Courts before it can be taken judicial notice of.

Incidentally, the Nigerian National Assembly affirmed the position of the Supreme Court in the *Cole* v. *Akinyemi*[43] to the extent that it amended the provision of the former Act to now read as follows: "A custom may be judicially noticed when it has been adjudicated upon once by a Superior court of record."[44]

The implication of Section 17 of the 2011 Act is that the aforesaid Supreme Court decision in *Orlu* v. *Gogo-Abite* (and similar cases) has been overruled legislatively and longer represents the position of the law. Therefore when a Superior Court of record has once pronounced on the existence of a custom as representing a set of rule regulating the affair of a community, all courts must judicially notice such a custom.

The concept of judicial notice of fact is not left out of new introduction into 2011 amended Act. It has widened the sphere of matters which the Court can now take judicial notice of. Thus, matters of common knowledge within the locality of the courts' forum and matters or facts which are capable of verification by reference to a document, the authority of which is not reasonably open to question may now be taken judicial notice of by the court. The relevant section provide that: Proof shall not be required of a fact the knowledge of which is not reasonably open to question and which is:

i) common knowledge in the locality in which the proceeding is being held, or generally; or

---

[38] (2010) 1 MJSC (pt ii) 186 at 221

[39] (1999) 3 NWLR (pt 596) 482

[40] *Ibrahim Olabanki & Anor v. Salami Adeoti Omokewu*

[41] *Ogunleye v. Oni* (1990) 2 NWLR (pt 135) 745, *Mogaji v. Cadbury Nig. Ltd* (1985) 2 NWLR (pt 71)

[42] (1985) 2 NWLR (pt 71)

[43] (1960) 5 F.S. C.84

[44] Section 17 Evidence Act 2011

ii) capable of verification by reference to a document the authority of which cannot reasonably be questioned.[45]

Notwithstanding the above, the Act further provide that the court may acquire, in any manner it deems fit knowledge of a fact to which subsection (1) of this section refers, and shall take such knowledge into account. The court shall give to a party to a proceeding such opportunity to make submission, and to refer to a relevant information, in relation to the acquiring or taking into account of such knowledge, as is necessary to ensure that the party is not unfairly prejudiced.[46]

Against the above explanation, a single decision of a court of competent jurisdiction on a point of custom or customary law is sufficient to have the effect of judicial notice.[47] However, it must be clear to the court from the previous decision on the particular custom that the people in that particular area looked upon the custom as binding on them and in relation to the set of circumstances similar to those under examination before the court.

It is herein contended that courts must take judicial notice of the fact that custom changes rapidly and that the continuous existence of a custom cannot always be taken for granted particularly at the lapse of a long period of time. Thus, a court will allowed a party to lead evidence to show that a custom, which has been judicially noticed has ceased to be a custom in the particular area.[48]

The fact that a particular custom or rule of customary law has been proved and accepted by the court to be applicable to a particular locality does not make it acceptable by the court to be applicable to another locality, unless a custom or rule of customary law is of such notoriety and has been so frequently followed by the court that judicial notice would be taken of the custom or rule of customary law without the requirement of evidence in prove.[49] Thus, a custom which by virtue of section 17 (1) of the Evidence Act, which is not judicially noticed must be proved by evidence in court.[50]

---

[45] Section 124(1) Evidence Act (Nigeria)

[46] Section 124(2); Evidence Act (Nigeria)

[47] Ibid; Section 17 (1)

[48] *Lewis* v. *Bankole*

[49] *Ntegwule* v. *Otuo* (2001) 6 NSCQR (pt ii) 132 at 105-1054

[50] *Iheanacho* v. *Chigere* (2004) 19 NSCQR 179 at 294

Chapter 5

Estoppel

Estoppel is an admission or something which the law views as equivalent to an admission, by its very nature. A bar that prevents one from asserting a claim or right that contradict what one has said or done before or what has been legally established as true.[1] It is so important and so conclusive that the party whom it affects is not allowed to plea against it or adduced evidence to contradict it.[2]

Estoppel is a rule of exclusion; it is a doctrine which bars or disallows a party to say and or from asserting or denying that certain statement or a particular fact is untrue, whether in reality it is true or not.[3] Estoppel is divided into Estoppel and Estoppel per res judicata. In *Omnia NIG LTD* v. *Dyktrade Ltd*[4]

> Estoppel has generally been defines as a disability whereby a party is precluded from alleging or proving in legal proceedings that a fact is otherwise than it has been made to appear by the matter giving rise to that disability.

Distinction between estoppel and res judicata

The distinction between *estoppels and re judicata* was described in the case of *Egesimba* v. *Onuzuruike*[5] and *Ukaegbu* v. *Ugoji*[6] Where the Supreme Court said:

> When a party pleads a judgment as estoppel, what he is telling the court is that the court should take the judgment into consideration in considering the totality of his present case before the court.

---

[1] Bryan A. G. *Black's Law Dictionary*, *op. cit.*, page 589

[2] *Egestimba* v. *Onuzuruike* (2002) 9-10 SC 1 at page 50

[3] *Agbogunleri* v. *Depo* (2008) 2 MJSC 70 at 85

[4] *Omnia NIG Ltd* v. *Dyktrade Ltd* (2007) 12 MJSC 115 at 146

[5] *Egesimba* v. *Onuzuruike* (2002) 9-10 Sc 1 at 50

[6] *Ukaegbu* v. *Ugoji* (1991) 6 NWLR (pt. 196) 127

Whereas, when he plea res-judicata he is saying that although he has already got judgment on say a piece or parcel of land he want the court to adjudicate on that matter that has already been adjudicated in his favour. These courts held that it is contradiction in term because he is asking the court to judge what has already been judged hence he said that res judicata oust the jurisdiction of the court.

It is settled and requirements of the law therefore, that to sustain a plea of res-judicata the party pleading it must satisfy the following conditionality to wit: [7]

i). that the parties (or their privies as the case may be) are the same in the present case as in the previous case;

ii). that the issue and subject matter are the same in the previous suit as in the present suit;

iii). that the adjudication in the previous case was by a court of competent jurisdiction;

iv). that the previous decision must have decided the issue finally between the parties.

See also *Afolabi v. Governor of Osun State*.[8] Note that failure to meet any of the conditions mentioned above means failure of the plea in its entirety.

Categories of estoppel

Estopel by record or estoppel by judgment

Estoppel by record or quasi record is popularly known as *estoppel per rem judicatam*. It presupposes that a final decision of a court of competent jurisdiction once pronounced between the parties cannot be contradicted by any of such parties in any subsequent litigation between them in respect of the same subject matter.[9] This is sub-divided into two: causes of action estoppel and issue estoppel, and it arises in any of the following ways:

1. Where an issue of fact has been judicially determined in a final manner between the parties by a Court/Tribunal having jurisdiction, concurrent or exclusive, in the matter and the same issue is directly in

---

[7] *Abubakar v. Bebejji Ltd* (2007) 4 MJSC 1 at 35 Para A-C

[8] *Afolabi v. Governor of Osun State* (2003) 7 SC 55 at 58

[9] *Agbogunleri v. Depo*, op. cit.

question in subsequent proceedings between the same parties. (Cause of action estoppel).

2. Where the first determination was by a Court having exclusive jurisdiction, and the same issue comes incidentally as a question in subsequent proceedings between same parties (Issue estoppel).

3. In some cases where an issue of fact affecting the status of a person or thing has been necessarily determined in a final manner as a substantial part of a judgment by a Court/Tribunal having jurisdiction to determined that status and the same issue comes directly in question in subsequent proceedings between any parties whatever.[10]

Note that, it is normal to find within a single cause of action, several issues which call for determination and are necessary for the determination of the whole case. As a general rule, once one or more of any such issues have been distinctly raised in a cause of action and determined between the same parties in a Court of competent jurisdiction, neither party, his privies, agents or servant is allowed to reopen or re-litigate any of such issues all over again in another action between the parties, agent or privies. This is based on the principle of law that a party is preclude from contending the contrary of any specific point which, having been once distinctly put in issue, has with certainty and solemnity been determined.[11]

What then is a cause of action?

A cause of action is a combination of facts and circumstances giving rise to a claim in court for a remedy. It includes all things which are necessary to give a right of action and every material fact which has to be proved to entitle the plaintiff to succeed.[12] In *Abubakar* v. *Bebeji*,[13] cause of action was defined to means:

> A cause of action arises from circumstances containing different facts that give rise to a claim that can be enforced in a Court of law, and thus leads to the right to sue a person responsible for the existence, either directly or by extension of such circumstances. There must in essence be a wrongful act of a party (i.e. the party sued) which has injured or given the plaintiff a

---

[10] Ibid. See also *Halsbury's Laws of England* Vol. 16, Fourth Edition. paragraphs 952 and 953

[11] *Ajiboye* v. *Ishola* (2006) 11 MJSC 191 at 201, see also *Lawal* v. *Dawodu* (1972) 1 All NLR (pt 2) 270

[12] *Union Bank PLC* v. *Umeoduagu* (2004) 6-7 SC 146 at 149

[13] *Abubakar* v. *Bebeji* (2007) 4 MJSC 1 at 27

reason to complain in a Court of law for remedy of consequent damages to the party aggrieved.

A cause of action as defined in Stroud's judicial Dictionary and set out in the case of *Savage & ors* v. *Uwechia*,[14] *by Fatayi Williams; JSC* (as he then was) is "The entire set of circumstance giving rise to an enforceable claim". The learned Supreme Court justice went on to say that "to our mind it is, in effect the facts combination of facts which give rise to a right to sue and it consists of two elements the wrongful act of the Defendant which gives the Plaintiff his cause of complaint and the consequent damages."

Thus, where a cause of action has been decided by a court of competent jurisdiction and satisfy the condition for its operation as stated in *Odutola* v. *Oderinde*,[15] it will operate as estoppel against any parties to litigate on same again.

On issue estoppel, within a cause of action, there may be several issues rose which are necessary for the determination of the whole case. The rule then is that once an issue has been raised and distinctly determined between the parties then as a general rule neither of the parties can be allowed to fight that issue all over again in the same or subsequent proceedings except in special circumstance.[16] In the case of *Odutola* v. *Oderinde*[17] Supreme Court held: "As there was no finding on the traditional history relied on before the Customary Court the present respondent who were the plaintiffs in that court cannot be estopped from relying on their traditional history in this subsequent proceeding". It means that issue estoppel regarding that traditional history is not available to the defendant/appellant.

Where a court has finally decided an issue or a cause of action, it operates as estoppel against subsequent suit. These are referred to, as estoppel by judgment, record or *estoppel per rem judicatam*.[18] A previous judgment is relevant to back a second suit on trial, thus the Evidence Act provides that:

---

[14] *Savage & ors* v. *Uwechia* (1972) 3 Sc 214 at 221, by Fatayi Williams, JSC Ibrahim v. Osim.

[15] *Odutola* v. *Oderinde, op. cit.*

[16] *Ogbogu* v. *Ugwuegbu* (2003) 4 SC (pt i) 69

[17] *Odutola* v. *Oderinde* (2004) 5 SC (pt11) 90 at 98

[18] Section 59; Evidence Act (Nigeria)

Every judgment is conclusive proof, as against parties and privies, of fact directly in issue in the case, actually decided by the court, and appearing from the judgment itself to be the ground on which it was based; unless evidence was admitted in the action in which the judgment was delivered which is excluded in the action in which that judgment is intended to be proved.[19]

Thus, a decision of a court is said to be final when it finally disposes of the rights of the parties. For instance, if the judgment/decision given by the Court is such that the matter in controversy between the parties would not be brought back to the Court for further adjudication, in such a case, such a decision or order is said to be final.

The only condition that may defeat such plea (estoppel by record) is absence of jurisdiction by the court, which enters judgment because, such a judgment is a nullity as was observed in *Lakami* v. *Adene*[20] per Kalgo JSC thus:

The importance of jurisdiction in all adjudicative exercise cannot be overemphasized and it is well settled that if a court is shown to have no jurisdiction to entertain a matter before it, the result will be that, all its proceedings on the matter, however well conducted, are a nullity and any decision reached thereon by the court is void *ab iinitio* and of no effect whatsoever.

The significance of estoppel by record is founded on two principles expressed in these Latin maxims:

i). *Interest rei publicae ut sit finis juris litium* (It is for the common good that there should be an end to litigation;

ii). *Nemo debit bis vexari proceadem causa* (No one should be sued twice on the same ground)

The judgment of courts are conclusive and binding only on parties to the suits, however there are judgments which are binding not only on the parties but also on non parties, on this basis judgments are divided into classes, namely, judgment *in rem* and judgment *in personam*.

Judgment *in rem*

This is a judgment of a court of competent jurisdiction that determines the status of a party or thing, or the disposition of thing as distinct from

---

[19] Ibid; Section 173
[20] *Lakami* v. *Adene* (2003) 4 Sc (pt ii) 92 at 96 per Kalgo JSC, *Ayman Ent. Ltd* v. *Akuma Ind Ltd*

particular interest in it by another party to the litigation. Such judgment in rem, is conclusive for and against all persons, whether parties, privies or strangers to the matter actually decided.[21] A privy was defined as that person whose title is derived from and who claims through a party.[22] It may also imply identity of successive interest or persons having interest in property. There are three kinds of privies, namely:

i)   privies in blood, such as testator and heir

ii) privies in law such as testator and executor or in the case of intestate succession, a successor and administrator;

iii) privies in estate, such as vendor and purchaser; lessor and lessee,[23] and so on.

Judgment *in rem* deals generally with matters of probate, admiralty, bankruptcy and status of person.[24] A declaration by the Supreme Court that *Shugaba Abdulrahman* is a citizen of Nigeria (a decree as to nationality) is a judgment in rem. A decree as to divorce or as to legitimacy of a child is a decree as to status and binding on the entire world, parties as well as non-parties.[25] See section 55 Evidence Act.

Judgment *in personam*

This is a judgment which determines the right of the parties or privies to or in the subject matter of dispute but does not affect the state of thing or person or disposition of a thing, such judgment only binds the parties and their privies.

Relevancy of previous judgment

Previous judgment is relevant to back a second suit or trial. This position if founded on the provision of the Evidence Act[26] which provide thus:

> The existence of any judgment, order or decree which by law prevents any court from taking cognizance of a suit or holding a trial is relevant fact

---

[21] Section 54 old Evidence Act, 2004 now section 173 Evidence Act (Nigeria)

[22] *Agbogunleri* v. *Depo* page 89, *op. cit.*; see also *Nwosu* v. *Udeaja* (1990) 1 NWLR (pt 125) 188

[23] Ibid. page 89

[24] *Adeshina Oke* v. *Shittu Atoloye* (1986) 1 NWLR (pt 15) 241 at 258

[25] Section 174 Evidence Act (Nigeria); provides that: "if a judgment is not pleaded by way of estoppels it is as between parties and privies deemed to be a relevant fact whenever any matter, which was or might have been decided in the action in which it was given, is in issue, or deemed to be relevant to the issue in any subsequent proceeding, such judgment is conclusive proof of the fact which is decided or might have been decided if the party who gives evidence of it had no opportunity of pleading it as an estoppels"

[26] Section 59 Evidence Act, *op. cit.*

when the question is whether such court is to take cognizance of such suit or to hold such trail.

When a court having jurisdiction over the subject matter in dispute enters judgment such a decision unless overruled, reviewed or set aside is final and conclusive evidence to the settlement affected by it.[27] The Supreme Court in *Balogun* v. *Ode*[28] defines final decision, per Mukhtar JSC thus:

> Final decision means a decision of a court that would finally determine (subject to any possible appeal or detail assessment of cost) the entire proceedings which way the court decided the issue before it.

Relevancy of a criminal judgment in civil matter

The general principle of law enshrined in the Nigeria Constitution[29] is that a person who shows that he has been tried by a competent court for a criminal offence and either acquitted or convicted shall again subjected to another trial for that offence or any similar offence except upon the order of a superior court. This provision is expressed in a Latin maxim *"autra fois convict and acutra fois aquit.[30]* Thus, the judgment is relevant to bar a subsequent trial. On the effect of *autra fois convict* and *acutra fois aquit,* the Supreme Court *in Chief Air Staff* v. *Iyen,[31]* per Niki Tobi JSC said:

> In criminal proceedings, an accused person who is discharged can be made to face a criminal trial at the whims and discretion of the prosecution. In other words, he does not breath the freedom of air forever or for all times. The prosecution has the power and discretion to return him to the dock the second time. The position is different, if an accused person is discharged and acquitted. Such a person cannot normally be made to face criminal trial on the same offence or offences. He will adequately meet such a charge with the plea of *autra fois convict and acutra fois aquit.*

However, it is trite that in any civil proceedings where the fact that a person has been convicted of any offence by a court of competent jurisdiction is relevant such judgment shall be admissible for the purpose of proving any issue in the proceedings that he committed the offence. But no conviction which has been quashed on appeal by a court of competent

---

[27] *Balogun* v. *Ode* (2007) 4 MJSC 76 at 92, see section 318 of the Constitution, *op. cit.*

[28] Ibid.

[29] Section 36(9) Constitution (Nigeria)

[30] *Chief of Air Staff* v. *Iyen* (2005) 21 NSCQR 645

[31] Ibid.

jurisdiction or in respect of which an appeal is pending shall be admissible in evidence by virtue of this section.[32]

If in any civil proceeding it is proved in accordance with subsection (1) of this section that any person has been convicted of an offence by a court of competent jurisdiction... that person shall be presumed to have committed the offence unless he proves to the contrary... without prejudice to the admission of any other evidence for the purpose of determining the facts upon which the conviction is based, the contents of any information, complaint or charge sheet according to that person has been convicted shall also be admissible in evidence for this purpose.[33] (section 63(2) (a) & (b) 2011.

A party who want to rely on a criminal proceeding to prove a civil case must give the defendant opportunity to cross examine on the fact stated in the criminal proceeding. Thus, a civil matter must be proved independently. In *Nwachukwu* v *Egbuchu*[34] it was held that the fact of conviction in criminal charge is not evidence and is inadmissible in civil proceedings.

However where the existence of such judgment, order or decree is a fact in issue or is admissible under some other provision of this or any other Act then the fact of previous conviction is relevant and admissible.[35] Note that no conviction that has been quashed on appeal by a court of competent jurisdiction or in respect of which an appeal is pending shall be admissible in evidence by virtue of this section. [36]

Courts' competency to determine a dispute

A judgment, to operate as estoppel must have been decided by a court having jurisdiction to hear and determine the issue or subject matter in dispute brought before it. In of *River State* v. *Specialist Consult*[37] it was held that a court is competent when:

i).   When it is properly constituted as regards number and qualifications of members of the bench and no member is disqualified for one reason or another and

---

[32] See generally sections 62 and 63 Evidence Act (Nigeria)

[33] Ibid; See section 63(2)(a) & (b)

[34] *Nwachukwu* v. *Egbuchu* (1990) 3 NWLR 439

[35] Section 62 Evidence Act (Nigeria)

[36] Ibid; Section 63

[37] *Rivers State* v. *Specialist Consult* (2005) 21 NSCQR 621 at 643-4

ii). The subject matter of the case is within its jurisdiction and there is no feature in the case which prevent the court from exercising its jurisdiction and

iii). The case came before the court initiated by due process of law and upon fulfilment of any condition precedent to the exercise of jurisdiction.

When the above conditions are satisfied, a court is said to have power or Jurisdiction to try the matter place before it for adjudication.

Other categories of estoppel
Estoppel by representation

When one makes a statement or admission that induces another person to believe something and that results in that person's reasonable and detrimental reliance on the belief.[38] The Evidence Act provides:

> When one person either by virtue of an existing judgment, deed or agreement or by his declaration, act or omission, intentionally caused or permitted another person to believe a thing to be true and act upon such belief, neither he nor his representatives in interest shall be allowed in any proceeding between himself and such person or such person's representative in interest, to deny the truth of that thing.[39]

For example; where M represents Y as his agent, he will be estoppel from denying M's authority. Estoppel by representation may arise through silence or by some conduct. Example, if a person is under a legal duty to speak but remain silent he is estoppel from denying what he ought to have spoken but kept quite. In *Abalogun v. Shell P.D Co*[40] the Supreme Court held that:

> No doubt it is now well settled that where one party has by his words or conducts made to the other a promise or assurance which was intended to affect the legal relations between them and to be acted on accordingly, then once the other party had taken him at his word and acted on it, the one who gave the promises or assurance cannot afterwards be allowed to revert to the previous legal relations if no such promise or assurance had been made by him. He must accept their legal relations as modify by himself even though it is not supported in point of law by any consideration but only by his words.

---

[38] Bryan A. G., *op. cit.*, page 590.

[39] Section 169 Evidence Act (Nigeria)

[40] *Abalogun v. Shell P.D Co* (2004) 5 SC (pt. 11) 19 at 88-89

The plaintiff was employed under a contract of employment to the effect that the plaintiff is to be retired at the age of 55 in 1996 by exhibit N a letter dated 31st January, 1995. By exhibit O, the defendant purportedly terminated the plaintiff's employment. The court found that there is absolutely nowhere in exhibit N that the defendant promised, assured or gave any guarantee to the appellant/plaintiff that he would remain in its employment until he reaches the retirement age of 55 years, the case was dismissed.

Estoppel by agreement
Where a party has entered into a solemn engagement by deed as to certain facts, neither he nor anyone claiming through or under him is permitted to deny such facts. The conduct required here is the entering of the agreement. It is not necessary to show that any representation has been made.[41]

Bailment, agent and licensee
The parties to a bailment, *agent* and *licensee* will be estoppel from denying the authority of the bailed to bail the good or agent's principal or Landlord.[42]

Tenancy
A landlord who has granted a lease to the lease will be estoppel from alleging his title during the continuance of the agreement. Also a tenant who is in occupation of premises may not dispute his landlord's title.[43]

Estoppel by standing
Simply means culpable inaction, it is failure to intervene when one's interest is radically involved. In *Kpansangi* v. *Shabako*,[44] the Court of Appeal held that:

> A person who knowingly stand by during litigation concerning the title to land in which he claims an interest in circumstance in which he might reasonably be expected to apply to be joined as a party, may find himself bound by the judgment even though, he was not a party to the suit in which the judgment was given.

---

[41] *Okonkwo* v. *CCB* (2003) 2-3 SC 104, see also section 169 Evidence Act

[42] Section 171 Evidence Act (Nigeria)

[43] Ibid; Section 170

[44] *Kpansangi* v. *Shabako* (1993) (pt. 291) 5 NWLR 67

Chapter 6

Presumption

A presumption is not a fact but a provisional estimate of facts. It is defensible but nevertheless secure until actually defeated: it remains in place unless and until it is displaced by destabilizing developments. It imposes on the party relying on the presumption the burden of proving basic facts. Thus, once the basic facts are found to exist, the presumption imposes on the party against whom it is directed the burden of proving nonexistence of the presumed fact or its more probable than its existence. Therefore, a presumption is a conclusion which may be or must be drawn from a given set of facts by courts until contrary is proved or taking of something for granted, that which is presumed, assumption, assumed probability, supposition or expectation.[1] Thus:

i.   Presumptions work on occasion to remove the need for proof. They are mostly of significance in relation to civil cases.

ii. Factual presumptions are common sense logical inferences from a state of affairs.

iii. Irrebuttable presumptions of law are provisions of the substantive law, such as the provision that a child of ten and over has criminal liability.

iv. Rebuttable presumptions of law cover situations where once foundational facts have been proved by a party a particular state of affairs will be assumed to exist. Evidence Act (Nigeria)

However, neither the Evidence Act nor any other statute of general application defines the word presumption, but a large number of provisions of the Act are devoted to presumption as to some documents or matters or the others. Presumptions are basically classified into two:

---

[1] Alan Tylor; 39

presumption of fact and Presumption of law. In the Black's law Dictionary[2], presumption is defined as:

> A legal inference or assumption that a fact exists based on the known or proven existence of some other fact or group of facts.

Generally presumption is of two categories that is; presumption of law (which is equally divided into two, rebuttable presumption of law and irrebuttable presumption of law) and presumption of facts. The two categories are explained in the following order.

Presumption of law

A "presumption of law" or "legal presumption", is "a rule of law that courts and judges shall draw a particular inference from a particular fact or from particular evidence unless and until the truth" (perhaps it would be better to say "soundness") of the inference is disproved. A legal presumption is thus a supposition to the effect that, by "legal prescription", it is to stand until refuted. A legal presumption has, as its basis, reasonably and appreciably truthful facts supported by legal logic and/or reasoning enabling the court to assume its correctness unless rebutted.[3]

Presumption of law is an inference which the court must deduced from a given set of facts such inference been stipulated by law. Presumption of laws is further classified into two rebuttable presumption of law and irrebuttable presumption of law.

Rebuttable presumption of law

In rebuttable presumption of law, contrary evidence may be offered to disprove and displace the presumption provided these other evidence is acceptable by the court. The Evidence Act provides:[4]

> Whenever it is provided by this Act that the court may presume a fact it may either regard such fact as proved unless and until it is disproved or may call for prove of it.

---

[2] Garner; *Black's Law Dictionary*

[3] See e.g. Nicholas Resher, *Presumption and the Practices of Tentative Cognition,* (Cambridge University Press; 2009) Sir Courtenay Ilbert art; *Evidence, Encyclopedia Britanica,* (11th edition Vol. 10, Cambridge 1910) pp. 11-21 at 15). see Butt W. Jones, "The Law of Evidence, Civil and Criminal," Vol 1, 5th edition (San Francisco, Whitney 1958)

[4] Section 145 (1) Evidence Act (Nigeria)

Examples of rebuttable presumption of law

i) Presumption of Innocent

Where a person is accused of committing an offence he is presumed innocent unless it is proved otherwise. This is in line with the spirit and letters of section 36 (5) of the Nigeria Constitution 1999.[5]

ii) Presumption of Death

Under the Evidence Act[6] a person is presumed death if two conditions are proved to the satisfaction of the court that is:

a. The person was absent for 7 years or more; and

b. Those who would have naturally heard of him had not heard of him. Such persons include Parents, husband or wife, guardian or closer relations or children.

It is a presumption that arises on the unexpected disappearance and continuous absence of a person for an extended period of time.[7] The presumption is also applicable to a situation where two or more persons died at the same time in a circumstance, which is uncertain, who survive the other for the purpose of title to property. In this circumstance, they are presumed to have died in order of seniority.[8]

iii) Presumption of Negligence (Res ipsa Loquitor)

This is a common law presumption. It manifests where a thing is shown to be under the control of the defendant or his agent or servant and an accident occurred in the situation, which in the ordinary causes of a thing would not have happen if those who have the management take proper care. In this situation, there is said to be negligence. It thus affords reasonable evidence in the absence of explanation by the defendant that the accident arose from want of care.[9]

The doctrine of *res ipsa loquitur* is premised or predicated on the mere fact of the event happening which is based on two rebuttable presumptions, that the event happened as a result of a want of duty of care somebody owes his neighbour, and secondly that somebody is the

---

[5] *Obiakor* v. *The State* (2002) 6 SCNJ 193 at 202

[6] Section 164 (1) Evidence Act (Nigeria)

[7] Bryan A. G. *Black's Law Dictionary*, 1224

[8] Section 164 (2) Evidence Act (Nigeria)

[9] *Aliyu* v. *Aturu* (1999) 7 NWLR (pt 612) 536

defendant. For *res ipsa loquitur* to apply, the event which gives rise to the negligent must tell its own story of lack of duty of care.[10]

iv) *Presumption of Regularity*[11]

In the case of *NAF* v. *James*[12] the Supreme Court said. Presumption of regularity apples where there is no evidence to contrary and things are presumed to have been rightly and properly done. This is expressed in the criminal law maxim latin phrase. *omia preasumuntarite acta rite sesse acta*. This type of presumption is very commonly resorted to and applied, especially with respect to official acts. In the case of *Nwachukwu* v. *State*[13] the Supreme Court per Iguh JSC said:

> There is therefore a general presumption of law to the effect that the formal requisites for the validity of all judicial or official acts were complied with so long as they are shown to have been done in a manner substantially regular. The position of the law is summarized by the Latin maxim *omnia prae sumuntar rite sesse acta*, which means that all acts are presumed to have been done rightly and regularly until the contrary is proved. This presumption of law is commonly applied particularly to judicial and official acts and the onus of proving the contrary lies on him who alleges such contrary position.

For example in the case of *Ugwu* v. *State*[14] the court said: it must be clearly stated again that the act of applying for and the grant of leave to prefer a charge against an accused person is both an official and judicial acts. In this respect Section 150(1) of the Evidence Act provides as follows: "When any judicial or official act is shown to have been done in a manner substantially regular, it is presumed that formal requisites for its validity were complied with." Furthermore, apart from what is called presumption of regularity of official acts as embodied in the provisions of the Evidence Act, there is the presumption that, where there is no evidence to the contrary, things are presumed to have been rightly and properly done. This is expressed in the common law maxim in the Latin phrase as

---

[10] *Ojo* v. *Gharoro* (2005) 25 NSCQR 712 at 751

[11] Section 168 (1), (2), (3) & (4) Evidence Act (Nigeria)

[12] *NAF* v. *James* (2002) 12 SC (pt 1) 1 at 11

[13] *Nwachukwu* v. *State* (2002) 7 SC (pt i) 124 at 133 paragraph 30-40. See also the case *Ogunye* v. *State* (1999) 4 SC 30 at 42 and *FRN* v. *Bankole* (2014) NWLR (pt 1418) 337

[14] (2013) LPELR 20177 (SC), See also; *Kahi* v. *State* (1998) 13 NWLR (Pt.583) 531; (1998) LPELR 1655; *Amala* v. *The State* (2004) 12 NWLR (ft.888) 520; (2004) 6 SCM 55; (2004) 18 NSCQR 834; *Peter Locknan & Ors* v. *The State* (1972) 5 SC 22

follows: *"Omnia praesumuntur rite ac sollemniter esse ease acta."* (All things are presumed to have been rightly and regularly done.) This particular presumption is very commonly resorted to and applied especially with respect to official acts.[15]

iv) Presumption of Marriage

It is formerly a common law presumption to the extent that the court presumes a marriage where there is marriage ceremony under customary law or under the Marriage Act and where a man and a woman are living together as husband and wife.[16] However, this presumption has now been incorporated into the Evidence Act. Consequently, it is allowed that court presume a marriage where in a proceeding the question as to whether a man or woman is the husband or wife under customary or Islamic law. The court shall unless the contrary is proved, presume the existence of a valid and subsisting marriage between the two persons where evidence cohabitation as husband and wife by such man or woman is given to the satisfaction of court. [17]

vi) Presumption of Legitimacy

By virtue of section 84 Matrimonial Cause Act, court may presume the legitimacy of a child where the child is born during the continuous of a marriage or born within 280 days after dissolution of marriage and the woman remain unmarried.[18]

vii) Presumption of Sanity

Every person is presumed to be of sound mind at any time, which it comes into question until the contrary is proved.[19] In *Guobadia* v. *State*,[20] the accused person admitted killing the deceased both in evidence and statement to the police but raised the defence of insanity. The defence was rebutted and the accused person was convicted for murder.

For instance in *Popoola* v. *State*[21] from the evidence adduced by the Prosecution revealed that, on the 29th day of January, 2004 at about noon,

---

[15] See *Ogbuanyinya* v. *Okudo* (1990) (No.2) 4 NWLR (Pt.146) 551 at6 570; *Nwachukwu* v. *The State* (2002) 7 sc (Pt.1) 124; *Akpan* v. *State* (2001) 11 SCM 66; (2002) 5 SC (Pt.11) 110. *Shitta Bey* v. *Attorney General of the Federation* (1998) 10 NWLR (Pt.570) 392; (1998) 7 SC (Pt.11) 121

[16] Section 5 (a) of the old Evidence Act 2004 has been repealed in the 2011 Act.

[17] Section 166 Evidence Act (Nigeria)

[18] Ibid; Section 165

[19] Section 27 Criminal Code Act

[20] *Guobadia* v. *State* (2004) 2 Sc (pt 11) at 6

[21] (2013) LPELR 20973 (SC)

the Prosecutrix (Bukola Adebajo) was urinating at the school farm of the Abeokuta Grammar School, Abeokuta, Ogun State when the Appellant accosted her and threatened to report her to the school authority on the ground that students had been barred from defecating in the school farm. The Prosecutrix (PW1) pleaded with him but the Appellant demanded for money which the Prosecutrix said she did not have and in the process of further threat of reporting the Prosecutrix, the Appellant grabbed PW1 and dragged her further into the farm, overpowering her, he raped her before fleeing the scene. The incident was later reported to the School Vice-Principal who took PW1 to the hospital and reported the matter to the police. The Appellant could not be found for arrest but on the 24th day of July, 2004 at about 9.20am at a place called Mortuary Junction in Abeokuta, PW1 saw the Appellant and she called her mother by phone who came over and got the Appellant arrested. He made a confessional statement the same day wherein he admitted the commission of the crime and he was charged to Court. He raise a defence of insanity however, no evidence was adduced by the defence as to the hospitalization of the Appellant at any point relevant or anytime at all. Nothing was said about any medical consultation made to any doctor and what such had thrown up. All that was proffered by the defence, through the evidence of DW1 and DW2 was that about June of 2003 before the incident the Appellant had been at a prayer house due to mental illness and getting normal absconded no more no less. The Appellant did not testify for himself. The Supreme Court on the presumption of sanity held:

> Whether the presumption of sound mind is rebuttable; and whether it is an issue of fact to be settled on evidence "The law is settled that every person is presumed to be of sound mind and to have been of sound mind at any time in question until the contrary is proved. [22] The word "presume" implies the possibility that the thing being presumed may be rebutted.[23] It follows that the presumption that an accused was of sound mind at the time of the alleged offence can be rebutted. It is an issue of fact to be settled on evidence. Arising from the presumption of soundness of mind is the burden placed on the accused who sets up a defence of insanity to lead evidence to prove same.[24]

---

[22] See *Oladele* v. *State* (1993) 1 SCNJ 60.

[23] See *Karimu* v. *State* (2005) 4 ACLR 438 at 443.

[24] *Ugwu* v. *State* (2013) LPELR 20177 (SC), Per NGWUTA, J.S.C. (P. 30, Paras B-D), see also *Okon* v. *the State* (2010) All FLR (pt 530), 1262 at 1269

viii) Presumption of Ownership

In *Kyari* v. *Alkali*[25] it was held that section 143 of the Evidence Act merely create a rebuttable presumption of ownership and no more. It operation can have no place but is automatically dislodge when another person proved better title to the property in dispute. Accordingly, where a person in possession of a piece of land is said to be a trespasser the onus is on the person asserting such allegation to establish that he has a better titled to the land than the person in possession. A person in possession is generally presumed to be the owner of the property. In *Dada* v. *Bankole*[26] the Supreme Court per Ogundare JSC citing with approval the case of *Veronica Graham* v. *Hona Esumai*[27] said:

> The presumption in section 145 (now section 143) of Evidence Act is a rebuttable presumption and it is rebuttable if on the totality of the evidence lead in both side, the trial judge is not satisfied that the case in hand is a proper case for him to exercise his discretion to grant a declaration. It is perfectly legitimate for a trial judge to hold that the evidence taken as a whole (meaning any presumption in favour of the claimant) does not satisfy him that a case for declaration has been made out.

Generally a rebuttable presumption of law indicates conclusion that is; the presumption stands until duly set aside, such as the model of the presumption of innocence. However a rebuttable presumption of law can be defeated by appropriate evidence to the contrary. A presumption of this kind and nature is sometimes called an argument from ignorance and sometimes an argument in ignorance. In any case, ignorance is not a ground or premise for which to reason but a circumstance in which one reasons.[28]

Irrebuttable Presumption of Law

An irrebuttable presumption of law is an inference which the court shall deduce from a given set of facts and no contrary evidence shall be admitted to dislodge it. The Evidence Act[29] provides that:

---

[25] *Kyari* v. *Alkali* (2001) 6 NSCQR 817 at 845

[26] *Dada* v. *Bankole* (2008) 3 MJSC 1 at page 23

[27] *Veronica Graham* v. *Hona Esumai* (1984) 11 SC 123 at 149

[28] Jones, B.W., *The Law of Evidence, Civil and Criminal*, Vol. 1, 5th ed. (San. Francisco: Baneroft Whitney, 1958).

[29] Section145 (3) Evidence Act (Nigeria); section 30 Criminal Code.

> Where one fact is declared by this Act to be conclusive proof of another, the court shall, on proof of that one fact, regard the other fact proved and shall not allow evidence to be given for the purpose of disproving it.

Legal presumptions are generally mandates based on rules that do not merely "authorize" but "require". Instructively "an irrebuttable presumption" may be described to be an inference required by a rule or law drawn as to the existence of some other established basic facts and as such conclusive prove of the fact presumed. Consequently, it is an "irrebuttable presumption" of law in the sense that a rule of law requires the conclusive assumption to be made.

A presumption of law must be distinguished from a presumption of fact. The distinction usually distillable by these two classes of presumption is that a presumption of law is an arbitrary rule of law that when a certain fact or facts appear, a certain other fact is, for the purpose of the case, deemed to be established, either conclusively or until contrary evidence is introduced. While a presumption of fact is merely a logical inference or conclusion which a judge of facts is at liberty or has discretionary power to draw or refuse to draw.[30]

For instance the concept of Constructive Notice is a presumption of law, making it impossible for one to deny the matter concerning which notice is given, while under the concept of implied notice which is a presumption of fact, relating to what one can learn by reasonable inquiry, and arises from actual notice of circumstances, and not from constructive notice.

However examples of such conclusive presumptions include:

- A child below 7 years is presumed to be incapable of committing an offence under section 50 Penal Code and section 30 Criminal Code;

- A male person under the age of 12 years is presumed incapable of having carnal knowledge of a woman;

- Every judgment is conclusive proof of matters and or issues decided therein. The matter or issue is said to be *res judicature*.

Although a presumption has, as its integral part, potential defeasibility, but certain legal principles are sometimes categorized "as conclusive presumptions." Just as stated above, that a child of less than seven years cannot commit a crime or that a crime exists only with the

---

[30] *Joseph Adelu* v. *The State* (2014) 13 NWLR (pt 1425), 465 at 469 (SC)

establishment of circumstances "beyond reasonable doubt". But these indefeasible "presumptions" are presumptions in name only.[31] In fact, they are incontestable legal postulates. Strictly speaking the idea of an "irrefutable presumption" is a contradiction in itself. Thus, such legal rules of ineligibility as (1) that a wife is incompetent to testify against her husband or (2) that a minor is too immature to vote or to enter into a valid contract are not "presumptions" but "stipulations". Unlike "presumptions", they are not defeasible but stand, come what may, as conclusive or irrebutable "presumptions".[32]

Presumption of Fact

A presumption of fact is a logical inference drawn from proved fact. This inference though recognize, it is not stipulated by law and so the court may draw such inference from a particular set of facts until contrary is proof. The justification for this presumption can be drawn from the Evidence Act[33] which provides that:

> Whenever it is directed by this Act that the court may presume a fact, it may either regard such fact proved unless and until it is disproved or call for proof of it.

Examples of Presumption of Fact

Presumption of facts is usually rebuttable, and these presumptions may include the following:

i) Presumption of intention

The presumption was developed by court. A man is presumed to intend all the natural consequences that may likely flow directly from his deliberate action or omission.[34] In *Nungu v. R*,[35] the accused hit the deceased with wooden half of an axe and the victim died. It was held that, it would not be reasonable to conclude that the accused did not intend the killing of the deceased or he did not believe that his action can cause death. He must in our view intend the natural consequence of his act.

---

[31] Richard A. Epstein, Pleadings and Presumption, (1973-4), 40, University of Chicago Law Review), pp. 556-82

[32] Ibid.

[33] Section 145 (1) Evidence Act (Nigeria)

[34] Section 27 of the Criminal Code Act

[35] *Nungu v. R.* (1953) 14 WACA 309, see also the case of *The State v. Abigail Njoku* (2010) All FWLR (pt 523) 1924 at 1937-1939

The law presumes that a man intends the natural and probable consequences of his acts. And the test to be applied in these circumstances is the objective test namely, the test of what a reasonable man would contemplate as the probable result of his act.[36] In Ali v Central Bank of Nigeria[37] the appellant/accused person was alleged to have struck the deceased with an Axe on the head which led to his death. He appealed against his conviction on grounds that the evidence was insufficient evidence to sustain his conviction relying on the evidence of tainted witness. In determination of the accused action the Supreme Court held that:

> A person intended the natural and foreseeable consequences of his action, an intention to kill can also be deduced from the nature and type of weapon used. In the instance case, where the appellant struck the deceased on the head with an Axe, the trial court rightly inferred that he intended to kill the deceased and convicted him thereof.

ii) Presumption Guilty Knowledge

Under the doctrine of recent possession of stolen property otherwise a presumption of guilt knowledge, the presumption that follows is, the person in possession is either the thief or received the property know it to have been stolen.[38] It could not have been otherwise for if a person is found in possession of property, which was property reported to have been recently stolen, with or without violence from another person, it is open to a trial court to convict that person of the offence.[39] Consequently, guilty knowledge is already indicated once stolen items were found in the appellant's possession soon after the robbery incident complained of.

It will therefore, be a clear case for the invocation of the presumption in Section 167 (a) of the Evidence Act, being the Nigerian statutory version of the English doctrine of recent possession.[40] In this perspective, an offence of receiving stolen property under section 427 of the Criminal Code or dishonestly receiving stolen property under sections 317 Penal

---

[36] *Ibikunle* v. *State* (2007) 3 MJSC 184 at 200-201

[37] (2015) All FWLR (pt 796) 559

[38] *Oseni* v. *State* (1984) 11 SC 44; *Alarape* v. *The State* (2001) FWLR (Pt.41) 1873; *Nwaebonyi* v. *State* (1994) 5 NWLR (Pt.342)

[39] *Isibor* v. *The State* (2002) LPELR - 1553 (SC) 22-23, G-C; *R* v. *Loughlim* 35 CR App. 69; In *Re Karimu Atanda* v. *The State* [1983] 6 SC 1" Per OKORO, JSC p., 50

[40] *Eze* v. *The State* (1985) LPELR - 1189 (SC) 11-13, C-C., *Aremu* v. *State* [1991] 17 NWLR (Pt.210) 1; *State* v. *Nnolim* (1994) 4 SCNJ 48; *Aiyeola* v. *State* (1969) 1 All NLR 309; *Adesina and Anor* v. *The State* (2002) LPELR -9722 (SC); *Oseni* v. *The State* [1984] 11 5C44

Code by the provisions of the law requires that the offender must have the requisite guilty knowledge that the property had been stolen. [41] The Evidence Act provides:

> The court may presume the existence of any fact which it deems likely to have happened, regard being had to the common course of natural events' human conduct and public and private business, in their relationship to the facts of the particular matter, the court may presume that - (a) A man who is in possession of stolen goods soon after the theft is either the thief or has received the goods knowing them to be stolen, unless he can account for his possession. [42]

Incidentally the Supreme Court in *Okoroji* v. *The State* [43] has identified the facts from which inference of knowledge that a property is stolen can be drawn as including:
1. the manner of receipt or delivery of the goods allegedly stolen;
2. the time of delivery; and
3. the price paid for the property or goods.

These principles can be understood from the facts of *Ekpo* v. *State*. [44] In the instance case the prosecution's case against the appellant was that between 22nd and 25th March, 1993, at Fergies International Ltd. Work Site, Uyo, he received from the 1st and 2nd accused 3 trips of chippings (15m3) valued at ₦8,500 knowing the same to have been stolen. He was found guilty of the offence and sentenced to 2 years imprisonment without option of fine. The court held that in this particular case, the manner of receipt and delivery of the chippings are open to suspicion when the goods were sold by the employee of the company to the purchaser at half the going price without the evidence of the actual price paid documented and only revealed by the *ipse dixit* of the buyer. The sale taking place at the work site of the company was shrouded in secrecy because of lack of the knowledge of the transactions outside the world of the seller and the purchaser. To crown it all evidence that the security men of the company who were keeping watch over the chippings had been cowed into total subservience by the seller acting in concert with a collaborator who was also a top official of the company and the 2nd accused at the trial not only

---

[41] *Eze* v. *State* (1985) 3 NWLR (pt. 13) 429

[42] Section 167(a) Evidence Act (Nigeria)

[43] (2002) 5 NWLR (Pt. 759) 21; (2001) FWLR (Pt. 77) 871, 890

[44] (2002) LPELR 10396 (CA)

ensured that the watchdog of the company could not lift a finger but also
lent a crescendo to the aura of silence that beclouded the sale and delivery.

In *Wale Banjo* v. *State*[45] the Appellant/Accused, Wale Banjo, together
with two others were charged with conspiracy to commit armed robbery
and armed robbery contrary to section 5 (6) and 1(2) (C) of the Robbery
and Firearms (special provisions) Act cap 398 Laws of the Federation of
Nigeria 1990 as amended by the Tribunal (certain consequential
amendments, etc.) Act 1999. The appellant/accused was found in
possession of some of the robbed items so soon after they were robbed.
There was no explanation from the appellant/accused as to how he came
into possession of the stolen item. The Supreme Court affirmed that the
conviction and sentence of 21 years imprisonment passed on the appellant
is absolutely correct and same is hereby affirmed. The Court held:

> Being in possession of a stolen items or robbed items is a prima facie
> evidence that the accused participated in the robbery. That being the case,
> the onus is on him to give satisfactory account/evidence as to how the
> good or goods got to his possession, failing which the court would be right
> to convict him for the offence of robbery or theft (stealing).[46]

In *Mohammed* v. *the State*[47] the learned trial judge believed the
evidence of PW1 who said she identified the appellant and the 2nd accused
being part of the gang of armed robbers who while armed with guns and
cutlasses invaded her home on 15/2/99 and robbed her and her household
of many dresses and household items. The appellant and 2nd accused were
caught soon after the robbery in the neighbourhood with bags which 1st
PW identified as hers and the items stolen from her. The learned trial
Judge found that 1st PW's evidence was corroborated with the evidence of
2nd-6th Prosecution witnesses. In reviewing the evidence at the trial, the
lower court in its judgment said at pages 327-328 of the records: "The
recovery of the robbed items belonging to the 1st PW, 2nd PW, 4th PW,
5th PW and 7th PW inside the four bags carried by the appellant and his
companion less than two hours after the robberies linked the appellant
with the robberies. His plea of alibi did not supply the particulars of the
alibi in terms of the address of the mosque and the person(s) with him at
the mosque at the material time for the police to investigate or verify. The

---

[45] (2013) LPELR, 20746 (SC)

[46] Ibid.

[47] (2015) LPELR 24397, (SC)

police were, in the circumstances, not expected to go on a wild goose chase in respect of the plea of alibi without particulars put forward by the appellant. The presumption of recent possession of the robbed goods under Section 149(a) of the Evidence Act availed the respondent.

It is instructive to note especially from above case that the proximity of the time of possession to the theft seems to be an essential requirement of the presumption whether the appellant is the thief, or received them with knowledge that they are stolen goods.[48] As can be equally seen in the Supreme Court decision in *Madagwa* v. *the State;*[49] in this case the appellant was found as an occupant of the stolen vehicle less than two hours after it was stolen at gun point from P.W.2. This case is similar to the case of *Iliyasu Sumaila* v. *The State*[50] where Ejembi Eko J.C.A held: "The PW1 identified the appellant as one of those who robbed him. Six hours after the robbery the appellant was found with the motorcycle and the telephone handset. There could be no better instance of the doctrine of recent possession in Section 149(a) of the Evidence Act (now Section 167(a) Evidence Act, 2011 than this. The doctrine runs thus; the man who is in possession of stolen goods soon after the theft is either the thief or is a receiver of stolen goods knowing them to have been stolen unless he gives proper account on how he came into possession of the goods. This is a presumption of facts, and is rebuttable.[51]

The significance of defendant explanation in rebuttal
An explanation by an accused of the way in which a stolen property came into possession which might reasonably be true and which is consistent with innocence, although the court may not be convinced of its truth, would displace the presumption under Section 167(a) of the Evidence Act 2011.[52] In this connection, the Court may infer guilty knowledge where the accused gives no explanation at all about how he came to be in possession of the property recently stolen or where the explanation he has given is untrue. It is only where the court is in doubt about whether the accused knew or did not know that the property was stolen that the court will discharge and acquit him. In this particular case, each of the respondents

---

[48] *Botu* v. *the State* (2014) LPELR 23225 (CA)

[49] (1988) 5 NWLR (pt 92) 50

[50] (2012) LPELR 19724 (CA)

[51] See also, *Eze* v. *The State* (1985) NWLR (Pt 13) 429

[52] *State* v. *Nnolim* (1994) 5 NWLR Pt 345 Pg 394 at Pg.410

was unable to give true account or explanation of how he came into possession.[53]

For example in *Mohammed* v. *the State*[54] the appellant did not give probable account of his possession of the goods or items found with him and openly identified in his presence by the victims of the robberies as their respective items. His evidence on the matter was evasive. Accordingly the court below was right to invoke the presumption of recent possession under Section 149 (a) (now section 167(a) 2011) of the Evidence Act to hold that the appellant was one of the robbers that robbed assorted items from the victims that testified for the respondent in the court below.

iii) *Presumption of Continuance*[55]

One of the most common applications of this presumption is the presumption in favour of continuance of human life. It is also applicable in respect of the offence of Bigamy under section 330 Criminal Code or section 248 Penal Code to the extent that spouse is free to marry another person if the other spouse has been absence for 7 years and was not heard of. It also relevant for the determination of title to property (or succession) where two or more persons have died in circumstances in which it is uncertain which survive the other, thus they are presumed to have died in order of seniority or as relate to presumption of age.[56] Similarly it applies to husband and wife who if it is presumed that they are married at a particular time they are presumed to remain married.[57]

iv) *Presumption of Cause of Business*[58]

It is presumed, in case of business, public, official or private business that the normal course of the business has been followed.

iv) *Presumption of Withholding Evidence*[59]

Where evidence, which could be produced, is not produced the court may presume that it would be unfavourable to the person who withheld it. In

---

[53] *Salami* v. *The State* (1983) 3 NWLR Pt 85 Pg. 670; *Kolawole* v. *State* (2015) LPELR 24400 (SC), (P. 48, paras D-E); See also *Ogoala* v. *The State* (1991) 2 NWLR (Pt.175) 509

[54] (2015) LPELR 24397, (SC), Per AKA'AHS, J.S.C. (Pp. 40-42, paras. F-E)

[55] Section 167 (b) Evidence Act (Nigeria)

[56] Ibid; Section 164(1), (2) & (3)

[57] Ibid; Section 166

[58] Ibid; Section 167 (c)

[59] Ibid; Section 167 (d)

Aigureghiah v. *State*[60] the court examined whether there was withholding of evidence to determine the cause of the deceased's death. The deceased was treated at two different hospitals and was discharged; subsequently the deceased took ill and was admitted to UBTH but later died. In the cause of proceedings no evidence was given as to the nature of the decease ailment and treatment at the hospitals. The Supreme Court held that:

> The evidence of treatments and ultimate death and medical certificate of death issued by UBTH was withheld by the prosecution. The court further held that the withheld evidence would have provided crucial clues and answers on the issue of whether the injuries lingered on until the deceased's death and whether or not new ailments intervened. This evidence was available to the prosecution but it was withheld.

Conditions for the application of the doctrine of withholding evidence were stated in *Awosibe* v. *Sotunbo*[61] that the court must be satisfy that:
  a) The evidence exist;
  b) The evidence can be produced;
  c) The evidence has not been produced;
  d) That the evidence has being withheld by the person who could produce it.[62]

Exemptions
a. The presumption deals with failure to produce or call evidence and not failure to call particular evidence.

b. The presumption cannot be invoked so as to shift the burden of proof in criminal cases from prosecution to the accused person.[63]

c. The presumption can be invoked where a party failed to call a material witness whose evidence will one way or the other tilt the balance of probability i.e. in civil cases where the only evidence in a transaction is that of the party who fails to call him.

vi). Presumption of Document Creating Obligation
Where a document creating an obligation is in the hand of obligor (debtor), it is presumed that the obligation has been discharged.[64] It is however a

---

[60] *Aigureghiah* v. *State* (2004) 1 SC (pt. 1) 63 at 75

[61] *Awosibe* v. *Sotunbo* (1986) 5 NWLR (pt. 47)

[62] *Alhaji Sufianu* v. *Isiaka Hassan* (2014) SC/44/2002

[63] *Onah* v. *State* (1995) 3 NWLR (pt. 12) 236

rebuttable presumption to the extent that a creditor (obligee) may prove that the debtor (obligor) stole the document or got it by false pretence, duress, undue influence or fraud to dislodge it.

Generally, presumption whether of fact or law within the concept of a *"prima facie case"* is very closely connected with a legal duty i.e. *"burden of proof"*. To make out a prima facie case for one's contention, the case has to be made out in a way that "reasonable presumption" should be in its favour and the burden of proof will now be on the opposing party. The term "Presumption" by its very essence is of provisional character demanding the actual truth. Simply put "presumption, speaking strictly and precisely, is an anticipation of something yet unproved.

---

[64] Section 167 (e) Evidence Act (Nigeria)

Chapter 7

Burden of Proof

From the outset and in considering burden and standard of proof the law places on disputed parties in court litigations, it is necessary to elucidate the differences between a civil case and criminal case, which generally form the fulcrum of litigation in court. The Nigeria legal system consists mainly of two very different types of cases, civil and criminal. Crimes are generally offences against the state, and are accordingly prosecuted by the state. Civil cases on the other hand, are typically disputes between individuals regarding the legal duties and responsibilities they owe one another. The following are important differences between a civil case and criminal case:

1. Crimes are considered offences against the state, or society as a whole and threaten the peace, security and peaceful coexistence of people in society. In view of this, even though one person might murder or commit armed robbery on another person, murder or armed robbery are considered offences to everyone in society. Accordingly, crimes against the state are prosecuted by the state, and the prosecutor (not the victim) files the case in court as a representative of the state. However, if it were a civil case, then the wronged party would file the case.

2. Criminal offences and civil offences are generally different in terms of their punishment. Criminal cases are punished with jail term or even death sentence, civil cases are generally only result in monetary damages or orders to do or not do something. Note that a criminal case may involve both jail term and imposition of compensatory punishments in the form of fines.

3. The standard of proofs in civil and criminal cases is different. Crimes must generally be proved beyond a reasonable doubt, whereas civil cases are proved by lower standards of proof such as "the preponderance of the evidence" (which essentially means that it was more likely than not that something occurred in a certain way). The

difference in standards exists because civil liability is considered less blameworthy and because the punishments are less severe.

4. A defendant in a criminal case is entitled to legal representation, and if he or she can't afford one, the state must provide. A defendant in a civil case may defend himself/herself in person or by procurement of a legal practitioner if he/she chooses and must pay for his/her service.

5. The protections afforded defendants under criminal law are considerable (such as the protection against illegal searches and seizures). Many of these well-known protections are not available to a defendant in a civil case.

6. In general, because criminal cases have greater consequences, the possibility of jail and even death, criminal cases have many more protections in place and are harder to prove than civil cases.

7. Similar conduct can occasion both civil and criminal Liabilities. Although criminal and civil cases are treated very differently, many people often fail to recognize that the same conduct can result in both criminal and civil liability. An assault or inflicting grievous bodily pain on another can produce civil and criminal liability.

Against the above background, proof in the law of evidence is known as; the observation of facts and circumstance that convince a Court or Tribunal of the truth of some allegations or claims asserted or denied.[1] More succinctly put, it (proof) describes the duty imposed on parties to court's proceedings (civil or criminal) to establish by evidence the existence or not existence of fact is established to the satisfaction of the Court or Tribunal. The Evidence Act provides:

> Whoever desires any court to give judgment as to any legal right or liability dependent on the existence of facts which he asserts shall prove that those facts exist.[2]
> When a person is bound to prove the existence of any fact it is said that the burden of proof lies on that person. [3]
> The burden of proof in a suit or proceeding lies on that person who would fail if no evidence at all is given on either side. [4]

---

[1] Alan Tylor, *Principles of Evidence*. (2nd ed., Cavendish Publish Limited London, 2000) pp. 13-23
[2] Section 131(1) Evidence Act (Nigeria)
[3] Ibid Section 131(2)
[4] Ibid Section 132

According to Phipson[5] the phrase burden of proof is used to describe the duty which lies on one or other of the parties either to establish a case or to establish facts upon a particular case. Most significantly the burden of proof rests with the party who asserts the positive and not on the party who affirms the negative. The maxim is "he who asserts must prove" operates.

Thus, a man cannot be expected to prove negative assertion. This proposition is summed up in Latin maxims as follow: *ei incumbit protabio qui dicit non-qui nagati, cum per rerum neuturam factum negantiis probation nulla sit* ("proof lies upon him who affirms, not upon him who denies, since by nature of things, he who denies a fact cannot produce any proof").[6] On burden of proof generally (civil or criminal), the Supreme Court in the case of *Ogbu* v. *Wokoma*[7] held that:

> It is settled law that in civil cases, the onus of proof is not as fixed on plaintiff as it is on the prosecution in criminal cases. Thus in civil cases, where the general burden of proof in the sense of establishing his case lies on the plaintiff, such burden is not as static as in criminal cases. Therefore, there will be instances in which on the state of pleadings, the burden of proof will be on the defendant also as the case progresses. Such a situation will arise when it may become the duty of the defendant to call evidence on proof or rebuttal of some particular points, which may arise in the case.

Burden of proof in criminal cases

The burden of proof in criminal cases is placed upon the prosecution to establish by credible evidence the guilt of a defendant person beyond reasonable doubt and it remain so and never change, if on the whole, there is any doubt, the defendant may be entitled acquittal. This principle of law is provided under the Evidence Act thus:

> If the commission of a crime by a party to any proceeding is directly in issue in any proceeding civil or criminal it must be proved beyond reasonable doubt.[8]

---

[5] *Phipson on Evidence op. cit.*, 156, Steve Uglow, *Evidence Text and Materials* (Sweet & Maxwell, London, 1997); 59-82

[6] *Nsefik* v. *Manu* (2007) 10 NWLR (pt 1043) 502

[7] *Ogbu* v. *Wokoma* (2005) 24 NSCQR 1 at 19-20

[8] Section 135(1) Evidence Act (Nigeria); see the cases of *Obiakor* v. *State* (2002) 6 SCNJ 193 at 202 and *Igabele* v. *State* (2006) 6 NWLR (pt 975) 100

> The burden of proving that any person has been guilty of a crime or wrongful act is, subject to section 139 of this Act, on the person who asserts it, whether the commission of such act is or is not directly in issue in the action.[9]

For instance in *Bello* v. *State*[10] it was held by the Supreme Court that; in all criminal trial, an accused person does not have to utter a word. The duty is on the prosecution to prove the charge against the accused person beyond reasonable doubt. The prosecution cannot go below proof beyond reasonable doubt to ground conviction of an accused standing trial in Nigerian courts, otherwise the constitutional presumption of innocence will be tempered with and breached, which is null and void.

Instructively, because the rationale behind criminal law is to punish offenders, thus it is common position that it is better for hundreds of criminal to escape punishment than for an innocent individual to be punished. In this perspective, the constitution affords a defendant of criminal allegation the right to be presumed innocent until the otherwise is proved. Therefore, the court will start by presuming a defendant in criminal litigation innocent unless the contrary is proved.[11]

Note that even where a defendant has any justification or excuse at common law such as accident, self-defence or alibi as an answer to a charge, there is no burden on him to establish same in line with the above stated constitutional protection. If proof placed on the accused person to establish,[12] the onus is not on the accused to prove such defence but on the prosecution to disprove. The accused person only has what is called evidential burden, which means duty of adducing evidence or raising a defence of alibi, self-defence, or accident and duty shall be discharged on the balance of probabilities.[13] The Evidence Act provides:

> Where in any criminal proceeding the burden of proving the existence of any facts or matter has been placed on upon a defendant by virtue of the provision of any law, the burden shall be discharged on the balance of probabilities.[14]

---

[9] Ibid Section 135(2)

[10] *Bello* v. *State* (2007) 10 NWLR (pt 1043) 564 at 587-588

[11] See section 36(5) of the Nigerian Constitution, 1999 which provides; "

[12] *Ozaki* v. *State* (1990) 1 NWLR (pt. 124) 94-95

[13] *Ubani* v. *State* (2003) 12 SC (pt i) 1

[14] Scetion 137 Evidence Act (Nigeria)

This can be underscored from the Supreme Court position in *Kadir* v. *State*[15] where it was held that the onus is on the prosecution to negate any defence raised by an accused person who can only be discharged if the prosecution called such quality and quantity evidence as to negate the defence beyond reasonable doubt. Similarly, in *Ogidi* v. *State*[16] the Supreme Court said:

> In our administration of criminal justice the burden is on the prosecution to proof his case against the accused beyond reasonable doubt it is the duty of the prosecution to establish the guilt of the accused person the burden never shift. This is emphasized by the constitutional right of the accused to be presumed innocent as provided under section 36 (5) of 1999 constitution of Nigeria.

Notwithstanding, the prosecution is deemed to have discharged this burden by adducing a prima facie evidence against the defendant. Thereafter, if no evidence is forth coming from the defence, the court decides whether or not the prosecution has proved its case beyond reasonable doubt.[17] This in line with provision of the Evidence Act that:

> If the prosecution proves the commission of a crime beyond reasonable doubt the burden of proving reasonable doubt shifted on to the defendant.[18]

In all cases of crimes the court is duty bound to afford a defendant the constitutional benefit of the presumption innocent, which means that the burden lies on the prosecution and not for the defendant to produce evidence.[19] It is instructive to note that at times an allegation of a crime may be made in civil proceedings and the issue arise upon whom the burden or onus of prove lies and how is discharged. This is explained by the Supreme Court in the case *Akinkugbe* v. *Ewulum*[20] per Aderemi JSC said:

---

[15] *Kadir* v. *State* (1991) 8 NWLR 134-137

[16] *Ogidi* v. *State* (2005) 21 NSCQR 302 at 318

[17] sections 135(2) & 135 (3) Evidence Act (Nigeria)

[18] Ibid. Section 135(3)

[19] *Okorogba* v. *State* (1992) 2 NWLR (pt. 222)

[20] *Akinkugbe* v. *Ewulun* (2008) 6 MJSC 134 at 152

The law is sacrosanct that if the commission of a crime by a party to a civil case is directly in issue, the party must prove it beyond reasonable doubt and such crime must be set down specifically in his pleading.

From the above, it is clear that the burden of proof is on the one who assert, thus, burden of proof of any particular fact lies on the person who wishes the court to believe in its existence. Unless it is provided by any law that the proof of that fact shall lie on any particular person but the burden may in the course of a case shift from one side to the other.[21]

It is of no use for the court to insist on hearing from the defence if after hearing from the prosecution witnesses the court is convinced that no any *prima facie* case is made against the accused, since onus does not shift. Invariably, the defendant is entitled to be discharged even without saying any word. As to who bears the burden of proof, everything will depend on the nature of evidence given before the court and the court can elicit either from the evidence of the prosecution or that of the defence.

The above proposition can be demonstrated from the case of *Uzoka* v. *State*.[22] In that case the accused persons were police officers manning Ibadan-Lagos express way. The deceased and two others came in a pick-up van carrying some tires and invoices suspected to be fake. The police were tricked and allowed them to pass. On discovering by the police that they were tricked, the accused and his colloquies were chased and caught up near Sagamu and were stopped. Conversation ensued and before the deceased gave an answer the accused opened fire on the deceased. The issue for determination was whether the accused defence involves the assertion of an explanation for his conduct namely defence of accidence and or intention. It was held that it is not for the accused to establish the explanation for his conduct. Omololu Thomas JSC observed that:

In my opinion therefore the prosecution has failed to discharge his burden as far as the crime charged is concerned. But this is not the end of the story as do not go off or discharged on its own. And from the totality of evidence before the court it was the accused/appellant's gun that was discharge. The discharge of the gun in the circumstance must be due at least to gross criminal negligence of the accused/appellant. The accused was discharge of murder but a conviction of manslaughter was substituted.

---

[21] Section 136 Evidence Act 2011, see also *Koiki* v. *Magnusson* (1999) 5 SC (pt ii) 30

[22] *Uzoka* v. *State* (1990) 6 NWLR (pt. 159) at 680

Burden of proof upon the Accused

One of the consequences of the presumption of innocence is the placing of burden of proof on the prosecution. It is the responsibility of the prosecution to establish the guilt of the defendant. As a result if the defendant raises a defence then it is the responsibility of the prosecution to disprove the defence, not the responsibility of the accused to prove his defence. If an accused argues that he is unfit to plead then he must prove that unfitness on the balance of probabilities. There are however, exceptions to the rule that the prosecution bears the burden of proof in relation to every issue arising in the course of a criminal trial.

The special circumstances under which the burden of proof is thrown upon the accused person are contained in the Evidence Act and some other statutes. For instance, notwithstanding the fact that a defendant is presumed innocent, the Nigeria Constitution[23] went further to provide that,

> Nothing in this section shall invalidate any law by reason only that the law imposes upon that person the burden of proving particular facts.

The concept of presumption of innocence is fundamental to the Nigerian legal system and is internationally recognised as an essential safeguard. It is the cornerstone of the criminal justice system. An accused person is presumed innocent until proved guilty. The burden of proving this guilt is on the prosecution and it must be proved beyond a reasonable doubt. [24] The presumption of innocence is a vital, constitutionally guaranteed, right of a person accused in a criminal trial and that the right has been expressly recognized in all of the major international human rights instruments currently in force" In fact Article 6(2) of the European Convention on Human Rights states that *"everyone charged with a criminal offence shall be presumed innocent until proved guilty according to law."*

Exceptions

The exceptions to the rule on burden of proof on the prosecution are as explain hereunder.

---

[23] Section 36 (5) Constitution (Nigeria)

[24] Sheppard, S., The Metamorphoses of Reasonable Doubt: How Changes in the Burden of Proof Have Weakened the Presumption of Innocence' (2003) 78, *Notre Dame Law Review,* pp. 1165–250

Defence of Exemption

Here the burden of proving the circumstances bringing a defendant within any exception, exemption or qualification to the law creating the offence with which he is charged is placed upon him.[25] Therefore, where a defendant raises a defence that he is exempted from any law or has any qualification, he has to prove to the court such exemption or qualification. This can be found in the Evidence Act that provides:

> Any exception, exemption, provision, excuse, qualification whether it does or does not accompany in the same section the description of the offence in the legislation creating the offence may be proved by the defendant, provided that the prosecution is not required to specify or refuse any of the exception mentioned in this section and if specified or denied, no proof in relation of the matter so specified or denied shall be required on the part of the prosecution.[26]

Defence of Intoxicant or Insanity

The burden of proof is on the defendant to prove the defence of intoxicant and insanity.[27] In *Nnabo v. State*,[28] the Supreme Court said that:

> The law is that every person is presumed to be of sound mind and to be of sane mind at all times until contrary is provided. The Supreme Court further held that the defence of insanity can only avail the accused person if he can show that he was insane at the time he was committing the offence. It must be prove that at the time of committing the act he was labouring under such defect of reason due to disease of mind and either does not know the nature and quality of the act or he was doing what was wrong section 27 Criminal Code.

> The court further held that it is not for the prosecution to disprove insanity where the accused adduced no evidence of insanity. The prosecution should only prove sanity in reply to the evidence of insanity by the defence.

Arguably, it must be noted that the burden of proof on the defendant relying on defence of insanity is less than the burden cast on the Prosecution to prove his guilt beyond reasonable doubt. The burden of

---

[25] Section 139(1) Evidence Act (Nigeria)
[26] Ibid, Section 141 Evidence Act (Nigeria)
[27] Ibid, Section 137(3) (c) 28 and 29 of Criminal Code and Section 50 of the Penal Code
[28] *Nnabo v. State* (1990) 9 SCNJ 145

proof is satisfied on a balance of probability or preponderance of evidence.[29]

Fundamental points to be kept in view when considering the evidence adduced by a defendant in his defence of insanity "In the consideration of the evidence available to or adduced by an accused person in his defence of insanity, the following radical and fundamental points have been held to be important to be borne in mind and kept in view are:

1. The law presumes every person, including any person accused of crime, sane until the contrary is proved.....(see Section 27 of the Criminal Code).

2. The Prosecution does not set out to prove what the law presumes in its favour.

3. An accused person who raises insanity as his defence has the onus of proving such insanity cast on him. The standard of such proof is not as high as that cast on the prosecution. It is not proof beyond reasonable doubt but it is proof of *reasonable probability, proof sufficient to create a reasonable doubt in the mind of a fair minded jury as to the sanity of the accused*

It is settled law that insanity is a question of fact to be determined by the trial court which ought to take into consideration each and every admissible piece of evidence where available together with the whole of facts and surrounding circumstances of the case. Particularly, it must take into consideration such vital facts like, the nature of the killing, the conduct of the accused before and immediately after the killing and any past history of mental abnormality of the accused.[30]

Knowledge

Any fact, especially within the knowledge of any person the burden of proving that fact lies on him.[31] Example: Where B is arrested by X a (police officer) for driving without driver's licence. The fact B has a driver's Licence is on B and not X (the police officer).

Another example is for instance where defendant X was arrested in possession of packets containing drugs but claimed not be aware of their contents. It is trite that once possession of the packages is proved the onus

---

[29] Section 137 Evidence Act (Nigeria), see also, *Ugwu* v. *State* (2013), Per NGWUTA, J.S.C. (P. 30, Paras. F-G)

[30] *Ani* v. *The State* (2002) 10 NSCQR 461 at 464

[31] Section 140 Evidence Act (Nigeria)

shifts to the defendant to prove lack of knowledge of the contents of the packages.

Thus the prosecution is only obliged to proof that a defendant had, and knew he had a package in his control and that package contained something. The prosecution must also prove that the package contained the controlled substance alleged. However the burden of proof then rested with the accused to bring themselves within the defence.

Burden of proof placed on the defendant by other statutes

a) By virtue of section 417 of the Criminal Code, the burden of proof is on an accused person found in possession by night, without lawful justification any instrument of house breaking to proof such lawful justification.[32]

b) By virtue of section 168 of the Custom and Exercise Act, if a custom officer found a person anywhere in Nigeria in possession of goods which are chargeable with import duties, the onus of proving that the duty had been paid or there was no intention to defraud the government of any duty is cast upon the defendant.

Note however, that where there is doubt in the mind of the court either as to the procedure adopted or failure to address a very important latent issue that assail or circumscribes a criminal case, the court should acquit and discharge the accused person.[33] The Evidence Act provides:

> The burden of proof placed by this Part upon the defendant charged with a criminal offence shall be deemed to be discharged if the court is satisfied by evidence given by prosecution, whether on cross-examination or otherwise, that such circumstances in fact exist.[34]

Burden of Proof in Civil Cases

In civil cases the burden of proof rests on the party who substantially asserts the affirmative, that is, either upon the plaintiff or defendant. It essentially lies on the party against whom judgment of court would be given if no evidence were produced on either side, regard being had to any presumption that may arise on the pleading.[35] The general principle is

---

[32] Ibid See section 167(b)

[33] *Shande* v. *State* (2005) NSCQR (pt ii) 766 at 777

[34] Section 139(2) Evidence Act (Nigeria)

[35] Ibid section 133

expressed in the latin maxim *eiqui affirmat non eque negat imcumba probation.* In *Obasi Bros Merchant Co. Ltd* v. *Merchant Bank of Africa Security Ltd;*[36] the Supreme Court said that:

> The burden of prove in civil cases rest upon the party whether the plaintiff or defendant who substantially asserts the affirmative of the issue. It is an ancient rule founded on consideration of good sense, and it should not be departed from without good reason. It is fixed at the beginning of the trial by the state of pleadings and it is settled as a question of law remaining unchallenged throughout the trial exactly where the pleadings place it and never shifting in any circumstances whatever. If, when all evidence by whosoever introduced, is on the party, who has this burden and has not discharge it, the decision must be against him.

The standard of proof in civil cases is by preponderance of evidence or balance of probability.[37] In *Adeleke* v *Iyanda*,[38] the court held that "*it is a principle of law that civil cases generally are decided on balance of probabilities.*"

Standard of Proof
The standard of proof is a question of law, i.e. it is an abstract norm which (similarly to the existence of certain prerequisites for a given crime) is defined by a legal rule, whereas evaluation of evidence is a question of fact, i.e. in this context it is a decision of how the evidence in a particular case relates to the norm. The standard of proof as the general norm must therefore be distinguished from its application in a particular case.

Criminal cases
The standard of proof in criminal case is proof beyond reasonable doubts. The Evidence Act[39] provides; "if commission of a crime by a party to any proceedings civil or criminal is directly in issue it must be proved beyond reasonable doubt" In *Obiakor* v. *State*[40] it was held that:

> In all criminal prosecution it is the duty of the prosecution to prove its case beyond reasonable doubt it is not essential to prove the case with absolute

---

[36] *Obasi Bros Merchant Co. Ltd* v. *Merchant Bank of Africa Security Ltd* (2005) 22 NSCQR 275 at 284; see also Ewo v. Ani (2004) 1 SC (pt11) 115 at 131

[37] Section 134 Evidence Act (Nigeria)

[38] *Adeleke* v. *Iyanda* (2001) 6 NSCQR (pt 11) 799 at 816

[39] Section 135 Evidence Act (Nigeria)

[40] *Obiakor* v. *State* (2002) 6 SCNJ 193 at 202

certainty but the ingredients of the offence charged must be proved as required by law to the satisfy of the court.

The meaning of the phrase reasonable doubt was given judicial interpretation by *Pat Acholonu JSC*, in *Buhari v. Obasanjo[41] thus* where on the phrase "beyond reasonable doubt" said:

> It is proof that precludes every reasonable hypothesis except that which tends to support, and verily it is a proof that is consistent with the guilt of the accused person or against whom the allegation has been made. Therefore, it can be said that for evidence to attain the height that could bring about a conviction it must exclude beyond reasonable doubt, every other hypothesis or conjecture or proposition or presumption except that of the guilt of the accused. If the evidence is wobbly, thermative or vague, or is compatible with both innocence and guilt, then it cannot be described as being beyond reasonable doubt.

The requirement of standard of proof presupposes that evaluation of evidence in criminal cases can be regarded as determination of whether or not strong evidence of the defendant's guilt has been proved. It must demonstrate that the expressed decision to prosecute is so strong that the prosecutor's statement of the criminal act charged constitutes the only reasonable explanation of the facts of the case; or to express it in more positive terms, that the evidence is so strong that the defendant's guilt may be regarded as certain or proved beyond reasonable doubt. If, on the other hand, the doubt is 'reasonable', the defendant must be declared innocent. A reasonable doubt means in this context a doubt which has the following characteristics:

a. It is rational, i.e. it can be logically justified,
b. It is concrete, i.e. it is founded on the facts of the case, and,
c. It is relative, i.e. the determination of reasonableness has been made within the scope of the nature of the case.

In each case, however, it is required that no concrete doubts are present with regard to the correctness of the prosecutor's statement of the criminal act charged. The required standard of proof is therefore the same in all criminal cases, what distinguishes them is not the quality criterion but the requirement of evidence necessary for the court to be satisfied beyond reasonable doubt.

---

[41] *Buhari v. Obasanjo* (2005) 23 NSCQR 442 at 703

Civil cases

In civil cases the standard of proof is that of preponderance of probability or balance of probabilities which must be in favour of the person asserting the affirmative.[42] In civil cases where there is allegation of crime it must be proved beyond reasonable doubt.

To 'establish by a preponderance of the evidence' means to prove that something is more likely so than not so. In other words, a preponderance of the evidence in the case means such evidence as, when considered and compared with that opposed to it, has more convincing force, and produces in your minds belief that what is sought to be proved is more likely true than not true. This rule does not, of course, require proof to an absolute certainty, since proof to an absolute certainty is seldom possible in any case.[43]

If the evidence is such that the tribunal can say 'we think it more probable than not' then the burden is discharged, but if the probabilities are equal it is not. If the fact finder is inclined to believe the plaintiff more than the defendant, even to the slightest degree, then he or she must find for the plaintiff. In other words, it is sufficient if the plaintiff's allegations are more probably true than not.[44]

Traditionally, the doctrinal discussion has emphasized that the standard of proof in civil matters is expressed by reference to the evidence or probabilities ("objectively"). However, as the judge instructions for the civil standard of the preponderance of the evidence the belief or state of mind of the fact finder is what counts ("produces in your minds belief that what is sought to be proved is more likely true than not true").[45]

The difference between the criminal and civil standard of proof lies in the degree of belief (or conviction) required for finding for the party bearing the burden of proof. This degree of belief is much higher in criminal cases than it is in civil cases.[46]

---

[42] *Adeleke* v. *Iyanda* (2001) 6 NSCQR (pt 11) 799 at 816

[43] Wright, R. W., 'Proving Facts: Belief versus Probability', in H. Koziol and B. C. Steininger (eds.), *Tort and Insurance Law* (Vienna: Springer Vienna, 2009), 80.

[44] Lord Denning in Miller v. Minister of Pensions

[45] T. Anderson, D. A. Schum and W. L. Twining, Analysis of Evidence, Law in Context, (2nd ed., Cambridge: Cambridge University Press, 2006), p. 243;

46 Wright, R. W., 'Proving Facts: Belief versus Probability', p. 81

Chapter 8

Confession and Admission

Confession

Confession is an admission made at any time by a person charged with a crime stating or suggesting the inference that he committed the crime[1] and the confession if voluntarily, are deemed to be relevant facts as against the person who makes it.

Voluntariness thus is a condition precedent to admission of a confession though it does not become inadmissible merely because the maker (defendant) denies having made it.[2] In this respect, a confession contained in a statement made to the police by a person under arrest is not to be treated differently from any other confession, so long as it is made voluntarily.[3] Similarly, it is immaterial to whosoever the confessional statement is made as shown in the Supreme Court position in *Nwachukwu* v. *State*[4] that:

> The person to whom a confession or admission is made by a party to a proceeding or accused person is generally immaterial and a statement in the nature of confession or admission made by a person, even if it is to himself and over heard by someone else may be received in evidence if it amount to a confession or admission.

When a confession is direct, positive and unequivocal as to the admission of guilt by a defendant, the statement is enough to ground conviction of the accused.[5] In *Alao* v. *State*[6] the Supreme Court propounded six (6) tests for the determination of the truthfulness of a confessional statement thus:

---

[1] Section 28 (1) and (2) Evidence Act (Nigeria)

[2] *Hehimiyien* v. *State* (2013) LPELR 20764 (CA)

[3] *Shade* v. *The State* (2005) 6 SC (pt ii) 1 at 6.

[4] *Nwachukwu* v. *State* (2007) 11 MJSC 29

[5] *Salawu* v. *State* (1971) NMLR 735; *Yusuf* v. *State* (1976) 6 SC 164; *Olalekan* v. *State* (2001) 18 NWLR (pt 746) 793 and *Nwachukwu* v. *State* (2007) 11 MJSC 29 at 62

[6] (2015) All FWLR (775) 262 at 282

1. is there anything outside the confessional statement to show that it is true;
2. is the confessional statement corroborated;
3. are the relevant statements of fact made in it true, as far as can be tested;
4. was the accused who had the opportunity to commit the offence;
5. is the confession possible; and
6. is the confessional statement consistent with other facts which have been ascertained? [7]

Retraction of a confessional statement by a defendant in evidence on oath is of no moment as it does not adversely affect the situation unless it can be shown to be involuntarily made.[8]

It is however desirable to have outside the accused person's confession, some corroborative evidence no matter how slight. Especially where circumstances which could make the confession probable (true and correct) are not generally disposed to without testing the truth thereof.[9] The position will however be different where the admissibility of a confessional statement is challenged on the ground that it was not made voluntarily. In the later case it will be incumbent on the trial court to call upon the prosecution to establish the voluntariness of the statement by conducting a trial within a trial.[10]

Where a confessional statement appears to court and in its opinion, made pursuant to an inducement, threat or promise in relation to the offence charged is not admissible. Particularly a promise from a person in authority that the defendant would gain an advantage is not relevant and admissible.[11]Iguh JSC in *Nwachukwu* v. *State*[12] on admissible confessional statement said:

> ...a free and voluntary confession of guilt by a prisoner, whether judicial or extra judicial, if it is direct and positive and is duly made and satisfactorily proved, is sufficient to warrant a conviction without any corroborative evidence. So long as the court is satisfied with the truth of a confession

---

[7] Ibid p. 282 – 283; *Golden Diebe* v. *State* (2007) All FWLR (pt 363) 83; *Onochie* v. *The Republic* (1966) NMLR 307; *Ikpase* v. *A. G. Bendel* (1981) 9 SC 7; *Akpan* v. *State* (1992) 6 NWLR (pt 248) 439; *Nwachukwu* v. *State* (2002)

[8] *Onyejekwe* v. *State* (1992) 4 SCNJ 19; *Akpan* v. *State* (2001) 7 SCNJ 567

[9] *Iliyasu* v. *State* (2015) All FWLR (pt 793) 1961 at 1983

[10] See *Gbadamosi & Anor.* v. *The State* (1992) 11/12 SCNJ 268, *Ojegele* v. *State* (1988) NWLR (Pt.71) 414

[11] Section 29 Evidence Act (Nigeria)

[12] Iguh JSC in *Nwachukwu* v. *State* (2002) *op. cit.*

which is free and voluntary and itself fully probable, such confession alone is sufficient to support conviction without corroboration.

In *Kolawole* v. *the State*[13] the Supreme Court held that"...a voluntary confession of guilt, if fully consistent and probable, and is coupled with a clear proof that a crime has been committed by some persons, is usually accepted as satisfactory evidence on which the court can convict. It is now trite that a confessional statement is admissible if it is direct and positive and relates to his own acts, knowledge or intention, stating or suggesting the inference that he committed the crime charged. In quite a number of cases decided by this court, where on the production of a confessional statement or any statement, it is challenged by the defence on the ground that the accused did not make it at all, such an objection does not go to the admissibility of the statement and the trial court is entitled to admit the confession in evidence as a statement the prosecution claims to have obtained from the accused person and thereafter to decide or find as a matter of fact whether or not the accused person in fact made the statement at the conclusion of the trial.[14]

Admission

Admission is defined in *N.A.S.L.* v. *UBA*[15] as a statement made by one of the parties to an action which amounts to a prior acknowledgement by him that one of the material facts relevant to the issues is not as he now claims. The position is that facts admitted require no further evidential proof. Admission on the other hand is:

i).   Statement made by a party to the proceeding, or by an agent to such party, whom the court regarded, in the circumstance of the case, as expressly or impliedly authorized by him to make them are admission.[16]

ii).   Statement made by parties to suits, suing or sued in a representative character are not admission unless they were made while the party making them held that character.[17]

---

[13] (2015) LPELR 24400 (SC), (P. 48, paras D-E); See also *Ogoala* v. *The State* (1991) 2 NWLR (Pt. 175) 509, *Federal Republic of Nigeria* v. *Dairo* (2015) All FWLR (pt 776) 486 and *Adeyemi* v. *State* (2015) All FWLR (pt 790) 1201 at 1230

[14] See *Godwin Ikpasa* v. *Bendel State* (1981) 9 SC 7 at 28, *Pele Ogunye* v. *The State* (1999) 5 NWLR (Pt.604) 518.

[15] *N.A.S.L.* v. *UBA* (2005) 23 NSCQR 127 at 139

[16] Section 21(1) Evidence Act (Nigeria)

[17] Ibid; Section 21(2)

According to the Act statement made by under-listed persons is admissible if made while the person that makes it is in the character wherein it was made:

i)   Statement made by a person who has any pecuniary or proprietary interest in the subject matter of the proceeding and who made the statement in their character of persons so interested.[18]

ii) Statement made by persons from whom the parties to the suit have derived their interest in the subject matter of the suit.[19]

iii) Statement made by persons whose position or liability it is necessary to be proved as against any party to the suit.[20]

iv) Statement made by a person to whom a party to the suit expressly referred for information in reference to a matter in dispute.[21]

In civil matter admission does not operate as estoppel nor is conclusive against a person to whom it is made. In *Nigeria Bank of Commerce* v. *Integrate Gas into*[22] per D.O. Edozie said:

> It is trite law that in civil cases admission by a party are evidence of facts asserted against but not in favour of such a party, although, they are not estoppels or conclusive against the party against whom they are tendered. Admissions are therefore no estoppels and are not conclusive against a party against whom they are tendered. The party has the right to explain the circumstance or show that the admissions were due to misconception or ignorance of the real facts or other circumstances which sufficiently explain them.

Admissions generally are not conclusive proof of the matters admitted, but they may operate as estoppel under the provision of *part viii* of the Evidence Act.[23]

---

[18] Ibid, Section 21(3)(a)

[19] Ibid, Section 21(3)(b)

[20] Ibid, Section 22

[21] Ibid, Section 23

[22] *Nigeria Bank of Commerce* v. *Integrate Gas into* (2005) 21 NSCQR 240 at page 261-262 said per D.O Edozie

[23] *Oladiti* v. *Raimi* (1999) 10-12 SC 109; *Nicholas* v. *Daniel* (1999) 5 SC (pt i) 114; *Fagunwa* v. *Adibi* (2004) 19 NSCQR 415 at 434; *Saburi Motors* v. *Royal Enterprises* (2004) 4 SC (pt ii) 67

Chapter 9

Corroboration

The law does not prescribe any number of witnesses a party should produce before he gets judgment in his favour. The general rule is that a court may attach whichever weight it chooses to any of the items of evidence presented before it, and it does not have to look for corroboration. In *Usiobafo* v. *Usiobafo*[1] the Supreme Court said:

> In the evidential scene in the context of probative value, it is not the number of witnesses that matter but the quality of the evidence given. And so, a situation may arise where a single witness gives credible evidence while a number of witnesses may not because they are bundle of contradictions. Therefore emphasis should be on the quality of evidence given rather than the quantity.

For instance in the case of *Ngorka* v. *State*[2] the appellant complained on the issue of the prosecution failure to call a vital witness, Caroline Azubuike listed as a witness in the prosecution's list of witnesses. The Supreme Court stated the position of the law as follows: "it is sufficient to say in this connection; that the law imposes no obligation on the prosecution to call a host of witnesses. All the prosecution needs to do is to call enough material witnesses to prove its case and in doing so, it has discretion in the matter. If the evidence of a witness is very essential to the defence of the accused, it is for the accused to call him. He should not expect the prosecution to call the witness since the prosecution is not expected to perform the function of the prosecution and the function of the defence.[3]

In another example of *Ogbodu* v. *The State*,[4] it was held that the prosecution was not bound to call the son of the Appellant who was present when the crime was committed if the prosecution felt that his

---

[1] *Usiobafo* v. *Usiobafo* (2005) 21 NSCQR 746 at 759
[2] (2014) LPELR 22532 (CA)
[3] *Asariyo* v. *The State* (1987) 4 NWLR (PT 67) 709; and *Nwaeze* v. *State* (1996) 2 NWLR (PT 425) 4 at 15, see also *Adje* v. *The State* (1979) 6 – 9 SC 18 @ 28
[4] (1987) 2 NWLR (PT 54) 20

evidence was not vital to its case. The defence might call him if it desired, nothing stopped it from doing so.[5] It therefore follows that the law does not impose an obligation on the prosecution to call some specific witnesses to prove its case. All it needs do is to call enough material witnesses to prove its case. It does not lie in the mouth of the defence to urge the prosecution to call a particular witness.[6]

However, as a general rule, in criminal cases a person can be convicted of any offence on the evidence on oath of a single adult witness just as a plaintiff in civil cases can so succeed on the evidence of a single witness without any supportive evidence.

Definition

Corroboration evidence pertain to any independent testimony which confers in some material particular to the evidence in need of corroboration and which if in criminal case must implicate the accused person. In every piece of evidence requiring corroboration what is to be look for is any independent testimony in support of the evidence. That:

a) the offence is committed.
b) the accused is implicated in it.[7]

However in any proceedings Criminal or civil there is[8] no particular number of witnesses stipulated by law to prove or disprove any. In fact a defendant can be convicted of any criminal offence on the evidence of a single adult witness, just as a plaintiff in civil suit can succeed on the evidence of a single witness without confirmation by the testimony of another person, this position of law, without prejudice, is not without any exceptions, this shall be discuss latter.

Nature of corroboration

The word 'corroboration' is derived from the Latin word 'corroboratus', part of the word 'corroborare' which has itself been derived from another Latin word 'robust'. It is also meant "to support or enhance the believability of a fact or assertion" by the presentation of additional information that confirms the truthfulness of the item. The evidence which is used for the purpose of corroboration is termed as corroborating

---

[5] *Eze* v. *State* (2013) LP ELR CA/OW/2011
[6] See *Olanyinka* v. *State* (2007) 9 NWLR (PT 1040) 561; *Nwaeze* v. *State* (1996) 2 NWLR (PT. 425) 1 at 15
[7] *Ogunbayo* v. *The State*, ibid.
[8] Section 200 Evidence Act (Nigeria)

or corroborative evidence which may be defined as that kind of "evidence which strengthens, adds to, or confirms already existing evidence." Hence, corroborative evidence is some evidence other than the one which it confirms, establishes, or makes more certain. It is additional in nature but confirmatory in quality.

The most important case regarding the nature of corroborative evidence is *Rex v.. Baskerville*[9] which is followed in numerous common law jurisdictions across the world Nigeria inclusive. The judgment in this case was pronounced by the Court of Criminal Appeal, United Kingdom, with respect to approver's evidence. But taking into account the rationale and cogency of the judgment, it is treated as a precedent in all circumstances requiring corroboration of any evidence. Its relevant portion explicating the rules of corroboration is reproduced here in detail:

1. The corroboration must be by some evidence other than that of an accomplice; and, therefore, one accomplice's evidence is not corroboration of the testimony of another accomplice.

2. The corroborative evidence must be evidence which implicates the accused, that is, which confirms in some material particular not only the evidence that the crime has been committed, but also that the accused committed it. In other words, the corroboration must be both as to the *corpus delicti* and as the identity of the accused.

3. It is not necessary that the story of the accomplice should be corroborated in every detail of the crime, since, if this were so, the evidence of the accomplice would be unnecessary.

4. The corroboration need not be direct evidence that the accused committed the crime; it is sufficient if it is merely circumstantial evidence of his connection with the crime.

In *Sale Dagayya v. State*,[10] corroborative evidence is explained thus:

> Corroboration entails the act of supporting or strengthening a statement of a witness. Corroboration does not mean that the witness corroborating must use the exact or very like words, unless the matter involves some arithmetic's. That will reduce the straightforward adjectival matter to a pedantic level.

---

[9] (1916) All ER Rep 38 or (1917) 12 CAR 81
[10] *Sale Dagayya v. State* (2006) 25 NSCQR 775 at 799

Corroboration is not a technical term of art. It means no more than evidence tending to confirm, support and strengthened other evidence sought to be corroborated. Corroboration need not consist of direct evidence that the accused person committed the offence, or does it amount to a confirmation of the whole account given by the witness, provided it corroborates the evidence in some material to the charge[11].

In any cases where corroborative evidence is required and such evidence is not gotten, any verdict/judgment recorded in the absent of such corroboration will be quashed. Similarly, evidence which is not corroborated if treated as such any verdict recorded in the circumstance, will be quashed. The followings are circumstances usually, in criminal cases where the court may, on issue of evidence, require corroboration.

1) **Evidence of an accomplice**

According to the Act,[12] an accomplice is a competent witness against a defendant and conviction is not illegal merely because it proceeds upon uncorroborated testimony of an accomplice. In the case of *Utteh* v. *State*[13] the Supreme Court opined that in law, the term accomplice includes, a participant in the actual crime charged (participant criminals) or a receiver of property in respect of which the accused is accused of stealing or where a person is charged with a particular offence in a particular occasion and evidence is admissible and has been admitted of having committed crime of identical type on other occasion, a proving system or intent or negative accident, parties to such other similar offences.

A witness is only an accomplice if he is a person who might, on the evidence before the court against an accused person, be convicted of the offence for which the accused is charged. Generally, an accomplice is a suspect witness hence, the requirement of corroboration is important to his testimony. In *Onuka* v. *State*,[14] the Supreme Court said that:

> Corroboration must be independent testimony, which affects the accused by connecting or tending to connect him with the crime. In other word it must implicates him that is, which confirm that the crime has been committed but also the prisoner committed it.

---

[11] *Ogunbayo* v. *State* (2007), *op. cit.*

[12] Section 198 Evidence Act 2011

[13] *Utteh* v. *State* (1992) 2 NWLR (pt 223) 257 at 269

[14] *Onuka* v. *State* (1988) 7 SC (pt 11) 25 at 41-42

Note that, the fact that a person knows that another was going to commit a crime (i.e. witness the commission of a crime) and does not prevent its commission or a person is a victim of a crime cannot be regarded as an accomplice. The term accomplice includes:

i)   Person who is participant *criminis* in respect of the actual crime charged, whether as principals or accessories, before or after the fact, in Felony, or persons committing, or procuring or aiding and abetting in the case of misdemeanours.

ii) On trial for larceny or receivers as regards the thieves from whom they receive the goods

iii) Where a person is charged with a specific offence on a particular occasion, and evidence is admissible and has been admitted, of his having system or intent, accident parties to such other similar offence.[15]

Since an accomplice is a suspect witness whose evidence requires corroboration, it is not for the trial court to pick and choose which part of his evidence could be believed and which part requires corroboration. The court can convict once it is satisfied that the accomplice's evidence is reliable even without corroboration but, once he is in doubt as to the truth of the evidence, it is unsafe to convict an accused person based on any part of that evidence. The reason being that one lie in an accomplice testimony makes the whole of his evidence suspect.[16]

In R v. Linzee[17] where two Army officers were charged before a court-martial with assaulting a suspect in their custody, and in addition to the alleged victim, the prosecution called a soldier who had witnessed and was said to have been a participant in the assault, it was held by the court Martial Appeal Court that it was proper to regard the soldier as a tainted witness and that there should be a warning and the desirability of looking for corroboration of his evidence.

The kind of corroboration required is not confirmation by independent evidence of everything the accomplice relates, his evidence would be unnecessary if that were so. What is required is some independent testimony which affects the prisoner by tending to connect

---

[15] Archbold (1962): *Criminal Pleading Evidence and Practice.* Sweet & Maxwell, London. Page 531-534
[16] *Amadi* v. *State* (1993) 8 NWLR (pt 644) at 661
[17] *R. v. Linzee*

him with the crime.[18] Note that the wife of an accomplice is not necessarily an accomplice, and her evidence may therefore be good corroboration.[19]

2) Tainted Witness

A tainted witness has been classified as one who is either an accomplice or by the evidence he gives, whether as a witness for the prosecution or defence, may and could be regarded as having some purpose of his own to serve.[20] In *Ojo* v. *Gharoro*,[21] tainted is defined per Niki Tobi JSC as:

> The word tainted in the context of our law of evidence is bereft of it ordinary 20th century dictionary daily meaning of impurity, undesirability, decay, infection and what have you. On the contrary, it has and carries the element of bias for the particular reason of nearness or closeness in relationship and deliberate and undeserved expression of favour to a particular person.

The evidence of a tainted witness must be regarded with considerable caution and the trial court should warn himself before a verdict of guilt is made on the uncorroborated evidence of such witness. His evidence cannot be allowed to stand, if founded upon scraggy reasoning or perfunctory performance, it is so in all criminal cases and particularly in capital offences.[22]

In *Orisakwe* v. *State*,[23] the Supreme Court accepted the reason of the trial Courts that, the fact that PW i is coming from the same village with the deceased, does not rendered his evidence inadmissible, nor was the evidence of PW I tainted by reasons only of his coming from the same village as the deceased.

3) Evidence of Co-defendant

The evidence of an accomplice is different from that of a co-defendant whose evidence though on his own behalf incriminates another co-accused, thus it does not render him an accomplice.[24] Such evidence will be considered in the special circumstance in which it is given. See the case of See *Okosi* v. *State*.[25] The Evidence Act[26] provides:

---

[18] Archbold *op. cit.*, page 532-533

[19] *R.* v. *Wills* (1916) 1 K.B. 933

[20] *Ali* v. *State* (2015) All FWLR (pt 796) 559 at 589 and *Oguonzee* v. *The State* (1998) 4 SC 110 at 133

[21] *Ojo* v. *Gharoro* (2005) 25 NSCQR 712 at 744

[22] *Igabele* v. *The State, op. cit.*

[23] *Orisakwe* v. *State* (2004) 5 SC (pt ii) 140 at 166-167,

[24] Section 199 Evidence Ac 2011

[25] *Okosi* v. *State* (1989) 2 SC (pt1) 126 at 133

Where defendants are tried jointly and any of them gives evidence on their own behalf, which incriminates a co-defendant, the defendant who gives such evidence shall not be considered as an accomplice.

The Supreme Court in *Oyakhire* v. *State*[27] on the evidence by an accused person (defendant) which implicate a co-accused person (defendant), said:

The settled principle is that a statement made by an accused person to the police may amount to an admission of the offence for which he is charged and such a statement and the fact admitted therein are admissible only against the maker of the statement not a co-accused. But where the accused goes into the witness box and repeats, on oath, the contents of his statement to the police, they become evidence for all purposes, admissible in law and can be acted upon by the court against a co-accused.

It is however said that the court is expected to regard such evidence of a defendant against a co-defendant, suspiciously and with caution and must be admitted with circumspection. The law does not impose a duty on the court to warn itself before convicting on it; however, such evidence requires no corroboration. The requirement of warning applies only to the evidence of an accomplice within the provision of section 198 (1) of the Evidence Act. Thus, evidence of co-accused on oath is admissible against other accused persons as a particular case may present.[28]

4) Evidence of Children

There is no age limit given for a person to be called as a witness. Competency generally is not a matter determined on age but that of intellectual capability of a person to testify in court and it is for the court to determine.[29] Children of any age are competent to give evidence provided they are possessed of sufficient intellect to be able to understand the question put to them and give rational answer to the question.[30]

Children can give evidence on oath if they understand the nature of oath and can also give an un-sworn testimony if they are unable to

---

[26] Section I99 Evidence Act 2011, Ozaki v. State (1990) 1 NWLR (pt 124) 92 at 117

[27] *Oyakhire* v. *State* (2006) 10 MJSC 62 at 74 paragraphs A-D

[28] *Kolawole* v. *State* (2015) All FWLR (pt 778) 864 at 882, see also *Oyakhire* v. *State* (2006) 12 SCM (pt i) 369 or (2007) All FWLR (pt 344) 1

[29] *Solola* v. *State* (2005) 22 NSCQR pt I 254 at 280-281

[30] Section 175) Evidence Act 2011

understand the nature of oath but understand the importance of telling the truth.[31]

Sworn evidence of a child needs no corroboration especially when he has attained the age of 14 years.[32] Although, such evidence may require that court warn itself with great caution in admitting it. However, where a child of 14 deliberately give false evidence in such circumstances the he would, if the evidence had been given on oath have been guilty of perjury, he shall be guilty of an offence under section 191 of the Criminal Code and on conviction shall be dealt with accordingly.[33] Un-sworn evidence of a child requires corroboration; a person cannot be convicted of an un-sworn evidence of a child unless such evidence is corroborated. The Supreme Court in *Solola* v. *State*[34] held that the evidence of a child given on oath need not be corroborated. "A child who does not understand the nature of an oath is even competent to give unsworn evidence if in the opinion of the court such a child is possessed of sufficient intelligence to justify the reception of his evidence.

Though, it is trite that an un-sworn evidence of a child cannot be corroborated by an un-sworn testimony of another child.[35] But the sworn evidence of another child or an adult can serve as sufficient corroboration.

5) Agent Provocateur

An Agent provocateur is a person, specifically a police or other witness who did not know that an offence was going to be committed but in fact provoked or joined in the commission of it in order that the accused may be apprehended. An agent provocateur is only a spies and such a person is called agent provocateur. The evidence of an agent provocateur must be suspect and it is the duty of a court which admit such evidence to warm itself that it is not safe to convict upon it expect it is corroborated. In *R* v. *Murphy*,[36] Lord McDermott CJ said:

> Detection by deception is a form of Police procedure to be directed and used sparingly and with circumspection, but as a method it is as old as the constable in plain cloth and regrettable though the fact may be, the day has not yet come when it would be safe to say that the law and order could

---

[31] Ibid, Section 209

[32] Ibid, Section 209(2) & (3)

[33] Section 209(4) Evidence Act 2011

[34] (2005) 11 NWLR (pt 937) 460

[35] *Okoh* v. *State* (1988) 1 NWLR (pt 69) 172

[36] *R* v. *Murphy* (1953) N I 138 at 147 to 148, Lord Mc-Dermott CJ

always be enforced and the public safely protected without occasional resort to it.

6) Treason and Treasonable Offences.

By virtue of the Evidence Act[37] no person charged with treason and treasonable offences mentioned in section 40, 41 and 42 of the Criminal Code can be convicted for the offence except:

i. Evidence is given in open court of two witnesses one witness to one over act of the accused each; or
ii. The accused plead guilty to the offence charged.

7) Other Offences Requiring Corroboration
i) Perjury

The Evidence Act[38] requires an independent evidence of a witness to sustain conviction of concealing or prosecuting the commission of perjury. Section 119 of the Criminal Code provides that:

> A person cannot be convicted of counselling the offence of perjury (as define in section 117) or counselling or procuring the commission of it upon the uncorroborated testimony of one witness.

ii) Exceeding Speed Limit

The Evidence Act[39] provides that a person charged under Road Traffic Act with driving at a speed greater than allowed maximum cannot be convicted solely on the evidence of a witness, such evidence must be corroborated by independent evidence.

However an innovation introduced in the 2011 amended Act is to the effect that evidence of a duly authorized officer of a relevant authority who at the time of the commission of the offence operating any mechanical, electronic or other device for recording of speed of a moving vehicle, the record of such device being additionally tendered against the defendant shall not require further corroboration.[40]

iii) Sexual Offences

A person cannot be convicted of named sexual offences upon the uncorroborated testimony of a witness. The offences are, defilement of girl

---

[37] section 201(1) & (2) Evidence Act 2011

[38] Ibid, Section 202

[39] Section 203 Evidence Act 2011

[40] Ibid, proviso to section 203

under 13 years, 16 years of age and of an idiot, either by threat or fraud or administering drugs. (See sections 221, 223 and 234 of the Criminal Code or section 273 of the Penal Code.) *Okoyomon* v. *State* [41] *State* v. *Maigemu* [42] H.C

It is now settled that evidence in corroboration must be an independent testimony, direct or circumstantial, which confirm in some material particular, not only that an offence is committed but that the accused committed the offence. [43] However, corroboration may be desirable (especially in sexual offences) it is settled that whether a particular evidence, need be corroborated is for the trial judge to decide. In *Ogunbayo* v. *State*,[44] the Supreme Court cited the case of *Reekie* v. *The Queen* [45] said:

> In the case of a sexual offence it is eminently desirable that the evidence of the complainant should be strengthened by other evidence implicating the accused person in some material particular. It is true that there is nothing in law to prevent the court from convicting on the corroborated evidence of the complainant, but it is an established rule that the presiding judge must direct himself and the assessors in such a case on the desirability of their being corroboration of the complainant's evidence.

In *Ogunbayo* v. *The State*,[46] the accused person was charged and convicted for the rape of a 13 years old girl (PW 1) without her consent contrary to section 357 of the Criminal Code cap 29 Vol. 11 Laws of Ogun State. The evidence of PW 2, the father of the complainant and PW 5 Medical Doctor were admitted to have provided adequate corroboration for the conviction of the accused. The Supreme Court said that corroboration is not a strict rule of law that an accused person charged for rape cannot be convicted on the uncorroborated evidence of the prosecution.

Dying Declaration

It pertinent to note that the well settled rule of law is that a dying declaration may form a sole basis of conviction without any corroboration

---

[41] *Okoyomon* v. *State* (1973) 1 All NLR (pt.1) 16

[42] State v. Maigemu (1978) NMLR 117 H.C

[43] Ogunbayo v. State *op. cit.*

[44] Ibid p. 46 Para B-F

[45] *Reekie* v. *The Queen* (1954) 14 WACA 501 at 502

[46] *Ogunbayo* v. *The State*, pp. 45 - 46

provided the same inspires judicial confidence.[47] On the other hand, the courts seek corroboration of dying declarations when they appear to be motivated, prompted or tainted by any other infirmity. This judicial practice is termed as a rule of prudence which has acquired sanctity almost equivalent to a rule of law. It only declares relevancy of dying declaration as an admissible piece of evidence. Most of the time declarations of dying men are hearsay evidence because they are not generally adduced in the court by their makers. The Act provides:

> A statement made by a person as to the cause of his death, or as to any of the circumstances of the events which resulted in his death in cases in which the cause of that person's death comes into question is admissible where the person who made it believed himself to be in danger of, approaching death although he may have entertained at the time of making it hope of recovery.[48]

> A statement referred to in sub-section (1) of this section shall be admissible whatever may be the nature of the proceeding in which the case of death comes into question.[49]

Arguably, it is trite law that it is not safe to convict a defendant merely on the evidence furnished by a dying declaration without further corroboration because such a statement is not made on oath and is not subjected to cross-examination and because the maker of it might be mentally and physically in a state of confusion and might well be drawing upon his imagination while he was making the declaration.

Confessional Statement

It is settled law that a defendant in criminal cases can be convicted solely on his confessional statement. Notwithstanding, it is desirable to have some evidence outside the confession of the defendant which would make it probable that the confession was true in other words corroborated.

In *Popoola* v. *State*[50] the accused was alleged to have raped one Bukola Adebajo, a secondary school girl within the school farm on or about the 29th day of January 2004. The Prosecution called four witnesses

---

[47] See section 40 Evidence Act 2011

[48] Section 40(1) Evidence Act 2011

[49] Ibid Section 40(2), Dying declaration by virtue of section 45 of the Evidence Act 2011 (as amended) is also relevant a will, that testator as to his testamentary intention where the will is lost, whether the existing will is genuine or not.

[50] (2013) LPELR 20973 (SC)

and tendered two exhibits 1 - 1A, the Yoruba and English version of the appellant's confessional statement and Exhibit 2, the Medical Report. The appellant did not testify but called two witnesses who gave evidence on his behalf.

The Supreme Court while upholding the judgment of lower court held that: In the case at hand, where there is no medical report but the confessional statement of the appellant is direct, cogent, positive, and in fact lends strong support to the evidence of the Prosecutrix. It stands to reason therefore that the corroboration desired is in place and the requirement of the law complied with. The confessional statement of the appellant corroborates the evidence of the PW1 that the Appellant raped her. In a trial for rape, evidence of corroboration could come from the accused himself.[51]

Similarly, in *Thomson v. State*[52] which is an appeal against the judgment of the Robbery and Firearms Special Tribunal sitting at Ikot Ekpene, Akwa Ibom, the accused were convicted and sentenced to death for the offence of armed robbery contrary to Section 1(2)(a) of the Robbery and Firearms (Special Provisions) Decree No.5 of 1984. One of the main issues on appeal was whether an accused person can be convicted on his confessional statement. The court held that there is no evidence stronger than a person's own admission or confession. Such a confession is admissible in evidence. The court further held that although an accused person can be convicted solely on his confessional statement, it is desirable to have some evidence outside the confession which would make it probable that the confession was true.[53]

Generally it is trite and by rule of law or practice requiring an evidence to be corroborated or regulation the manner in which uncorroborated evidence is to be treated, a statement rendered admissible as evidence by the Act shall not be treated as corroboration of evidence given by the maker of the statement.[54]

---

[51] See also the cases of *Ezeigbo* v. *The State* (2012) NCC 7 436 at 447 para. H." Per NGWUTA, JSC (P. 31, Para. E) See *Iko* v. *The State* (2001) SCNJ 39.

[52] (2013) LPELR 20206

[53] *Dibie* v. *State* (2007) 9 NWLR Pt.1038 Page 30, *Nwaebonys* v. *State* (1994) 5 NWLR Pt.343 Page 130

[54] See section 34(2) Evidence Act 2011

Chapter 10

Competency and Compellability

Who may be a witness in court? The answer to this question involves the consideration of two concepts, Competency and Compellability. Every person is a competent witness under our judicial system, thus, such a person is fit and proper person to testify. However a witness may be competent but not compellable. Therefore, when a person is non-compellable witness, it is at his discretion to give evidence or he may refuse to give evidence unless where a legislation provide for compelling a witness to appear and testify in court.[1] But all compellable witnesses are competent witnesses. If any compellable witness refused to give evidence he can be convicted for contempt of court. The Evidence Act provides that:

> All persons shall be competent to testify unless the court considers that they are prevented from understanding the questions put to them, or from giving rational answers to those questions by reason of tender year, extreme old age, disease whether of the body or mind or any other cause of the same kind.[2]

Notwithstanding the fact that a witness is competent or even compellable it is expedient that such witness possess credible character to testify as to the facts only within is knowledge. The credibility of a witness depends upon the following:

i) **Knowledge**
Although a witness may be perfectly disinterested or even a man of integrity and veracity, and has a just sense of the moral obligation of the oath he has taken, still the degree of credit to be given to his testimony depends upon his real knowledge of the facts to which he testifies. A man may be deceived in a fact from depriving his knowledge of it through a

---

[1] Section 246 – 254 Administration of Criminal Justice Act, 2015 (Nigeria)
[2] Section 175 Evidence Act 2011

false medium or from defects in his power of observation or from his attention being occupied more by the circumstances accompanying it, that by the fact itself at the time of its occurrence, or from a thousand other circumstance, which if candidly stated, might be satisfactorily answered and accounted for by the other party so as to convince the witness himself that he laboured under a mistake.[3]

Where there is doubt the question then is, whether the evidence given by a witness is not founded on some misconception, it is the duty of the counsel who cross-examine him to question him as to the sources of his knowledge, his reason for believing the fact to be as he has stated, his reasons for recollecting it, the circumstances attending its occurrence, whether it was light or dark, and whether it was near or distance at the time it occurred, and the like, so that the jury may be able to judge the degree of confidence they should place in the witness testimony.[4]

Disinterestedness

A witness to be perfectly credible must not be in the slightest degree biased or partial to one party or the other. Therefore, if it appears that the witness is prejudiced against the party against whom he appears, or has before expressed sentiments indicative of such prejudice, or if it appears that a prosecution is pending against him for the same or a similar offence, and he comes to disprove some of the facts charged in the indictment against the prisoner all these are circumstance which detract proportionately from his credit that the prosecutor will derive an advantage from a conviction of the prisoner if not objection to his competency: as has been seen it goes to his credit. A father is a competent witness for his son, and a son for his father; and husband and wife for each other but the interest arising from the relationship detracts proportionately from the credit of the witness.[5]

ii) Integrity

The fact that a witness has been convicted of crime affects only his credit, and not his competency. Whether a witness has or has not been convicted, witnesses may be called to speak as to his general character, although not as to any particular offence of which he may be guilty: in order to impeach the credit of a witness for veracity, witnesses may be called by the other

---

[3] Archbold, *op. cit.,* page 560

[4] Ibid. pages 560-563

[5] Ibid. pages 560-563

side to prove that his general reputation is such that they would not believe him upon his oath. They need not have heard him on oath.[6]

The credit of a witness may be impeached by the means of the evidence of persons who swear that from their knowledge of the witness believe him to be unworthy of credit on his oath. The impeaching witness may not, in examination-in-chief, give reasons for his belief, but he may be asked for his reason in cross-examination, and his answers in cross-examination cannot be contradicted.[7] This principle does not permit the calling by one side of a doctor to discredit the evidence of a witness for the other side by testifying that he was suffering from a disease of the mind so that his testimony was unreliable.[8]

All other questions the answers to which would have a tendency to expose him to a criminal charge, or to a penalty or forfeiture, as to which for the purpose of impeaching a witness's character not only may be put, but must be answered, although the answers may degrade the witness's character. If the witness be examined as to the offence or improper conduct imputed to him, and deny it, his denial is conclusive. If the question is merely collateral to the point in issue, and it is not permissible to call witnesses or offer other evidence to contradict him but if the question is relevant to the point at issue, and the witness denies the thing imputed, he may be contradicted.[9]

iii) Veracity

The character of a witness for habitual veracity is an essential ingredient in his credibility of a man who is capable of uttering a deliberate falsehood, this, in most cases capable of doing so under the solemn sanction of an oath.[10] If, therefore, it appears that he has formerly said or written the contrary of that which he has now sworn (unless the reason of his having done so is satisfactorily accounted for), his evidence should not have much weight with a jury; and if he has formerly sworn the contrary, the fact (although no objection to his competency) is almost conclusive against his credibility.[11]

---

[6] Ibid. pages 560-563
[7] See section 223 Evidence Act 2011
[8] Ibid. pages 560-563
[9] Ibid. pages 560-563
[10] Section 223 (a) Evidence Act 2011
[11] Ibid. pages 560-563

While previous statement may be put to an adverse witness to destroy his credit and thus render his evidence given at the trial negligible, such statements are not admissible evidence of the truth of the facts stated. This principle applies equally to statements made on oath as well as to the un-sworn statement

A consideration of the probability of a fact also may aid in forming a judgment of the credit that should be given to a witness for veracity. If he tells of a fact having occurred which is contrary to common experience and observation, it will require that his integrity, veracity, and means of knowledge should be indisputable to induce any one to believe it: but if, on the contrary, the fact stated by him is very likely to have happened, persons may be induced to believe it, without very scrupulously inquiring into his character for integrity, veracity, etc. the strength of the evidence should always be great in proportion to the improbability of the fact to be established by it.[12]

The incompetency that can affect a witness from testifying in court includes immaturity or defect of intellect and it may arise from infancy, idiocy or drunkenness, these disabilities and conditions are:

i) Infancy
It is not so much age that is the determinant factor of infancy's competency to testify because, a person of the same age, may differ in their mental capacity. Thus, the court will first decide, whether an infant understand question put to him and give rational answer to it to determine his competency.[13] This is usually done, by putting series of questions to the child, like, what happened to a person who tells lies? What is the importance of oath? Thus, if the child gives rational answer to the question, he is a competent witness.[14]

ii) An Idiot
is a person who does not possess understanding from his birth and such in-competency is permanent he cannot be a competent witness.

iii) Deaf and Dumb
A deaf and dumb cannot speak but, he may give evidence in any manner in which he can make it intelligible. For example, by writing or by signing in

---

[12] Ibid. pages 560-563
[13] Sections 175 & 209 Evidence Act 2011
[14] Section 209 Evidence Act 2011

the open court. So is dumb person is competent a witness, evidence given shall be deemed to be oral evidence. The Evidence Act provides:

> A witness who is unable to speak may give his evidence in any other manner in which he can make it intelligible, as by writing or by signs; but such writing must be written and the signs made in open court. Evidence so given shall be deemed to be oral evidence.[15]

iv) A Lunatic (Insane Person)
This is an incompetent witness because of the loss of his reason but, his competency may be restored during lucid intervals. A person of unsound mind is not incompetent to testify unless he is prevented by mental infirmity from understanding the questions put to him and give rational answer to them.[16]

v.) Drunkard
A drunkard is competent to be called as a witness when the effect of the drug/alcohol disappears, except he does not understand the questions put to him nor gives irrational answer to them.

vi) Extreme old Age
Aged persons are competent witnesses except they do not understand question put to them and give rational answer to them.

Competency of Various Classes of Witnesses
1) Children Evidence
There is no age limit given for a person to be called as witness, competency is not a matter of age but that of intellectual capability.[17] Two conditions determine the competency of a child to testify as a witness in court, that is:

1. the child understands the questions put to him and give rational answer to the questions;[18]
2. the child understands the nature of oath and the importance of telling or speaking the truth.[19] The court can determine this by asking him questions about God and what happens to any person who tells lies on oath.

---

[15] Section 176 (1) & (2) Evidence Act, *op. cit.*

[16] Section 175 (2) Evidence Act 2011

[17] *Solola* v. *The State* (2005) 22 NSCQR pt I 254 at 280,

[18] Section 175 (1) Evidence Act 2011

[19] Ibid. Section 209

The two conditions are rightly enforced in civil proceedings if the child does not understand the nature of oath is incompetent to be called a witness. In criminal proceedings the matter is classified as follows:[20]

Sworn Evidence

Sworn evidence of a child under the Evidence Act[21] is admissible on oath if the child understands the nature of oath or even the duty of speaking the truth. The fact that a child cannot give evidence on oath because he does not understand the nature oath does not make him incompetent witness.

However, a defendant cannot be convicted of an offence on an un-sworn testimony of a child unless the testimony is corroborated by some other evidence implicating the accused person. The corroborative evidence must be from an independent source.[22]

In *Solola* v. *The State*[23] the accused was charged and convicted of murder, the testimony of a 12 years old child who sworn on the Holy Quran to the effect that the accused, his father asked him to call the deceased his playmate (a boy with hunch back) under the pretext that they wanted to send him on an errand, that he conveyed the message to the deceased in the presence of his father and delivered the deceased to the accused and leave. After waiting for sometimes without seeing the deceased he approached his father the 3ʳᵈ accused but was told that the deceased had left for home, he also testified that he observed that his father who used to give him ₦5.00 for school then gave ₦10.00 that day. The accused contention on appeal was that the evidence of the child DW ii by the combined effect of sections 155 and 183 were not admissible. The Supreme Court held that, *"the evidence needs no corroborative evidence and as such he is a competent witness."*

The un-sworn evidence of a child requires corroboration under sub-section (3) of section 209. A child gives un-sworn evidence if he does not understand the nature of oath. The un-sworn evidence which also requires corroborative evidence cannot be used to corroborate the un-sworn evidence of a young child.

In *Sambo* v. *State*,[24] the accused a legal practitioner was charged with committing the offence of rape against a 10 years old girl contrary to

---

[20] Section 175 & 209 Evidence Act op cit

[21] Ibid.

[22] Ibid. see, Section 209(3)

[23] *Solola* v. *The State* (2005) 22 NSCQR (pt i) 254

[24] *Sambo* v. *State* (1993) 6 NWLR (pt 300) 399

section 283 of the Penal Code. At the trial the prosecution called four (4) witnesses, the child, the complainant, her sister, IPO and a medical officer. The un-sworn evidence of the child who knows the nature of oath but does not know the consequences of telling lie affirmed to speak the truth. His testimony was admitted in evidence and the evidence of the other three witnesses was held to have provided necessary corroboration. In *Sale Dagayya* v. *State*[25] the Supreme Court per Niki Tobi, J S C held that:

> Once a witness is a child, by the combined effect of section 154 and 182 (1) & (2) of the Evidence Act, the first duty of the court is to determine first of all, whether the child is sufficiently intelligent to understand the questions he may be asked in the course of his testimony and to be able to answer rationally. This is tested by the court putting on him preliminary questions which may have nothing to do with the matter before the court, (2) if, as a result of these preliminary questions, the court comes to the conclusion that the child is unable to understand the questions or to answer them intelligently, then the child is not competent witness within the meaning of section 154 (1). But if the child passes this preliminary test then the court must proceed to the next test as to whether, in the opinion of the court, the child is able to understand the nature and implication of an oath. (3) if after passing the first test, he fails this second test, then being a competent witness, he will give evidence which is admissible under section 182 (2), though not on oath. If, on the other hand, he passes the second test so that, in the opinion of the court, he understands the nature of an oath, he will give evidence on oath.[26]

2) Sovereign and Diplomatic Immunity

The Sovereign, Foreign sovereigns and those entitled to diplomatic privilege are competent witness but not compellable. In Nigeria the following class of persons enjoys immunity to testify in court they include, Head of States (President), Military Governors (Governors) and Foreign Diplomats. Under section 175 (1) Evidence Act they are competent but not compellable witnesses to attend court during the tenure of their office under section 308 (1) of the Nigeria Constitution 1999. But they can waive the immunity granted. This type of immunity is also granted to UN, WHO, ILO, EU, and AU members.

---

[25] *Sale Dagayya* v. *State, op. cit.*

[26] Niki Tobi, J S C at pages 793-794

(3) Official and Privilege Communication

i) No Justice, judge, Grand Kadi, or President of Customary Court and Appeal shall be compelled to answer questions as to his own conduct in court as to anything which came to his knowledge in court except upon:

   a.   An order of the High Court State or Federal Capital Territory Abuja or Federal High Court; or
   b.   May be examine as to matter that occur in his presence while he was so acting[27]

(ii) No Magistrate or police officer or any other public officer authorized to investigate or prosecute offences under any written law, or public officer employed or about the business of any branch of public revenue shall be compelled to say where he got any information as to their commission of any offence and or offence against public revenue.[28] In *Igabele* v. *State* [29] the Supreme Court said:

> An investigation police officer is not bound to disclose his source of information this is the purport of section 166 Evidence Act.

iii) No one shall be permitted to produce any unpublished official records relating to the affair of the State or give evidence derived from them, except:

   a.   Upon the direction of the President and or Governor, or
   b.   Permission of the head of the department concerned.[30]

iv) No public officer shall be compelled to disclose communications made to him in official evidence when he considers that the public interests would suffer by the disclosure.[31] How where he is directed by court to so do it shall be disclose to the judge alone in chambers.[32]

4) Legal Practitioner

is a competent witness but shall not be compellable to disclose any communication made to him in the course and for the purpose of his employment.[33] Similarly he cannot be compelled to disclose the content or

---

[27] Section 188 Evidence Act 2011

[28] Ibid. Section 189

[29] Igabele v. State (2006) 6 MJSC 96 at 110

[30] Section 190 Evidence Act 2011

[31] Ibid. Section 191

[32] See the proviso to section 191

[33] Ibid. section 192

condition of any document he became acquainted or disclose any advice given to his client all in the course of and for the purpose of his professional engagement between him and his client, unless and except with his (client's) consent. The rule applies to interpreters and the clerk of legal practitioners.[34] The principle justifiably applies to communication made either:

a. To enable the client obtain or to give legitimate legal advice, event or content of a document.

b. With reference to litigation which is actually taking place or was in the contemplation of the client.[35]

In similar paradigm a client shall not be compelled to disclose communication between him and his legal practitioner unless he offers himself as a witness.[36] The general principle on which the statutory provision of legal practitioner and client confidentiality is grounded was stated by Holden J[37] thus:

> Every client is entitled to feel safe when making disclosures to his solicitors or counsel, and there are cases establishing firmly that counsel cannot be called to give any evidence which would infringe the client's privilege of secrecy.

However, where such communication is in furtherance of an illegal purpose or facts observe by the legal practitioner in the course of his employment that any crime or fraud has been committed, he is competent to give evidence or disclose such communication 192(1), (2) & (3) Evidence Act. In *Abubakar* v. *Chuks*[38] the Supreme Court per Onnoghen said:

> It is very clear that the principle of client's privilege is based on secrecy of the information disclose by the client to his solicitor or advice given by the solicitor to the client to the effect that what is done in secret must remain secret...

---

[34] Section 193 Evidence Act 2011

[35] Ibid. Section 192 (1)

[36] Ibid., section 195

[37] *Iris Winifred Horns* v. *Robert Richard* (1963) NNLR 67 at 68 quoted in *Abubakar* v. *Chuks* (2008) 2 MJSC 190 at 215.

[38] *Abubakar* v. *Chuks* (2008) 2 MJSC 190 at 215-216

On the principle behind the privilege, Aderemi JSC[39] further observed, it has become a well settled principle that no counsel or solicitor shall accept a brief where it is clear that the services to be rendered flow out of or are closely connected with the previous services he had rendered to the opposing side. So also is that a solicitor is not permitted to disclose the contents or the conditions of any document with which he has become acquainted on the course of and for the purpose of such employment. This privilege is that of the client and not of the legal practitioner and as such, it can only be waived by the client. The right of confidentiality guaranteed by this provision is absolute. This is so, because even the courts cannot generally, compel counsel to disclose information given to him by his clients in confidence.

5) Bankers
A banker or an officer of a bank is a competent but not compellable witness in any legal proceedings the bank is not a party to produce banker's book, the content of which can be proved in any manner provided under sections 89 and 90 of the Evidence Act. Or to appear as a witness to prove the matters, transaction and account recorded, unless by order of the court made for special cause.[40]

Competency of Parties in Court Proceedings
i. Civil proceedings
The Nigerian Evidence Act[41] provides for situations when spouses may be competent and compellable witnesses. Section 178 provide thus:

> Subject to the proviso contained in section 165 of this Act, in all civil proceedings the parties to the suits and the husband or wife of any party to the suit shall be competent witness.

ii. Criminal proceedings
A defendant is a competent and compellable witness for the prosecution or the defence for certain offences. But in all other criminal cases, the accused is an incompetent witness for the prosecution.[42] The Act provides:

---

[39] Ibid. pages 221 -223

[40] Section 177 Evidence Act 2011

[41] Ibid., Section 178

[42] Section 179 Evidence Act 2011

Subject to the provision of this part of this Act, in criminal case the accused person, and his or her wife or husband and any person jointly charge with him and tried at the sense time, is competent to testify.

iii. Competence of a person charged to give evidence

The Evidence Act[43] provides that; every accused person charged with an offence shall be competent witness for the defence at any stage of proceedings whether the person is charged solely or jointly with any other person. However this provision is subject to two limitations. An accused person shall not be called as a witness except:

a. Upon his own application;[44] and
b. When the only witness of fact of the case called by the defence is the person charged he shall be called as a witness after the close of evidence for the prosecution.[45]

Instructively a defendant charged and being a witness in pursuance to this section may be asked question during cross-examination notwithstanding the fact that it would tend to implicate him as to the offence charged. [46]

In a criminal trial where an accused person is before the court without a counsel, he cannot be compelled to give evidence, the court should inform him of the three alternative opened to him that:

i). He may make a statement from the witness box or other place (dock) where other witnesses give their evidence.[47]
ii). He may give evidence from the witness box after being sworn and he is liable to cross-examination.[48]

The general position of the law is that where two or more persons are charged with the commission of an offence, and the evidence against all the defendants is the same or similar, to the extent that the evidence is inextricably woven around all the accused persons, the discharged of one must as a matter of law, affect the discharge of the others, this is because if one or more of the accused persons is discharged for want of convicting evidence, that must automatically affect all the others in the light of the

---

[43] Section 180 of the Evidence Act 2011
[44] Ibid.; Section 180 (a)
[45] Ibid.; Section 180 (c)
[46] Section 180(b) Evidence Act 2011
[47] Ibid.; Section 180 (d)
[48] Ibid.; Section 160 (e)

fact that the evidence against all the defendants is tied together, like Siamese twins at the umbilical cord with the mother.[49]

iv. Evidence of husband or wife, when compellable

However, in a specific situation a husband or wife either of is competent and compellable witness[50], this may include the following situations:

i. When a person is charged with an offence under any of the enactments contained in sections 217, 218, 219, 221, 222, 223, 224, 225, 226, 231, 300, 301, 340, 341, 357, to 362, 369, 370 and 371 of Criminal Code[51] or

ii. With an offence against the property of his her wife or husband[52] or

iii. With inflicting violence on his or her wife or husband the wife or husband of the person charged shall be competent and compellable for the prosecution or defence with or without the consent of the person charged. [53]

This does not mean that the husband or wife is compellable to disclose any communication made to his wife during the marriage. So also is the fact that failure of the husband or wife to give evidence shall not be subject of any comment by the prosecution.

---

[49] *Ebiri* v. *The State* (2005) 12 SC (pt ii) 29 at 35

[50] Ibid., Section 182(2)

[51] Ibid. section 182(1)(a)

[52] Section 182(1)(b); Evidence Act 2011, this is however subject to section 36 of the Criminal Code which provides 'when husband and wife of a Christian marriage are living together, neither of the incurs any criminal responsibility for doing or omitting to do any act with respect to the property of the other, except in the case of an act or omission of which an intention to injure or defraud some other person is an element, and except in the case of an act done by either of them when leaving or deserting, or when about to leave or desert, the other. Subject to the foregoing provisions husband and wife are each of them criminally responsible for any act done by him or her with respect to the property of the other, which would be an offence if they were not husband and wife, and to the same extent as if the were not husband and wife. But in the case of a Christian marriage neither of the can institute criminal proceedings against the other while they are living together.

[53] Ibid. section 182(1)(c)

Chapter 11

Opinion Evidence

An opinion is what a person thinks, belief or inference about something or a witness's view about facts in dispute, as opposed to personal knowledge of facts themselves.[1] Witnesses may testify only to what they themselves did, said, heard or witnessed.[2] The expression also means what people in general think about something. It also conveys a professional judgment on the part of a professional.[3] As a rule a witness who is himself a party to the suit or a third party is only allowed to testify as to the facts known to him. Consequently as a general principle the law provides:

> The opinion of any person as to the existence or non-existence of a fact in issue or relevant to the fact in issue is inadmissible except as provided in section 68-76 of this Act. [4]

Therefore when a witness appears before a court of law he is only entitled to the facts known to him and not his opinion. He can only speak of what he knows and not what he believes. However there are cases where the court may not be properly equipped to draw the inferences without the help of those who have acquired skill and experience on the particular subject matter, under this circumstance, the evidence, based on opinion of an expert becomes relevant.

An expert therefore is 'a person with the status of an authority (in a subject) by reason of special skill, training or knowledge; a specialist'. Similarly, an expert witness has been described as 'one who has made the subject upon which he speaks a matter of particular study, practice or observation: and he must have a particular and special knowledge of the subject.'[5]

---

[1] Bryan A.G Black's *Law Dictionary*, *op. cit.*, page 1126

[2] Dennis, *op. cit.* pages 699-706

[3] Dagayya v. State (*supra*) 791-792.

[4] Section 67 Evidence Act 2011

[5] See the Shorter Oxford English Dictionary.

Persons who take on the role of an 'expert witness' has a different function. The job of the 'expert witness' is not simply to articulate their client's position; it is to assist the decision maker (a court, tribunal or other similar body) with the information about the specialist area which is necessary before a decision can be made. The expert cannot usurp the functions of the jury or judge sitting as a jury, any more than a technical assessor can substitute his advice for the judgment of the Court. It was held in *Davie* v. *Magistrates of Edinburgh*[6] that the duty of the expert witness:

> "...is to furnish the Judge or jury with the necessary scientific criteria for testing the accuracy of their conclusions, so as to enable the Judge or jury to form their own independent judgment by the application of these criteria to the facts proved in evidence. The scientific opinion evidence, if intelligible, convincing and tested, becomes a factor (and often an important factor) for consideration along with the whole other evidence in the case, but the decision is for the Judge or jury. In particular the bare ipse dixit of a scientist, however eminent, upon the issue in controversy, will normally carry little weight, for it cannot be tested by cross-examination nor independently appraised, and the parties have invoked the decision of a judicial tribunal and not an oracular pronouncement by an expert."[7]

It is these two limitations on the role of the expert witness which therefore define what the duties and responsibilities of an expert witness are. The primary duty of the expert witness is to the court and not to the client. The specialist skill, knowledge and experience of the expert witness is therefore to be used to assist the court. That gives rise to a number of consequences. If the witness is putting themselves forward as an expert it follows that the opinions that person expresses should be within that individual's area of expertise. They must be satisfied that the information they present is accurate and complete, that they have taken into account all relevant matters and not taken into account irrelevant matters. So far as taking into account all relevant matters is concerned, this also includes matters which might be contrary to the opinion they have formed. The factual information underlying any opinion evidence must be based on actual knowledge or on identifiable source of information. Where it is possible for there to be a range of reasonable opinion on any matter this should be acknowledged. The opinions the expert expresses should be the

---

[6] 1953 SC 34.
[7] Ibid; Lord President Cooper, page 40.

expert's own, formed independently, and not the views of either the client or of any other person. Where an expert witness is being asked to express a view about the actions of another professional or specialist then the expert witness must also understand the correct legal test which the court applies to that professional or specialist's acts.

However there are exceptions to this general principle of law contained in the Evidence Act.[8] The exceptions are broadly divided into opinion of expert and opinion of non-expert.

Competency of Experts

The term expert has been defined as, a person especially skilled in the subject he testified. Thus a person may be considered an expert in a field if he can show to the court that he possessed particular knowledge of same, it is the duty of courts to determine the competency of the expert. The Supreme Court in the case of *Sowemimo* v. *State*[9] held that:

> ...In certain cases evidence of opinion of an expert is relevant but he must be called as a witness and must state his qualification and satisfy the court that he is an expert on the subject in which he is to give his opinion and he must state clearly the reason for his opinion.

A person can be regarded an expert on a particular field even though he did not acquired systematic tutoring in the field but, provided that he has sufficient knowledge or experience in the particular field of study in which he is put up as an expert. (Note that the court must challenge the evidence of an expert when it is against the usage of mankind or it is against common sense. Note also that when there is a conflict of opinion of an expert and or among experts it is the duty of the court to resolve the conflict.)

In *Sowemimo* v. *State*[10] the witness gave two conflicting evidences as to his skill in a case of murder before the court, on one strength he said he was a pathologist and on strength, gave evidence that he was not but undergoing training to become a pathologist. The court held that the evidence of a medical doctor does not bind the court *particularly when the evidence is contradictory in some material facts.*

---

[8] Sections 68 to 76 of the Evidence Act 2011

[9] Sowemimo v. State (2004) 4 SC (pt 11) 20 at 31-34

[10] Sowemimo v. State (2004) 4 SC (pt 11) 20 at 31-34

Also in *Egesimba* v. *Onuzuruike* [11] the Supreme Court on the acceptance of expert evidence held that:

> The law does not require expert evidence in all cases for proof. An expert witness is only necessary if by the nature of the evidence scientific or other technical information, which is outside the experience, and daily common knowledge of the trial judge as judge of fact is required.

Responsibilities of an Expert Witness

It is instructive to note that an expert giving evidence in court has a purpose or purposes to serve. On this spectrum the case of *Makita (Australia) Pty Ltd* v. *Sprowles (2001) 52 NSWLR 705 at 739* which enumerated the list of duties and responsibilities of expert witnesses is relevant. Justice Heydon JA stated the conditions or duties as follow:

i.   Expert evidence should be the independent product of the expert uninfluenced as to form or content by the exigencies of litigation.

ii.   An expert witness should provide independent assistance to the Court by way of objective unbiased opinion in relation to matters within his expertise

iii. An expert witness should never assume the role of an advocate.

iv.   An expert witness should state the facts or assumptions upon which his opinion is based. He should not omit to consider material facts which could detract from his concluded opinion.

v.   An expert witness should make it clear when a particular question or issue falls outside his expertise.

vi.   Where expert evidence refers to photographs, plans, calculations, analyses, measurements, survey reports or other similar documents, these must be provided to the opposite party at the same time as the exchange of reports.

Against the above listed duties, an expert witness appearing before court to give evidence is only entitled to *the facts known to him, not his opinion* and he can give evidence only of what *he knows and not what he believes.* This represent the general rule, however there are cases where courts may not be properly equipped to draw inferences from facts and evidence before it without the help of those who have acquired skill and experience on the particular subject matter, under this circumstance, the evidence, based on opinion is admissible.

---

[11] Egesimba v. Onuzuruike (2002) 9-10 sc 1 at 59

These exceptions are specifically listed in the sections 68 to 76 of the Evidence Act, 2011, and can be divided broadly into opinion of expert and opinion of non-expert.

Relevance of Expert Opinion

The statutory framework for the admissibility of expert opinion requires that the opinion must first be relevant; that is, 'if it were accepted, [the opinion] could rationally affect (directly or indirectly) the assessment of the probability of the existence of a fact in issue in the proceeding'. [11] Under the Evidence Legislation, the opinion rule excludes evidence of an opinion 'to prove the existence of a fact about the existence of which the opinion was expressed'.[12] The exception to this exclusionary rule is s 79(1) which provides:

> If a person has specialised knowledge based on the person's training, study or experience, the opinion rule does not apply to evidence of an opinion of that person that is wholly or substantially based on that knowledge.

The importance of relevance could be highlighted on the basis of the fact that the tendering party is required to identify the fact which the opinion proves or assists in proving because the opinion rule assumes that evidence of an opinion is tendered to 'prove the existence of a fact'.

Failure to identify the assumptions for the opinion, or prove the factual basis or reasoning used to reach a conclusion, could make an opinion irrelevant and therefore inadmissible.[14] An opinion based on factual assumptions that are not established by evidence could render the opinion irrelevant to assess the existence of a fact in issue in a particular case; for example, an opinion about slipperiness based on the assumption of a wooden surface is clearly irrelevant in a case where the evidence unequivocally establishes that the plaintiff slipped on concrete.

Similarly expert opinion which satisfies s.79 can be excluded at the trial judge's discretion if its 'probative value' is outweighed by the danger that the evidence is 'unfairly prejudicial', 'misleading or confusing', or might 'cause or result in undue waste of time'. The lack of a factual or reasoning basis for an expert's opinion could give rise to the operation of ss 135 or 137. For example, an opinion based on factual assumptions that are not established by evidence could 'mislead' the trial of fact. An expert opinion which does not disclose its reasoning process could place the cross-examiner in a position where their task is to impeach the expert's conclusions without knowing how those conclusions were reached. This could risk the expert validating their opinion in cross-examination and create 'unfair prejudice'.

Therefore in Nigeria, the unreliability of an expert's opinion is not considered in assessing the opinion's 'probative value' the evidence is taken at its highest. For example, the credibility of the expert as a witness is not used to assess the 'probative value' of the expert evidence for the purpose of ss 135 and/or 137, although the unreliability of an opinion would be a factor used by the trial of fact to assess the opinion.

Instructively, an expert as earlier on stated is a person skilled in the subject matter he is called upon to testify not necessarily based on academic qualification or training but by experience, thus he is required, as enumerated in the case of *Shell P.D Co. Nig. Ltd* v. *Tiebo;*[12]
i) to state his qualification and experience;
ii) furnish the court with necessary criteria and scientific reason for his opinion.

These requirements assist the court in forming its own independent judgment and failure to satisfy the court with the basis of an opinion will affect the weight to be attached to the evidence. In contrast to lay witnesses, expert witnesses are permitted to express opinions and to draw inferences from facts.

An expert witness does not perform the function of advocate for the party relying on the opinion of the expert. Far from supporting the "client", such advocacy will tend to discredit the expert and taint or nullify the whole of that expert's evidence. Therefore expert opinion is relevant in the following situations.

1) Foreign Laws
The opinion of expert as to foreign law is relevant and admissible, but he must be a person well acquainted with such law. The Evidence Act does not define foreign law but this may include, Laws of Common Wealth Nations and portions of English laws that have not been received in the Nigeria Legal System. A person need not belong to the legal profession to be so called expert on foreign laws.[13]

---

[12] (1999) 6 NWLR (pt 299), p. 330
[13] Section 58 (1) Evidence Act, *op. cit.*

2) Science and Arts

Opinion expert on the point of science or art is relevant provided, he is especially skilled in the field where he is called to testify. Note that there is presumption of competency to determine the cause of death by medical doctor or nurse.[14]

The expert must give evidence on how he acquires his skill. In *Titidabale* v. *Sokoto Native Authority*[15] the evidence of a dispenser, who did not give evidence of his skill in determining the cause of death was held to be inadmissible.

In *Shonubi* v. *People of Lagos State*[16] Forensic medicine was described as a branch of medicine concerned with law, especially in criminal law. The forensic pathologist is doctor who is specialized in the examination of bodies when circumstances suggest death was unnatural. Forensic scientist use laboratory method to study body fluid (such as blood and semen) found on or near the victim and compare them with those from the suspect, they are also trained in ballistic and identification of fibers from clothing. In addition forensic expert may advice on blood group and genetic fingerprinting in legal investigation. What court requires of expert may be summed up as; impartiality, reliability, clarity, service which is to command credence and result must obviously be known to be completely objective and impartial. In the instance case,[17] pw 6 a trained forensic officer testified that preliminary test was conducted and he participated in it, he classified it and the result match only the appellant Kunle Shonubi. The procedure, he explained that he did some stages here in Nigeria and sent the exhibit to London for the other part and result was sent to the Police forensic service in United Kingdom who interpreted it compare it with what was done in Nigeria, the result came back with Kunle Shonubi's name among Nine (9) suspects. Forensic report of Pw 6 Exhibit E was tendered and admitted in evidence. The Supreme Court on whether it is expedient for the presence of an expert in court held:

> It is not necessary for forensic expert who analysis the crime and issue the report to come to court in person to tender the document for it to be admitted. What govern admissibility is relevance and the fact that the

---

[14] Ogunzee v. State (1998) 4 SCNJ 226

[15] Titidabale v. Sokoto Native Authority (1964) 1 Nig. L.T 123

[16] (2015) All FWLR (pt 801) 1422

[17] Ibid.

document is properly tendered in the form and by the person it should be produced through and if it is not opposed and consented to by the court such a party cannot object on appeal.[18]

3) Opinion as to native law and custom is relevant provided the person expressing the opinion is expert on the subject.[19]

The Evidence Act provides that the opinion of:

i)   Expert on such native law and custom is acceptable; or

ii) The evidence of native chiefs;

iii) Books and manuscripts recognized by native as legal authority will also be relevant. [20]

4) Opinion expressed in textbook

The opinion express in textbook is relevant and admissible in court; this can be done by tendering the textbook. Where an opinion is expressed and the person who expresses the opinion cannot be called, the party tendering it must put it through other expert on the same field. However this position seems not to be necessary by the combined effect of section 126(d) of the Evidence Act, 2011. It provides that:

> The opinions of experts expressed in any treatise commonly offered for sale, and the grounds on which such opinions are held, may be proved by the production of such treatise if the author is dead or cannot be found, or has become incapable of giving evidence, or cannot be called as a witness without an amount of delay or expense which the court regards as unreasonable.[21]

5) Opinion as to handwriting or finger impression

The opinion of expert and non-expert are relevant and admissible. The expert must be specifically skilled in identifying handwriting.[22]

In the realm of non-expert opinion, opinion of a person who is acquainted with the handwriting in dispute of party against whom is been contested is admissible. [23] A person is acquainted with handwriting according to the law is that the person:[24]

---

[18] Ibid., p. 1457

[19] Sections 70 & 73 Evidence Act, *op. cit.*

[20] Adedibu v. Adewoyin (1951) 13 WACA 199

[21] Section 162(d) Evidence Act 2011 (Nigeria)

[22] Section 72 Evidence Act 2011

[23] Ibid; Section 72(1)

[24] Ibid; Section 72(2)

1. Had seen the other person writes
2. Had received document purporting to be written by the other person in answer to document written by him or written under his authority to that person
3. Had document purporting to be written by that person habitually submitted to him

Irrespective of the above, a court may compare the handwriting with the one admitted.[25] This procedure is also applicable in prove of signature, seal or finger impression.[26] Similarly, the court may extract from any person in court for the purpose of comparing such writing, finger impression or seal.[27] Note that where a defendant does not give evidence he may not be so direct to write such word or figure or to make finger impression for the purpose of any comparison in court.

6) Opinion as to age
A witness may state his own age or state a fact by which it may be infer that a person is of certain age. This is relevant in civil and criminal cases (i.e. to determine whether an defendant is criminally liable).

7) Opinion as to relationship
When the court has to form an opinion as to the relationship between one person to another the opinion expressed by conduct as to such relationship or any person who is a member or family or any special means of knowledge on the subject matter is relevant fact and admissible.[28] Such opinion shall not be relevant to prove a marriage in proceeding for a divorce or in a petition for damages against an adulterer or in prosecution for bigamy.

8) Opinion as to Usage or Tenets
When court has to form an opinion as to usage and tenet the opinion of person having special knowledge on the usage and tenet is relevant and admissible as to the:
i) usage and tenets of anybody or family or charitable foundation;
ii) the Constitution and government of any religious or charitable foundation; or

---

[25] Ibid; Section 101(1)

[26] Teich v. Northern International market Ltd. (1987) 4 NWLR (pt 56) 44.

[27] Section 101(2)

[28] Section 75 Evidence Act 2011

iii) the meaning of words or terms used in particular districts or by particular classes of people.[29]

---

[29] Section 74 Evidence Act 2011

Chapter 12

Evidence of Character

In the decisions that we make about the conduct of others in daily occurrence of human lives, character is perhaps the most significant single factor. Human being's conduct and reaction go about their every day business on their expectations of what others will do. It is common sense that when asked to judge a man's conduct on a particular occasion, to enquire how he behaves on other occasions his character becomes an issue. Thus, character is simply a compendious summary of a person's past actions, good and bad. The conclusion about a man action may be expressed in terms of moral and mental qualities, but these are in turn determined only by what a person says and does. The law is principally concerned with the character of a person in the estimation of those who know him, which is his reputation.[1]

Character evidence is a term used in the law of evidence to describe any testimony or document submitted for the purpose of proving that a person acted in a particular way on a particular occasion based on the character or disposition of that person. The logical function of character evidence may be shown from the following illustration:

> If a man is accused of stealing, his reputation as a thief logically weighs heavily against him. There is a strong tendency, however, that character evidence will produce a dislike or hatred for the party against whom the evidence is tendered which may result in an adverse finding to vindicate the judges feeling and in disregard of culpability.

Under the Nigerian law, the word character has no single, well defined, technical and all encompassing meaning. Sometimes it means actual character, disposition, what a person is, and sometimes it means reputed character, reputation, community opinion as to character, what a person is supposed to be. When used in the sense of nature or disposition, sometimes it means the entire character, the "sum of the inherited and

---

[1] John Sopinka, Character Evidence in Civil Cases, (2014), 18(2) McGill Law Journal pp. 246 -257 at p. 247

acquired ethical traits which gave to a man his individuality," as when we speak of good or bad character generally; and sometimes it means a single trait of character, as when we speak of a person's honesty, chastity, or veracity. Sometimes it has reference to moral traits or qualities and sometimes not.

It is probably true, however, that in law, as in common speech, the word character usually means moral character, and actual character, as distinguished from reputation; though from the fact that reputation is in law the chief means of proving character, the words character and reputation are frequently but improperly used as if they were synonymous.

Character is what a person is, reputation is what the community thinks he is; but evidence of the general reputation of a person affords the basis for an inference as to the actual character; for behind a good reputation usually there lies a good character, and behind a bad reputation a bad character. Character evidence may be quite unrelated to the fact in issue thus it may have an overwhelming prejudicial effect on a party. It was perhaps because of this possible prejudicial effect on judges or justices that for a period of time in English legal history the use of character evidence was in disrepute, epitomized by the abolition of its use in criminal cases.

Evidence of Character in civil cases

Like any concept, the word character has no single and all encompassing well defined technical meaning. Sometimes it means actual character, disposition, what a person is, and sometimes it means reputed character, reputation, community opinion as to character, what a person is supposed to be.[2]

When used in the sense of nature or disposition, sometimes it means the entire character, the "sum of the inherited and acquired ethical traits which gave to a man his individuality," as when we speak of good or bad character generally; and sometimes it means a single trait of character, as when we speak of a person's honesty, chastity, or veracity. Sometimes it has reference to moral traits or qualities and sometimes not.[3]

---

[2] Torrance, David, "Evidence of Character in Civil and Criminal Proceedings" (1903). *Faculty Scholarship Series.* Paper 3923; http://digitalcommons.law.yale.edu/fss_papers/3923 HeinOnline -- 12 Yale L.J. 352 1902-1903
[3] Ibid.

It is probably true, however, that in law, as in common speech, the word character usually means moral character, and actual character, as distinguished from reputation; though from the fact that reputation is in law the chief means of proving character, the words character and reputation are frequently but improperly used as if they were synonymous.[4]

In civil cases facts must be proved by independent evidence, evidence of character of parties is generally irrelevant except where such character is relevant. The Act provides:

> In civil cases the fact that the character of any person concerned is such as to render probable or improbable any conduct imputed to him is irrelevant, except in so far as such character appears from facts otherwise relevant.[5]

Essentially, character is what a person is, reputation is and what the community thinks he is; but evidence of the general reputation of a person affords the basis for an inference as to the actual character; for behind a good reputation usually there lies a good character, and behind a bad reputation a bad character.

Evidence of character is admissible, under certain limitations and for certain purposes in civil as well as in criminal proceedings; and it is the object of this article to state briefly some of the prevailing rules governing its admissibility, and incidentally to note some of the variations from those rules prevailing in some jurisdictions.[6] The character sought to be proved may be that of a party to the proceeding, or that of a witness therein, or that of a person neither a witness nor a party to the proceeding.[7] Again character may be offered in evidence either:

1. to prove its existence as one of the facts in the case, or
2. to prove its existence as circumstantial evidence tending to prove some other fact therein.[8]

In the one case, character is a disputed fact which existence may be proved by evidence, but which is neither offered nor used as evidence of any other fact. While in the other case, it is offered as the basis of an inference to

---

[4] Ibid.
[5] Section 78 Ibid.
[6] Ibid.
[7] Ibid.
[8] Ibid.

some other facts in the case. The rules relating to the admissibility of character evidence may be conveniently considered as follows:

i.   Those relating to its admissibility to prove the character of a party or of a third person as one of the facts in the case;

ii.   Those relating to its admissibility to prove the character of a party or of a third person as circumstantial evidence in the case; and

iii.   Those relating to its admissibility to prove the character of a witness.

Examples of where Evidence of Character is Relevant

1) Where in the case of defamation the defendant set up a defence of justification, in that case the character of the plaintiff may become an issue.[9] In actions of slander and libel various questions have arisen with respect to the admissibility of evidence of character. The character of the defendant in such cases is not generally regarded as being in issue. However, the defendant could prove the plaintiff bad character in mitigation of damages. Whether the plaintiff in this class of cases can give evidence of his own good character in the first instance, "not to sustain it from attack but to prove its excellence," is a question upon which the courts have differed.

Evidence of the plaintiff's bad character is admissible in mitigation of damages on the ground that "a reputation already damaged in the very point in controversy is not so valuable commercially speaking as a reputation which is unspotted." But whether such evidence is admissible under the general issue alone, or whether bad character must be expressly pleaded in mitigation, are questions upon which the decisions have not been quite harmonious. The widely prevailing rule is that it need not be expressly pleaded, however such evidence can only be given with the leave of court, unless seven (7) days at least before the trial the plaintiff is furnished with particular of facts he intends to give evidence.[10]

After evidence of the plaintiff's bad character has been given, the plaintiff may of course give evidence of good character as bearing upon the question of damages. Whether the defendant, in mitigation of damages, may show the plaintiff's general bad character, or only his bad character in respect to the trait involved in the defamation, or may show both, are questions upon which the courts are not quite agreed. Upon principle it would seem that he should be permitted to do both, but it can hardly be

---

[9] Section 80 Evidence Act 2011

[10] Section 80 Evidence Act 2011 (Nigeria)

said that this is the prevailing rule. It is, however, well settled in this class of cases that good or bad character, whether general or in respect to some trait involved, can only be shown by evidence of general reputation, and not by evidence of specific acts.

2) The fact that the character of any person is such as to affect the amount of damages, which he ought to receive, is relevant.[11] (Reputation is social).

3) Where a party testify, his character becomes relevant as it affect credit because the character of witness is relevant as affecting credit being a witness.[12] The question whether impeaching and supporting evidence must be confined to evidence affecting veracity alone, or whether it may include evidence of general good or bad moral character is a subject of conflicting opinion. The fundamental trait desirable in a witness is the disposition to tell the truth, and hence the trait of character that should naturally be shown in impeaching him is his bad character for veracity. However, there has always been more or less support for the use of bad general character.

It should be noted that a mere conflict of testimony, however, is not such an assault upon the veracity of a witness as will justify the admission of evidence in support of veracity; nor will a mere attack upon the veracity of a witness by counsel in argument, be ground for the admission of evidence in support of the character of the witness.

4) In an action for breach of promise to marry evidence of plaintiff bad character may constitute a defence for the repudiation of the promise by the defendant and this is relevant. In an action for breach of promise of marriage, evidence of bad character is relevant and admissible, the section provides:

> In proceedings in which damages are claimed, any fact, which will enable the court to determine the amount of damages, which ought to be awarded, is relevant.[13]

In actions of breach of promise of marriage the character of the plaintiff is generally held to be put in issue, at least for certain purposes. Such an action impliedly asserts that the character of the plaintiff is good,

---

[11] Ibid Section 10 Ibid.

[12] Section 233 and 235 Evidence Act

[13] Section 10 Ibid.

and harm to it is recognized as one of the elements of damages therein. The plaintiff's want of "chastity is, under certain circumstances, a defence to the action. It may, as a defence, be shown not only by general unchaste reputation, but also by evidence of unchaste acts and conduct. In such a defence unchaste character clearly means actual character rather than reputed character. The defendant may also, in mitigation of damages, show the bad character of the plaintiff for chastity, and his or her general bad moral character by reputation evidence, and then the plaintiff may rebut this by similar evidence of good reputation for chastity, and for good moral character.

When under such a defence, evidence has been given of plaintiff's bad character for chastity, in either or both of the ways above mentioned, the plaintiff may, of course, give evidence to contradict the evidence as to particular acts or conduct, and also give evidence of general chaste reputation. Thus, the plaintiff may give evidence of her good character if the defendant makes an imputation against it in his pleading.

5) Malicious prosecution: In actions for malicious prosecution, harm to the plaintiff's character is usually one of the elements of damages involved in the case. Where this is so, the character of the plaintiff is held to be put in issue, and the defendant may give evidence of the plaintiff's general bad character, in mitigation of damages, while the plaintiff, in rebuttal, may of course give evidence of his general good character. Such evidence of good or bad character is confined to evidence of general reputation.

Again the character of a person may afford a fair basis for an inference as to some fact other than the conduct or acts of that person. For example; in an action against malicious prosecution, the character of the plaintiff may have a bearing upon the knowledge or belief of the defendant. In that case it presumed that reasonable grounds exist for instituting the prosecution against the defendant. Evidence of character for purposes like the foregoing is admitted in both civil and criminal cases, but the civil cases in which it is admissible are comparatively few and they will be first considered.

In all of the foregoing classes of cases where character is held, in effect, to be one of the facts to be proved in the case, its existence may be proved, not as tending to prove some other facts in the case, but simply as one of the facts involved in the issue. It is not regarded as an evidential fact nor used as such. Where a party testifies, his character is relevant and admissible particularly when it affects the credit of the witness.[14]

Evidence of Character in Criminal Cases

Evidence of Good Character

In substantially all criminal prosecutions, a defendant may give evidence of his good character in proof of his innocence; and that when he has done so, and not until then the State may give evidence of his bad character. If the accused fails to offer evidence of his good character no presumption arises that he is guilty of the offense charged, or that he is of bad character. Thus, in criminal proceedings evidence of good character of a person is relevant and admissible.[15] But note that such evidence is only helpful in doubtful cases and not when the case can be proved beyond reasonable doubt.

The good or bad character of a defendant in such cases can be proved only by evidence of general reputation, and not by evidence of particular acts or conduct. Thus, evidence of good character, in criminal as in civil cases, may be negative in its nature, for the best character is often the least talked about. The defendant may not only offer evidence of general good character, he may also offer evidence of specific traits of character; but such traits can only be proved by evidence of general reputation. The specific trait, offered to be proved, however, must correspond with the trait involved in the offense charged, or it will be inadmissible because irrelevant.

Evidence of Bad character

Evidence of bad character is generally irrelevant in criminal proceeding for the purpose of establishing the offence with which a defendant is charged.[16] Firstly, this is because accepting such evidence may prejudice the mind of court or trial of fact against the defendant. Secondly, accepting such evidence may lead to hasty conclusion that the defendant committed the offence.

However, the admissibility of bad character should bound up with, and dependent upon probative value and the credibility of the evidence as a factor that the trial judge, exercising his or her discretionary function is entitled to take into consideration. Similarly for bad character to be

---

[14] Sections 223-224 Evidence Act (Nigeria)

[15] Section 81 Ibid.

[16] Section 82(1) Ibid.

admissible, of course, there must be an evidentiary link between the alleged similar prior acts and the accused as the perpetrator of them. Though, it is may not be entirely clear how strong the link needs to be (probably the civil standard).

Before evidence of bad character can be admitted as evidence of similar facts, there must be a link between the alleged similar facts and the accused. In other words there must be some evidence upon which the trial judge of fact can make a proper finding that the similar facts to be relied upon were in fact the acts of the accused. For it is clear that if they were not his own but those of another they have no relevance to the matters at issue under the indictment.

Exceptions

1) Where bad character of a defendant is a fact in issue, for instance where the accused person's bad character constitutes an element of the offence charge, evidence of bad character is admissible. [17] Examples of such offences are: offences of being a rogue or vagabond under Section 250 (1) Criminal Code, which requires proof that the accused is a disorderly person. See Section 249 Criminal Code. In this case, evidence of the accused previous conviction is relevant.

However, in prosecutions for homicide, where the accused claims that the killing was in self-defence, and the question arises whether the deceased was the aggressor, the character of the deceased for violence and turbulence, is held to be admissible, as circumstantial evidence bearing upon that question. [18] In this class of cases, it is of no consequence whether the accused at the time had knowledge of the character of the deceased or not.

In this class of cases also, when the question arises whether the accused did acted in reasonable apprehension of an attack, evidence of the character of the deceased as a man of violence, if known to the accused at the time, is admissible as circumstantial evidence bearing upon the question of reasonable apprehension.

2) A defendant may equally be asked questions to show that he is of bad character in circumstances mentioned in section 180(g)(i) & (2) of the Evidence Act, 2011, which provides:

---

[17] Section 82 (2) (a) Ibid.
[18] *Ugwagboe* v. *State* (2008) 7 MJSC 182 and *Musa* v. *State* (2009) 7 MJSC (pt ii) 52

A person charged and called as a witness in pursuance of this section shall not be asked, and if asked shall not be required to answer any question tending to show that he committed or has been convicted of or being charged with any offence other than that with which he is the charged, or he is of bad character,

(i) the proof that he or been convicted of such other offence is admissible in evidence to show that he is guilty of the offence with which he is the charged or

(ii) he has personally or by his legal practitioner asked question of the witness for the prosecution with a view to establish his own good character or has given evidence of his good character, or nature or conduct of the defence is such as to involve imputation on the prosecutor or the witness for the prosecution or

(iii) he has given evidence against any other person charged with the same offence.

When evidence of bad character is admissible evidence of previous conviction is also admissible. See section 82(4) Evidence Act, 2011. For example; in a charge for receiving stolen property, knowing it to have been stolen or being in possession of stolen property to prove guilty knowledge (but not fact of receiving the property) evidence may be given under Section 36 (a) & (b) Evidence Act, 2011 of:

i) Facts that other property stolen within the period of 12 months preceding the date for the offence charged was found or had been in possession of the accused is relevant, or

ii) The fact that within 5 years preceding the date of the offence charged the accused was convicted of an offence involving fraud or dishonesty. See Section 427 Criminal Code and Section 317 of the Penal Code.

Note that in cases where subsection 4 of section 82 applies, court shall only admit evidence of previous convictions which are related in substance to the offence charged. Similarly such evidence can be relevant and admissible if seven (7) days notice in writing has be given to the offender that the evidence shall be given in court.

3) Where an accused person either by himself or through his counsel ask prosecution witnesses questions to establish his good character, evidence of bad character is relevant. The prosecution may rebut the evidence.[19]

---

[19] Section 82(2) (b) Ibid.

4) Where an accused person in his evidence in-chief, gives evidence as to establish his good character, he has put his character in issue and therefore evidence of bad character is relevant in rebuttal.[20]

5) Where an accused person gave evidence of his good character, by virtue of Section 82 (2), evidence of the accused bad character is relevant and admissible to rebut the evidence of his good character.

6) An accused may be asked question to show his bad character including previous conviction in the circumstances mentioned in Section 180 (b) Evidence Act; that is when the accused person is a witness as provided by the Act thus:

> A person charged and being a witness in pursuance of this section may be asked any question in cross-examination notwithstanding that it would tend to incriminate him as to the offence charged.
> When the only witness to the facts of the case called by the defence is the person charged and shall be called as witness immediately after the close of the evidence for the prosecution.[21]

In notes 3, 4, 5 and 6 above the trait of character sought for in an accused is truthfulness, veracity, disposition to tell the truth, at the time of testifying. The existence of this trait is assumed or taken for granted to begin with; and until the veracity of the accused person is attacked in some way, evidence of his good character for veracity will not be received.

While it would be difficult to argue from a common sense point of view that character evidence is not logically relevant, the danger of its illogical use is considerable. The logical function of character evidence may be shown by the following illustration.[22] If a man is accused of stealing, his reputation as a thief logically weighs heavily against him. There is a strong tendency, however, that character evidence will produce a dislike or hatred for the party against whom the evidence is tendered which may result in an adverse finding to vindicate a judge's feelings and in disregard of culpability. Instructively the use of character evidence to prove a fact in issue may include:

---

[20] Ibid.

[21] Sections 180(b) & (c) Evidence Act 211

[22] John Sopinka, *Character Evidence in Civil Cases*, p. 250

1. The first is where it is tendered in proof or disproof of some other issue apart from character, or to show the doing or not doing of an act by the person against whom the evidence is tendered;

2. The second is where under the law and pleadings in the action it is one of the issues, or the issue to be resolved. For convenience the first kind of evidence may be referred to as secondary evidence of character and the second primary evidence of character.

In criminal cases evidence of the good character of the accused is most properly and with good reason admissible in evidence, because there is a fair and just presumption that a person of good character would not commit a crime. However, in civil cases such evidence is with equal good reason not admitted, because no presumption would fairly arise, in the very great proportion of such cases, from the good character of the defendant, that he did not commit the breach of contract or of civil duty alleged against him.

While the above statement deals with the introduction of evidence of good character the same prohibition applies with respect to evidence of bad character unless the evidence meets the rigid standards relating to the admission of evidence of similar acts.

The rationale for allowing character evidence in criminal cases is clearly based on its relevance. Such evidence is admissible; because it renders less probable that which the prosecution has averred is true. It is strictly relevant to the issue.[23] If the logical relevance of the evidence were the test of admissibility it would be difficult to rationalize its exclusion in civil cases and its admission in criminal cases. In tort actions such as assault, deceit and negligence evidence of good character on the part of the defendant would appear to be as relevant as the evidence of good character of the accused in a criminal case.

It is submitted that, while the courts appear to exclude character evidence in civil cases on the basis of irrelevance, the real rationale is the policy to restrain civil proceedings within manageable limits and to prevent unfairness to civil litigants who cannot be expected, without previous notice, to be prepared to protect themselves against imputations which may range over their whole career.

---

[23] See generally, section 82 Evidence Act 2011

Chapter 13

Examination of Witnesses

The oral adversarial trial is a firmly established feature in common law legal systems. Conventionally, evidence is given orally in court by witnesses, who are called and examined in chief by the party who tenders their evidence, then cross-examined by the opposing party, and re-examined by the party calling them.[1] There are at least two significant rationales for this historical and traditional preference for oral evidence:

1. That a party has the opportunity to hear, and challenge and test by cross-examination, the evidence adduced by the opposing party; and

2. That the court has the opportunity the see and hear the witness and have regard to his or her demeanour in the witness box, which can inform judgments about the credibility of the witness.[2]

This preference for oral testimonial evidence is reflected in and enforced by the hearsay rule. The effect of which is that a statement (oral or written) made otherwise than in the course of giving evidence in the proceeding is not admissible to prove the existence of a fact asserted or denied in the statement.[3] While there are numerous exceptions to the hearsay rule, its effect is that the starting point is that to prove a fact, a witness must give oral evidence of the fact in court.

Testimony should generally be given orally in open court. Thus, testimony is usually a form of responses to several questions of linked, rather than form of narrative. Testimony is simply defined as; uttered, communicated in spoken words, conducted by words of mouth or spoken verbal. To elicit oral testimonial evidence in court, the counsel (for either party in dispute) put questions to the witness during examination, though a judge may also ask the witness any question in the course of proceedings. In general there three types of examination methods of eliciting evidence

---

[1] Ellis S. M., The Best Evidence Rule – Oral, Testimony or Documentary Proof? (1995) NSW Law Journal, 67 – 94 at 69

[2] Ibid.

[3] Hunter J., Crain K., *Evidence, Advocacy and Ethical Practice*, (Butterworth, London, 1995) 66

from a witness in court proceedings, the method are discussed in the preceding parts. Significantly however, oral testimony of a witness must at all times limited only to relevant facts.[4] The evidence Act provides that:

> The order in which witnesses are produced and examine shall be regulated by the law and practice for the time being relating to civil or criminal procedure respectively and in the absence of any such law, at the discretion of the court.[5]

Pertinently, there is no rule of law which imposes any obligation on parties to a dispute to call a host of witnesses because parties have discretion to call only those witnesses to unfold his/her case.[6] However, where there is more than one witness present in court to testify, while a witness is testifying the other witnesses have to stay out of court till call in to testify. The procedure for this is as provided by the law that:

> On the application of either party, or of its own motion, the court may order witnesses on both sides to be kept out of court, but this provision does not extend to the parties themselves or to their respective legal advisers, although intended to be called as witnesses.[7]

It is important to state that the court may during any trial take such means as necessary to prevent communication with the witnesses in the court room or it precincts waiting for examination.[8] There are however some exceptions to the general rules as found in cases of trial based wholly or partly on affidavit and trial of children as provided under the" Children and Young Persons Act. It is pertinent to note that oral evidence in court is subject to certain procedural conditions namely:

1. Oral evidence of a witness in court proceedings must be given on oath;[9] except for the fact that:

---

[4] *Isheno* v. *Berger* (2008) 4 MJSC 104 at 120

[5] Section 210 Evidence Act 2011

[6] *Nkebi* v. *State* (2010) 1-2 MJSC 78 at 97, *Adeje* v. *the State* (1979) 6-7 SC 1, *Inusa Saidu* v. *the State* (1982) 4 SC 49, *Okonofue* v. *the State* (1981) 6-7 SC 1, *Okpolor* v. *the State* (1994) 6 NWLR (pt 358) 281 and *Udo* v. *State* (2006) 15 NWLR (pt 1001) 178, *Onafowokan* v. *State* (1987) 3 NWLR (pt 61) 538, *Effiong* v. *the State* (1988) 8 NWLR (pt 512) 362l, etc

[7] Section 212 Evidence Act 2011

[8] Ibid.; Section 213

[9] Ibid.; Section 205

a. A person, who has duly taken an oath but later discovered he has no religion, will not render the oath already taken invalid. [10]

b. Receive evidence of witness not oath of any person who declares that the taking of oath according to his religious belief is unlawful or who by reason of want of religious belief ought not, in the opinion of the court, to be admitted to give evidence upon oath.[11]

2. The witness must be cautioned before giving oral evidence that if he tell lie or wilfully mislead the court will be liable to be prosecuted and if found guilty will be seriously dealt with according to law.[12]

Note that the reason for evidence not given on oath must be specifically recorded in the minutes of proceedings.[13] The following are the types of examination in court proceedings.

Types or order of examination of witnesses in court
Examination in Chief

This is a method questioning witnesses with a view of obtaining material evidence from them. It is the function of the party calling the witness usually through counsel that examines in-chief. The functions of examination–in-chief are firstly; to lead the witness in logically presenting his story about disputed fact or issue before the court, and secondly; to obtain testimony in support of the facts which the party calling that witness is contending.[14]

Examination in chief must be strictly limited to relevant facts, that is as contained in pleadings (in case of civil matter) or as define by statute creating the act (in case of criminal proceedings). The question to be asked should be one that will enable the witness to independently narrate events without influence. Here the counsel leading the witness professes ignorance of the event or issue in order to engage the witness in narration of facts within his knowledge.

Against the above principle leading questions are not allowed. A leading question is a question that suggests the intended answer from the

---

[10] Section 207
[11] Section 208(1)
[12] Section 206
[13] Section 208(2)
[14] Section 214(1) and 215(1) Evidence Act 2011

witness being examined.[15] However, leading questions that is introductory in nature or undisputed or in the opinion of the court have already been sufficiently proved is allowed.[16] Leading question shall not be asked if objected to in examination in-chief except with the permission of the court.[17]

Hostile Witness

A witness is considered hostile when in the opinion of the court he shows that he is adverse to the party calling him and he is unwilling to tell the truth. If the court is satisfy that a witness is hostile, the court in his discretion may allow the party calling the witness to put leading question to him or cross-examine him, the party may not however attack the witness character directly but may prove previous inconsistent statement made by him.

Cross Examination

This is the second stage in the order of examining witnesses in court. After the party calling a witness has concluded examining him in chief, if the other party in the case asked question from him that is cross-examination.[18] The main purpose of cross examination is to extract from the witness evidence, which is favourable to the party cross examining him or evidence which destroy the case of the party producing the witness or to cast doubt upon the accuracy of the evidence already given by the witness. In this perspective the Act [19] provides that when a witness is cross-examined he may in addition to the questions herein before referred to, asked any questions, which tend:

1. To test his accuracy, veracity or credibility
2. Discover who he is and what is his position in life or
3. To stain his credit by injuring his character

A defendant giving evidence may be asked any question, but cannot be compelled to give answer to any question tending to show that he has committed or been convicted of or been charged with any offence previously. However, a judge may in his discretion disallow question that appear to the court offence to the witness or defendant, or considered:

---

[15] Ibid.; Section 221(1)

[16] Ibid.; Section 221(3)

[17] Ibid.; Section 221(2)

[18] Garner B. A., *Black's Law Dictionary*, (8th ed., Thomsom West, US, 1999), p. 405

[19] Section 223 Evidence Act 2011

a. to be indecent or scandalous[20]
b. to be intended to insult or annoy the witness or to be needlessly offensive in form; even though proper.[21]

In *Awara* v. *Alalibo*,[22] Ogundare JSC said: the evidence of a witness taken in earlier proceedings is not relevant in the case on trial except for the purpose of discrediting such witness on cross examination and for the purpose only. The court should come to a decision on the facts placed before it without regard to the result of another proceeding before another tribunal. See *Durosaro* v. *Ayorinde*[23] In the same paradigm failure to challenge evidence by cross-examination the adverse party is deemed to be conceding on issue affected.[24]

It is instructive to note that evidence elicited from a party or his witness(es) under cross-examination which goes to support the case of the party cross-examining constitute evidence in support of the case or defence. If at the end of the day the party cross-examining decides not to call any witness, he/she can rely on the evidence elicited from cross-examination in establishing his/her case or defence.[25] In such a case the adverse party cannot say that the party called no witness in support of his/her case or defence. However, one may say that the party called no witness in support of his/her case or defence but not evidence, because elicited from his/her opponent under cross-examination which are in support of his case or defence constitute his/her evidence in the case.[26]

In the same perspective there is a catch to this principle. The exception is that the evidence elicited under cross-examination must be facts pleaded by the party concerned for it to be relevant to the determination of the question/issue in controversy between the parties.[27] It is important to note that for cross-examination to stand its worth, it need not be extensive before it could be relevant and sufficient, provided the crucial facts raised in the evidence-in-chief are examined and addressed therein. It is only when a party completely refused to cross-

---

[20] Section 227 ibid.
[21] Section 228 ibid.
[22] *Awara* v. *Alalibo* (2002) 12 SC (pt.1) 77 at 117
[23] *Durosaro* v. *Ayorinde* (2005) 3-4 SC 14 at 19
[24] *ACME Builder Ltd* v. *Kaduna State Water Board* (1999) 2 SCNJ 25
[25] *Mrs Anike Akomolafe & ors* v. *Guardian News Paper Limited & 3 ors* (2010) 1 MJSC 93 at 105-109
[26] Ibid.
[27] Ibid.

examine a witness that such a party will be deemed to have accepted the testimony of the said witness.[28]

Re Examination

Re-examination is the second stage of examination by the party calling a witness after cross-examination. The purpose of re-examination is to clear ambiguities or to shed more light on any fact not clearly stated in the cross-examination. Re-examination must not be use for new matters if allowed by court the other party must be given the opportunity to cross examine the witness[29]. Leading question is not allowed during re-examination.

Refreshing Memory

A witness at any stage of examination in chief, cross-examination or re-examination may be granted permission to refer to some document so as to recall some matter. However he should not read aloud from the document but merely view it before he gives.[30]

When a witness has been asked and answered any question which is relevant to the inquiry only in so far as intends to shake his credit by injuring his character, no evidence shall be given to contradict him; if he answers falsely, he may afterwards be charged with an offence against section 191 of the Criminal Code and, on conviction shall be dealt with accordingly.[31] The Act provides that:

(a)   If a witness is asked whether he has been previously convicted of any crime and denies it, evidence may be given of his previous conviction.

(b)   If a witness is asked any question tending to impeach his impartiality and answers it by denying the facts suggested, he may be contradicted.[32]

The party calling a witness shall not be allowed to impeach his credit by general evidence of bad character, but he may, in case the witness shall, in the opinion of the court, prove hostile, contradict him by other evidence, or by leave of the court, prove that he has made at other times a statement inconsistent with his present testimony; but before such last mentioned

---

[28] *Ali* v. *State* (2015) All FWLR (pt 796) 559 at 583

[29] Section 214(3) Evidence Act 2011

[30] Ibid., Sections 239(1) – 247, see *Abike* v. *Adedosun* (1986) 3 NWLR (pt 30) 548

[31] Section 229 Evidence Act 2011

[32] Ibid.

proof can be given the circumstances of the supposed statement, sufficient to designate the particular occasion, must be mentioned to the witness and he must be asked whether or not he has made such statement.[33]

If a witness upon cross-examination as to a former statement made by him relative to the subject-matter of the trial, and consistent with his present testimony, does not distinctly admit that he has made such statement, proof may be given that he did in fact make it; but before such proof can be given the circumstances of the supposed statement sufficient to designate the particular occasion must be mentioned to the witness, and he must be asked whether or not he has made such statement.[34]

A witness may be cross-examined as to the previous statements made by him in writing relative to the subject-matter of the trial without such writing being shown to him, but if it is intended to contradict such witness by the writing, his attention must, before such contradictory proof can be given, be called to those parts of the writing which are to be used for the purpose of so contradicting him:

Provided always that it shall be competent for the court at any time during the trial, to require the production of the writing for its inspection, and the court may thereupon make use of it for the purpose of the trial, as it shall think fit.[35] The credit of a witness may be impeached in the following ways by any party other than the party calling him or with the consent of the court by the party who calls him.

(a) By the evidence of person who testify that they, from their knowledge of the witness, believe him to be unworthy of credit;

(b) By proof that the witness has been bribe, or has accepted the offer of a bribe, or has receive any other corrupt inducement to give his evidence;

(c) By proof of former statements inconsistent with any part of his evidence which is liable to be contradicted.[36]

The significance of cross examination was reiterated by the Supreme Court in the case of *Ali* v. *State*[37] (2015) All FWLR (pt 796) that; "for cross-examination to stand its worth, it need not be extensive before it could be relevant and sufficient. Provided the crucial facts raised in evidence in chief are examined and addressed therein. It is only when a party

---

[33] Section 230, ibid.

[34] Section 231, ibid.

[35] Section 232, ibid.

[36] Section 233, ibid.

[37] (2015) All FWLR (pt796) 559 at 583

completely refused to cross examine a witness that such a party will be deemed to have accepted the testimony of the said witness.

Chapter 14

PART I
Documentary Evidence

It remains exceptionally rare in the Nigeria administration of justice system for a case to be heard and decided without at least some testimonial evidence – that is, evidence given by a witness, either orally in Court or in a sworn statement (affidavit) placed before the Court. However, there is a far greater readiness to accept documentary evidence and in many commercial disputes documentary evidence predominates and is often decisive.[1] It is may be argued that the increased acceptance of documentary evidence resulted from recognition of two matters of human experience:

1. That documents brought into existence close in time to the events they record will often be more reliable sources than the recollections of witnesses related orally in court years later; and
2. That in commerce and public administration, records were routinely made of events and transactions, which were relied on as accurate for the purposes of public administration and commerce, and if they were regarded as reliable for those purposes, then they ought to be reliable for the purposes of the courts also.[2]

A document is literarily construed as a piece of writing, which furnishes evidence. A document is defined in the Evidence Act,[3] as including books, maps, plants, drawings photographs and any matter expressed or described upon any substance by means of letters, figures or marks or by more than one of these means, intended to be used or which may be used for the purpose of recording the matter.

Documentary evidence consists of any information that can be introduced at trial in the form of documents. While it is often thought of as

---

[1] Coady, CAJ, *Testimony – A Philosophical Study*, (Clarendon Press, 1992) 32 - 33
[2] Ibid.
[3] Section 2 Evidence Act, *op. cit.*

information written down on paper, such as letters, a contract or a will, documentary evidence more broadly encompasses information recorded on any media on which information can be stored. Under the Nigerian law of evidence, this includes information stored on computers and other media, such as e-mails, Web pages, and other data.

Documentary evidence may be offered as direct or circumstantial proof of a fact that is material to a case. For example, invoices from medical providers may be offered to prove economic damages in a personal injury case, the fact that a party was warned not to destroy evidence material to a claim may be proved with an e-mail in a spoliation case, and a contract provision and notes from its negotiation may prove that an individual is not a member of a shareholder class that was scheduled to receive distributions.

Classification of Document

Document is classified into public document or private document depending on their ownership and utility. Generally, the central focal point in the classification of document into private and public document relates to the admissibility, custody and relevancy of such document.

Public Document

According to the Evidence Act,[4] a public document is one, forming the Act or record of the Act of,
  i) Sovereign authority or the government
  ii) Document of official bodies and tribunals and
  iii) Of public officers whether legislative judicial or executives and of official bodies and tribunals either of Nigeria or elsewhere.
  iv) It will also include private documents kept for public purposes as where a statute provides for private document to be registered or filed with specific public officers for public purposes.

Private Document

All documents other than public documents are private documents. They are those emanating from private person or public person in their private capacities.[5]

On proof or admissibility of documents, public or private under Sections 109 and 110 of the Evidence Act, the Supreme Court in *Okonji* v.

---

[4] Section 102 Evidence
[5] Section 103 Evidence

Njokanna[6] said that the position of the law in relation to the question of admissibility of a document in evidence is that admissibility is one thing while probative value that may be placed thereon is another. However the court would first consider the following main criteria to determine the admissibility of a document in evidence namely:

a. Is the document pleaded?
b. Is the document relevant to the inquiry being tried by the court?
c. Is it admissible in law?

Proof of Document

the Evidence Act provides for the method of proofing a document, arguably, proof of content of document is different from proof of due execution of document, these shall be explained.

1) Proof of Content of a Document.

This may be done by primary evidence or secondary evidence.

A party who wants to rely on a document must bring to the notice of the court by introducing it in evidence basically by primary or secondary evidence depending on their classification. A private documents is proved by primary evidence while public are proved by special form of secondary evidence. Section 85 Evidence Act provides that *the contents of documents may be proved either by primary or secondary evidence.*

ii) Primary Documentary Evidence

This is the document itself produced for the inspection of the court. The following are primary evidence of documents:

1. Document executed in several parts each parts will be primary documentary evidence of the document.
2. Document executed in counterpart each counterpart being executed by one or some of the parties each counterpart is primary evidence in relation to a party executing them.
3. Where series of documents are made in one uniform process such as printing lithograph or photograph each is primary evidence of the counterpart of the rest. But where they are copies of common originals they are not primary evidence but secondary evidence of the copy of the original.[7]

---

[6] *Okonji* v. *Njokanna* (1999) 12 SC (pt 11) 150 at 156

[7] Section 86 (1) – (4) Evidence

If document is made through the same process or makes many copies of an agreement with carbon copy, each copy including the carbon copies will be primary evidence of the agreement provided they are all signed and executed by all parties. So an unsigned carbon copy will not be primary evidence of the signed copies. Similarly where copies of letters were types from the draft each copy of the letter is primary evidence of the content of the other copies including the top copy but not the draft.

ii) Secondary Documentary Evidence

This is described as substitution evidence adduced only, where primary evidence of a document is not available or it is not convenient to be produced in court, it is generally copy or oral expression of the original. The Evidence Act[8] provides for exceptional circumstances when secondary evidence of a document may be given:

a) When the original is shown or appears to be in the possession of a person against whom the document is sought to be proved or any person legally bound to produce and when after notice mentioned in section 91 such person does not produce. *Its secondary evidence is admissible.*[9]

    i.   Any secondary evidence including oral account is admissible.[10]

b) When the existence or condition or contents of the original has been admitted in writing by the person against whom it is to be proved or by his representative in interest.[11]

    ii.   The written admission is admissible as secondary evidence.[12]

c) When the original has been lost destroyed or cannot be found.[13]

    i.   Any secondary evidence including oral account is admissible.[14]

d) When the original is not easily moveable.[15]

    ii.   Any secondary evidence including oral account is admissible.[16]

e) When the original is a public document within the meaning of section 102 Evidence Act.[17]

---

[8] Section 89 Evidence Act 2011

[9] Section 89 Evidence Act 2011

[10] Ibid.; Section 90(1)(a)

[11] Section 89 Evidence Act 2011

[12] Ibid.; Section 90(1)(b)

[13] Section 89 Evidence Act 2011

[14] Ibid.; Section 90(1)(a)

[15] Section 89 Evidence Act 2011

[16] Ibid.; Section 90(1)(a)

[17] Ibid.; Section 89

    i.   Note that only certified copy of the document may be given but no other secondary evidence is admissible.[18]

f)   When the original is a document of which certified copy is permitted by this Act or by any law in force in Nigeria to be given in evidence.[19]

    i.   Note that only certified copy of the document may be given but no other secondary evidence is admissible.[20]

g)   When the original consist of numerous accounts or documents, which cannot be conveniently, examine in court and the fact to be proved is the general result of the whole collection.[21]

    i.   Note that oral evidence of the general condition may be given by an expert or a person who has examined it. [22]

h)   When the original is an entry in a banker's book the copy of the cutting in the book may be admitted.[23] By virtue of section 90(1)(e) secondary evidence cannot be given except it proved that:

    i.   Entry was made at the time of making one of the ordinary books of the bank.[24]

    ii.   Entry was made in the usual and ordinary course of business.[25]

    iii.   The book is in the control and custody of the bank, which proof may be given orally or by affidavit made by an officer of the bank.[26]

    iv.   Copy has been examined with the original entry and is correct, which must be given by some person who had examined the copy with the original entry, and may be given may be given orally or by affidavit.[27]

Note that before a secondary evidence of content of a document can be admissible a proper foundation for its admissibility must be laid as required by section 89 of the Evidence Act. However secondary evidence according to section 87 Evidence Act includes:

    i.   Certified copies given under provision of the Evidence Act

    ii.   Copies made from the original.

    iii.   Copies made from or compare with photocopies.

    iv.   Counterpart of document as against parties who sign them

---

[18] Ibid.; Section 90(1)(c)

[19] Ibid.; Section 89

[20] Section 90(1)(c)

[21] Ibid.; Section 89

[22] Ibid.; Section 90(1)(d)

[23] Ibid.; Section 89

[24] Section 90(1)(e)(i)

[25] Section 90(1)(e)(ii)

[26] Section 90(1)(e)(iii)

[27] Section 90(1)(e)(iv) see also the case of *Edokpolo v. Sem Edo* (1989) 4 NWLR 116

v.   Oral accounts of the content of document given by a person who saw the document.

2) Proof of Due Execution of a Document

Proof of execution of a document arises when a party is denying the execution of the document or that the signature, finger impression or seal appearing on the document is not his own, forged or that the content is different from the one he executed. In *Chitex Ind. Ltd* v. *Oceanic Bank*[28] the Supreme Court held that:

> Where document is challenged and impugned as unauthentic, the maker of the document should be called to support the document, otherwise no weight should be attached.

a) Public Document

Public documents are generally proved by secondary evidence but one of a special nature, the only admissible secondary evidence of a public document is certified true copy (CTC) and non-other type of the document or the part is required in the proceeding in court. Sections104 and 105 of the Evidence Act are relevant.

Section 104 Evidence Act provides that every public officer having the custody of a public document, which any person is entitled to inspect, shall give to that person on demand a copy of it on:

i.   Payment of legal fees

ii.   A certificate at court of such copies that is true copy

iii. Copy shall be dated subscribed by the officer with his name official title and seal whenever such officer is authorized by law to make use of a seal.[29]

The reason for authenticating public documents by a designated official was state in the case *of Onochie* v. *Ogogwu*[30] to include:

i.   To obviate the necessity of calling officials to come to testify as to the geniuses of copies made from the original documents or records of public nature.

ii.   To preserve those original documents or records from being removed from their proper place of custody through requests that they be tendered in court.

---

[28] *Chitex Ind. Ltd* v. *Oceanic Bank* (2005) 23 NSCQR 148 at 164

[29] Section 104(2) Evidence Act 2011

[30] *Onochie* v. *Ogogwu* (2006) 2 SC (pt ii) 153 at 167

Such copy shall be called Certified True Copy. By virtue of section 105 Evidence Act such certified copies may be produced in proof of the content of the public document or part thereof the public document of which they purport to be copies.[31] In the same vein, an officer who is by the ordinary course of his official duty is authorized to deliver a public document shall be considered to the custody of the document.[32]

b) Private Document

In the course of proceedings, whether criminal or civil, one of the important and most usually contending issues regarding documentary has to do with execution, dispute as to signature or hand writing. The execution of a document herein means signing or sealing by person whose signature or seals the document purport to bear. The Supreme Court in *Amadi v. Orisakwe*[33] held that; the position of the law is that in resolving issue of due execution of a document where the alleged maker denies his signature, the course or option opened to the court would be the following:

i). To receive evidence from the attesting magistrate if there is such an attestation and if it is possible to call the magistrate;

ii). To hear evidence from a person familiar with the signature of the alleged signatory or who saw him write the signature.

iii). To compare the signature admitted by the alleged signatory, to be his own with the one in contention[34].

iv). To direct the person to sign his signature for the purpose of enabling the court to compare the signature alleged to have been written by him.[35]

Essentially, the above stated procedure equally applies in proving a dispute over seal, handwriting and or finger impression. Thus, by virtue of section 101 such signature, seal, handwriting or finger impressions may be proved against whom it's contended to be his signature seal or handwriting if it is a document that requires no attestation by it can be proved by;

---

[31] *Okonjo* v. *Njokanna* (1999) 12 SC (pt 11) 150 at 156 see also See also section 106 of the Evidence Act 2011

[32] Section 104(3) of the Evidence Act

[33] *Amadi* v. *Orisakwe* (2005) 1 SC (Pt i) 35 at 41

[34] Section 101(1) Evidence Act 2011

[35] Ibid.; section 101(2)

i. Evidence that a person exist having the same name, address business or occupation as the maker of the document purport to have shown that such a document was written or signed by that person.[36]

ii. Evidence that a document exists to which the document the making of which is in issue purport to be a reply together with the evidencing of making and delivery to a person of such earlier document is admissible to show the identity of the maker of the earlier disputed document.[37]

iii. Opinion of any person acquainted with the handwriting of the person by whom it is supposed to be written or signed.[38]

iv. Opinion of expert

It is instructive to explain that as a general principle of law it is not essential requirement for a person who intends to prove due execution of a document or establish handwriting of such person/party against whom the document is to be proved if:

1. The person produces such document and claims an interest under it in reference to the subject matter in dispute

2. He is a public officer bound by law to produce it.

Proof of document the validity of which attestation is necessary

In certain instances validity of a document (such as wills or testament) depends on proper attestation the absence of which may render the document void or voidable. However to proof the due execution of such document in any proceedings, civil or criminal and where the validity attestation is essential requirement may none the less be proved in any manner in which it might be proved if no attesting witness is alive.[39] This may be achieved:

i. By showing that the attestation of one attesting witness at least is in his handwriting or signature and the hand writing or signature is that of the executor of the document.[40] or

---

[36] Ibid.; Section 94(1)

[37] Ibid.; Section 94(2)

[38] Ibid.; Section 72

[39] Section 96(1) Evidence Act 2011

[40] Ibid.; Section 96(2)

ii.   Where a party to an attested document admits its attestation by himself that shall be   sufficient prove of its execution.[41]

iii.   Where the attesting witness denied or does not recollect the execution of the document it execution may be prove by other evidence.[42]

Essential point to note on documentary evidence

Firstly, the language of the court is English, therefore where a document not written in English but it is sought to be tendered in evidence as prove of a disputed issues, it will be or is improper for a court to receive the document in evidence unless an English version of it is also tendered in evidence.[43] In the same paradigm it is equally not proper for a judge to interpret the document not written by himself. That will be the function of an official translator or any other competent witness which must be called in to interpret the document. The consequence of wrongly receiving such document is that the document will be removed from the record of proceedings.[44]

Secondly, it is trite law that an intelligent report through a public officer is a public document and presumed to contain true information. The document contain an intelligent report is admissible in evidence in accordance to the procedure contained in sections 105 and 106 of the Evidence Act.[45]

Thirdly, any unsigned document is worthless and void.[46] Though it may be relevant a document not signed does not have any efficacy in law, the document is worthless and a worthless document cannot be efficacious.[47]

Exclusion of Oral Evidence by Documentary Evidence

The trite principle of law is that once an agreement has been reduced in to writing and signed by the party the content of the document cannot be alter by oral evidence.[48] In *Ezemba* v. *Ibeneme*[49] the Supreme Court said:

---

[41] Ibid.; Section 97

[42] Ibid.; Section 99 Evidence Act, *op. cit.*; see also *Adenle* v. *Oludo* (2002) 9-10 sc 124 at 131

[43] *Ojengbede* v. *M.O Esan* (2001) 12 SCNJ 401

[44] Ibid.

[45] *Ntegquile* v. *Otuo* (2001) 6 NSCQR (pt.11) 032 at 1059

[46] *Omega Bank Nig Ltd* v. *O.B.C Ltd* (2005) 1 SC (pt 1) 49 at 73

[47] Ibid.

[48] Section 128 (1) Evidence Act (Nigeria)

[49] Ezemba v. Ibeneme (2004) 19 NSCQR 352 at 405

The best evidence rule as it relates to oral evidence will not apply where the oral evidence contradicts documentary evidence. This is because, since the documentary evidence was first in time, the oral evidence in the absent of admissible evidence that there was an agreement between the parties outside the document that oral evidence will be led to vary the documentary evidence will be admissible. The court will be entitled to hold in such a situation or circumstances that the oral evidence is an afterthought after all, documentary evidence is less prone to lying than oral evidence. If documentary evidence tells a lie it is by human conduct and the act, which makes it to lie is traced to and punished by our criminal law.

The Supreme Court also in *IMNL* v. *Pegofor Industries Ltd* [50] emphases that it is an established principle of law, where parties have reduced their agreement into a written document subject to some exceptions, oral evidence will not be allowed to contradict or alter the content of the document.

Exceptions
However oral evidence may be allow in all matters stated under section 128 (1) (a)-(e) as exceptional circumstances to prove,

    a. Fraud, intimidation, illegality or want of due execution;
    b. Separate oral agreement as to any matter on which the document is silent and not inconsistent with terms of the agreement;
    c. Oral agreement constituting a condition precedent to any obligation in the contract;
    d. Existence of distinct subsequent oral agreement to review or modifies the agreement; and
    e. Any usage or custom by which incidents not expressly mentioned in any contract is annexed to the contracts of that description.

In *Ezemba* v. *Ebeneme* [51] *per Niki Tobi (JSC)* states the grounds for exclusion of oral evidence to vary alter or contradict the content of a document to include:

1) That to admit inferior evidence when the law requires superior evidence would be to nullify the law and
2) When the parties have deliberately put their agreement into writing, it is conclusively presumed between them and their privies. It is also presumed that they intend the writing to form a full and final statement of their

---

[50] IMNL v. Pegofor Industries Ltd (2005) 22 SC (pt 1 38 at 43

[51] *Ezemba* v. *Ebeneme* (*supra*) per Niki Tobi (JSC)

intention and on which should be placed beyond the reach of future controversy, bad faith or treacherous memory.

While live witness testimony may be interesting to a judge, documentary evidence can be particularly compelling. Documentary evidence is not subject to an imperfect memory, exaggeration, or vague recollections. What you see is what you get, and documentary evidence can establish a claim for damages or a party's statements regarding a material issue with a precision that witness testimony lacks. Likewise, when used to impeach a witness who has the poor judgment to lie on the stand, documentary evidence can be very dramatic.

PART II
Computer and Electronically Generated Evidence

New technology and the evolution of communications systems have substantially transformed the process of exchanging information and products in all spheres of life: business, civil and military, exponentially increasing the creation of electronic documents in organizations.

It is an undisputable fact that global advancement in technology has made people increasingly computer literate and use computer and other electronic devices in every aspect of their lives. The advancement of computers has therefore created an entirely new source of evidence in court proceedings commonly referred to as 'electronic evidence. Electronic evidence is any electronic information/statement created on a computer that can assist litigant in establishing their assertions or denial in a disputed matter.

Instructively, electronic evidence is an information, which when given in court tends to prove facts or relevant facts in dispute between the contending parties. In any proceedings before a court of law evidence may be presented either orally or physically by means of documents that are admissible to assist the court to reach a conclusion. Accordingly, the concept of 'electronic evidence' in the context of the above-mentioned definition of evidence refers to *'information that is stored electronically on a computer, internet, handset (SMS Messages, E-Mail Messages), and that can be used as evidence at trial civil or criminal as the case may be.*[52]" The Evidence Act defines electronic or computer as:

---

[52] Byran G. A., *Black's Law Dictionary*

Means any device for storing and processing information, and any reference to information being derived from other information is a reference to its being derived from it by calculation, comparison or any other process.[53] and any device by means of which information is recorded, stored or retrievable including computer output are consider document. [54]

It is important to note that electronic evidence can reside in graphic and includes but not limited to; optical disks, floppy disks, remote internet storage, handheld devices, memory cards, network servers and emails. This kind of evidence may be created at any stage once a person starts to use and enter information into a computer. Electronic evidence as an information stored in electronic form must be relevant to the issues in a particular litigation and the relevant electronic evidence must be gathered in a method that will be both admissible and justifiable in court.

Classification of Computer/Electronic Evidence

1. Documentary evidence: Computer evidence may be classified as documentary such as a computer printout.

2. Real evidence: Computer evidence can be real evidence because the computer that generated the electronic evidence had been programmed to generate such information on its own without human interference.

3. Hearsay evidence: Computer evidence can also be classified under hearsay evidence because it is not directly seen from the computer and the only person who has direct knowledge of it is the person who created it.

4. Circumstantial evidence: Electronic evidence may also be classified as circumstantial evidence because it is not the originator of the evidence that provides the evidence in court but a third person; this makes it circumstantial evidence.

5. Physical evidence: Physical or real evidence this is because the computer and information retrieved out of it are all objects that can establish that a fact exist and can provide a link between a issues in dispute and litigants.

---

[53] Section 258(1)

[54] Ibid., sub-section (1)(e)

However, the facts of each case can always assist the court in determining which type of evidence electronically generated information represent.

Use of Electronic Evidence

In today's world, law enforcement officers attempting to extract electronic evidence and contracting parties in civil agreements or commercial transactions face growing challenges from more types of devices with greater data storage capacity. Electronic media that could be seized in relation to transactions or information or an offense include computers, laptops, flash drives, external storage devices, digital cameras, game units and cellular phones. The parties involved must deal with vastly more data. Data contained on digital devices can assist court in arriving at just decision, parties to civil or criminal (i.e. criminal investigation) matters to establish their cases in a variety of ways, described below:

1. Electronic evidence may be found on a computer or other electronic device directly related to the commercial transaction, or agreement generally or offence committed. For example, where law enforcement agencies investigating a child molestation complaint they may analyze a suspect's computer which can reveal for instance multiple pictures that may appear to show that the suspect molested a number of children. In another example, a small flash card from a digital camera found in the possession of a suspected car thief may contain images of stolen cars;

2. Electronic evidence can be used to show intent existed to enter into an agreement or to commit a crime (in legal terms, *mens rea*) or premeditation of an act. Many digital devices efficiently track user activity; it is also possible to recover deleted files, both of which may affect a criminal investigation or settlement of civil disputes. Physical evidence may already point to a suspect's guilt, and digital evidence can indicate that the crime was planned in advance.

For example, a man who is suspected of killing his wife because he had discovered she was having an affair claimed that he killed her accidentally during an argument that became violent. When a computer forensic examiner analysed his laptop, however, she found deleted Internet history files showing searches for "perfect murder" ,"getting away with murder", and "quick ways to kill someone" that occurred weeks and days prior to the crime. Based on this evidence of premeditation, the defendant could be charged with murder instead of manslaughter. The usage of electronic evidence in this perspective is supported under the similar fact evidence particularly the section which provides that:

> Any fact is relevant which shows or constitutes a motive or preparation for any fact in issue or relevant fact. The conduct whether previous or subsequent to any proceeding: of any party to any proceeding, or an agent to such party, in reference to such suit or proceeding or in reference to any fact in issue in it or a fact relevant to it; and of any person an offence against whom is the subject of any proceeding is relevant in such proceedings if such conduct influences or is influenced by any fact in issue or relevant fact. The word "conduct" in this section does not include statements, unless those statements accompany and explain acts other than statements but this provision shall not affect the relevance of statements under any other section. When the conduct of any person is relevant, any statement made to him or in his presence and hearing which affects such conduct is relevant.[55]

3. Another possible use for electronic evidence is in supporting or refuting witness, victim, claimant or suspect statements in cases of questionable credibility particularly under cross-examination. For example, a suspect in a homicide case denied knowledge about the firearm used to commit the crime. An examination of his cellular phone, for instance may show deleted images that can implicated the suspect.

4. Another useful application is to expand an investigation by revealing new crimes or suspects. For example, an identity theft investigation revealed that the suspect was part of a network that was sharing, selling and buying identity data. This resulted in an expansion of the investigation to other jurisdictions and led to additional arrests.

5. An often overlooked use of electronic evidence is data mining. By exporting information from multiple digital devices (such as call logs from multiple cellular phones or e-mails from computers) and importing that data into an analytical software package, investigators can diagram and visualize a criminal enterprise or a timeline of events. This graphical representation can make it easier for investigators to understand the complex relationships in a criminal enterprise or for a judge to understand criminal activity in a courtroom presentation, and could reveal possible connections between offenders.

---

[55] Section 6(1) – (4) Evidence Act (Nigeria)

The listed computer or electronic evidence as enumerated above are not exhaustive of its application but to they demonstrate the extent at which such evidence can be used relevant and admissible in civil and criminal matters.

Admissibility of Electronic document

There are two main problems associated with computer or electronically generated documents. First, computer or electronically generated documents are particularly susceptible to being altered. It is possible to make additions or deletions that are not apparent to viewers of the document. The second problem is that it is difficult to tell the difference between the original authentic record and copies of a computer or electronically generated document, which may have been altered.

Notwithstanding, document whether in the traditional form or computer or electronically generated is admissible in any court proceedings provided it is relevant. Admissibility of documentary evidence is generally is established on three main criteria and these are: that the document is pleaded; that the document is relevant to the matter in dispute or inquiry being tried by court; and it is admissible in law. However, for computer or electronically generated document to be admissible as relevant evidence, it must in addition to the stated criteria, fulfil all conditions of any statutory provisions that have made prescriptions on the procedure for its admission. [56] This has been elaborately provided for in the Act which provides that:

> In any proceeding, a statement contained in a document produced by a computer shall be admissible as evidence of any fact stated in it of which direct oral evidence would be admissible, if it is shown that the conditions in subsection (2) of this section are satisfied in relation to the statement and computer in question. [57]

Instructively for the admissibility of electronic or computer document under the Nigeria law, it is contingent that such evidence satisfies some other conditions stipulated in the Act. The conditions are that the computer or electronic document containing the statement must be that which was:

---

[56] *Ibrahim* v. *Okutepa* (2015) All FWLR (pt 785) 331 at 357

[57] Section 84(1) Evidence Act (Nigeria)

1. produced by the computer during a period over which the computer was used regularly lo store or process information for the purposes of any activities regularly carried on over that period, whether for profit or not by anybody, whether corporate or not, or by any individual;

2. that over that period there was regularly supplied to the computer in the ordinary course of those activities information of the kind contained in the statement or of the kind from which the information so contained is derived;

3. that throughout the material part of that period the computer was operating properly or, if not, that in any respect in which it was not operating properly or was out of operation during that part of that period was not such as to affect the production of the document or the accuracy of its contents; and

4. that the information contained in the statement reproduces or is derived from information supplied to the computer in the ordinary course of those activities.[58]

(3) Where over a period the function of storing or processing information for the purposes of any activities regularly carried on over that period as mentioned in subsection (2) (a) of this section was regularly performed by computers, whether:
   a. by a combination of computers operating over that period;
   b. by different computers operating in succession over that period:
   c. by different combinations of computers operating in succession over that period; or
   d. in any other manner involving the successive operation over that period in whatever order, of one or more computers and one or more combinations of computers, all the computers used for that purpose during that period shall be treated for the purposes of this section as constituting a single computer; and references in this section to a computer shall be construed accordingly.[59]

(4) In any proceeding where it is desired to give a statement in evidence by virtue of this section a certificate:
   a. identifying the document containing the statement and describing the manner in which it was produced;

---

[58] Section 84(2)

[59] Section 84(3)

b. giving such particulars of any device involved in the production of that document as may be appropriate for the purpose of showing that the document was produced by a computer:

i. Dealing with any of the matters to which the conditions mentioned in subsection (2) above relate, and purporting to be signed by a person occupying a responsible position in relation to the operation of the relevant device or the management of the relevant activities, as the case may be, shall be evidence of the matter stated in the certificate: and for the purpose of this subsection it shall be sufficient for a matter to be stated to the best of the knowledge and belief of the person stating it.[60]

Be that as it may; a party seeking to rely on documentary evidence be it electronic/computer or other form of paper document, which is relevant to an inquiry being litigated must produce the document before the court to examine, assess, and act on the same. Thus, where such documents are relevant it ought to be produced and tendered as they speak for themselves as against *ipsa delix* of a witness in respect of the transactions which may and be readily accepted by the courts.[61]

Computer/electronic evidence (Original or Secondary evidence)
Original or copy
As earlier noted, the fundamental rule of admissibility of documentary evidence is that a party wishing to rely on the contents of a document in proof of his or her case must tender an original or primary document before the court.[62] This is otherwise called the best evidence rule. However, a copy or secondary evidence of a document may also be tendered in court as an exception to the best evidence rule after certain conditions have been fulfilled.[63] In the realm of computer or electronically generated document, it is not always easy to determine what is considered to be the original document, which constitutes primary evidence in this sense, and sometimes the same document which is primary for one purpose may be secondary for another.

---

[60] Section 84(4)

[61] *UTB (Nig) Ltd* v. *Ajagbule* (2006) 2 NWLR (pt 965) 447 and *First African Trust Co. Ltd* v. *Partnership Investment Co. Ltd* (2003) 18 NWLR (pt 851) 35

[62] Section 88 Evidence Act (Nigeria)

[63] Ibid.; See section 89

This has made computer or electronic evidence more complex. As for instance it is not always clear what is an "original/primary" and what is a "copy/secondary". When information is first entered into a computer system, it is commonly stored in the system's memory (such as, read/write or Ram memory on a PC, which generally has the quickest access time). It is then usually quickly copied to a semi-permanent storage device such as a hard disk so that the system's core memory can be freed up of other tasks. At some point it may also be copied or moved to a magnetic tape or optical disk storage media for longer-term storage. The information, as stored in any of the foregoing digital storage mediums, is not perceived by humans and must be printed out in hardcopy form, or displayed on a computer monitor. The Act provides:

a. Information shall be taken to be supplied to a computer if it is supplied to it in any appropriate form and whether it is supplied directly or (with or without human intervention) by means of any appropriate equipment:

b. Where, in the course or activities carried on by any individual or body, information is supplied with a view to its being stored or processed for the purposes of those activities by a computer operated otherwise than in the course of those activities, that information, if duly supplied to that computer, shall be taken to be supplied to it in the course of those activities;

c. a document shall be taken to have been produced by a computer whether it was produced by it directly or (with or without human intervention) by means of any appropriate equipment.[64]

Against the above explanation and view from this perspective, the question is when can a record stops being an "original/primary" and becomes a "copy/secondary" during this process.' It is pertinent to note that there is nothing "sacrosanct" about the admission of electronic/computer evidence. Though the incorporation of electronic evidence has incorporated substantial changes to the Nigeria Evidence Act however, in analyzing the admissibility of such evidence, it is often best to treat it as originating from the most similar, non-electronic source as thoughtful application of traditional evidentiary principles will nearly always lead to the correct result. Therefore, while electronic evidence may present some unique challenges to admissibility and complicate matters of establishing authenticity and foundation, it does not require the

---

[64] Section 84(5)

proponent to discard his knowledge of traditional evidentiary principles or learn anything truly new. More so it is trite law that in any proceeding where it is desired to give a statement in electronically produced document it is sufficient to produce a certificate: identifying the document containing the statement and describing the manner in which it was produced; giving such particulars of any device involved in the production of that document as may be appropriate for the purpose of showing that the document was produced by a computer.[65]

Distinguishing Primary from Secondary Electronic/Computer Evidence
There are basically two major divergent approaches employ in determining what constitutes an 'original/primary' and what is a 'copy/secondary' of a document in the realm of computer or electronic evidence. The first approach is, an original document is a computer print-out or other output of data stored in the computer device. This is distillable from the letter of the Evidence Act which provides:

> Section 86(3)(4) Primary evidence means the document itself produced for the inspection of the court. Where a number of documents have all been made by one uniform process, as in the case of printing, lithography, photography, computer or other electronic or mechanical process, each shall be primary evidence of the contents of the rest; but where they are all copies of a common original, they shall not be primary evidence of the contents of the original.66

The second approach which is the opposite of the first approach and treats computer print-outs as copy/secondary evidence is underscored by the decision of the Nigeria Supreme Court in *Anyaebosi* v. *R T Briscoe*.[67] In a unanimous decision the held that:

> Computer print-outs are admissible in evidence under the provisions of the Nigerian Evidence Act, with the underlying assumption by all the members of the court that such evidence amounts to secondary evidence.

Instructively, the two methods above create difficulty in determining when a computer/electronic evidence is primary or secondary. This is especially so, when the Act provides that a computer print-out is an original but does legislate on the status of computer data from which the

---

[65] Section 84(4) Evidence Act (Nigeria)
[66] Section 84(3) & (4)
[67] (1987) 3 NWLR 84 (pt 59)

print-out originates. From the above it is difficult to understand a situation where a computer print-out could be considered to be an original document while the computer data which existed before is held to be a copy.

Beside, another problem which has seldom been addressed in the Nigerian evidence legislation, case law and in academic discussion is also the problem as to the status of the soft copy available on the computer monitor because hardware and software operation on the data input may result into two types of output namely, soft copy on the monitor and the printed hard copy. Consequently a soft copy stands in the middle of computer data and computer print-out and unless it is printed a computer print-out remains in the machine as either computer data or soft copy available to view on the monitor.

Thus, the relevant of secondary evidence of computer/electronic evidence's and admissibility as secondary evidence has been overlooked in the Act the question is thus left for the court interpretation. That is if copy or secondary evidence is admitted in the form of copies of the original document as provided in section 89 and 90 of the Act, then what will be status of a copy of a computer print-out, when the a printout is held to be an original and vice versa.

Authentication of Electronic or Computer Evidence

It is instructive to note that electronic/computer evidence is ordinarily complex thus before being admitted, such evidence must be authenticated – that is, the proponent of the computer or electronic evidence must make a showing sufficient to support a finding that the evidence is what it purports to be. Essentially a court need not find that the evidence is necessarily sufficient evidence that the judge can act upon it. Arguably, because of the common perception that electronic/computer records may be readily altered to appear to be something else therefore, "authenticity is often the central battleground for determining admissibility of electronic evidence."

Consequently, the proponent of electronic evidence often has to navigate through the tide of a judiciary that is highly sceptical of such evidence.

For instance, while some look to the Internet as a technological innovative vehicle for communication, the court may warily and wearily view it largely as one large catalyst for rumour, innuendo, and misinformation. There is no way claimant can overcome the presumption that the information discovered on the Internet is not inherently trustworthy. This is based on the fact that anyone can put anything on the Internet. More particularly there is inherent perception that web-site is usually monitored for accuracy and nothing contained therein is under oath or even subject to independent verification underlying documentation. Additionally, there is possibility for court holding an illusion that hackers can adulterate the content on any web-site from any location at any time. For these reasons, any evidence procured off the Internet is adequate for almost nothing, even under the most liberal interpretation of the hearsay exception rules.

However, courts may not seem incline to dismiss electronic/computer evidence based on the mere fact that such evidence is susceptible to alteration. Indeed, courts will admit, for example, such evidence, after a threshold showing of authenticity in line with provision of the Evidence Act.

Methods authenticating electronic evidence

It is pertinent to note that several ways are inherently provided in the Evidence Act applicable to identifying and authentication of electronically generated evidence for admission in proceedings. These methods are though more traditional forms of evidence in mind, most of the methods are easily applicable or adoptable for authenticating computer or electronic evidence. In view of the above background some of the relevant methods of authenticating electronic or computer evidence distillable from the provision of the Act are herein discussed.

1. Testimony of a Witness with Knowledge

A party intending to rely on electronic or computer evidence in support of his case may do so through testimony that the evidence "is what it is claimed to be. Just as it is obtainable for non-electronic documents, the witness providing such testimony may be the person who created the electronic document or maintains the evidence in its electronic form. This can be justified by the provision of the Act which states:

> In a proceeding where direct oral evidence of a fact would be admissible; any statement made by a person in a document which seems to establish that fact shall, on production of the original document, be admissible as evidence of that fact if the following conditions are satisfied:
>
> (a) if the maker of the statement either (i) had personal knowledge of the matters dealt with by the statement, or (ii) where the document in question

is or forms part of a record purporting to be a continuous record. made the statement (in so far as the matters dealt with by it are not within his personal knowledge) in the performance of a duty to record information supplied to him by a person who had, or might reasonably be supposed to have personal knowledge of those matters: and

(b) if the maker of the statement is called as a witness in the proceeding.[68]

Thus, a witness authenticating electronic or computer evidence must provide factual specificity about the process by which the electronically stored information is created, acquired, maintained, and preserved without alteration or change, or the process by which it is produced if the result of a system or process that does so. This proposition is supported by the Act which provides:

(4) In any proceeding where it is desired to give a statement in evidence by virtue of this section a certificate:
a) identifying the document containing the statement and describing the manner in which it was produced;
b) giving such particulars of any device involved in the production of that document as may be appropriate for the purpose of showing that the document was produced by a computer:[69]

It may be argued that failure to provide such testimony may result in the subjection of the electronic evidence inadmissible or affect the weight to be attached to the document. In this perspective, evidence of an expert in computer or electronic operation generally may be relevant or necessary.

2. Distinctive Characteristics and the Like

In distinctive characteristics method, a party may authenticate computer or electronic evidence using circumstantial evidence in conjunction with the appearance, contents, substance, internal patterns, or other distinctive characteristics of the evidence. For instance where a witness testifies that an e-mail or text message originated from the known e-mail address or screen name of another person, courts may find that the e-mail or text message is an authentic communication from the purported sender. Inference of the application of this method can be drawn from the Evidence Act which provides:

---

[68] Section 83 Evidence Act (Nigeria) see also Rules 903 and 1007; US Federal Rules of Evidence (Cornell University Law School, Information Institution, 2015)
[69] Section 84(4) Evidence Act (Nigeria)

The court may presume that a message forwarded from a telegraph office to the person to whom such message purports to be addressed corresponds with a message delivered for transmission at the office from which the message purports to be sent: but the court shall not make any presumption as to the person by whom such message was delivered for transmission.[70]

The court may presume that an electronic message forwarded by the originator through an electronic mail server to the addressee to whom the message purports to be addressed corresponds with the message as fed into his computer for transmission: but the court shall not make any presumption as to the person to whom such message was sent.[71]

Note however, that this method of authentication is not entirely complete proof; because, network administrators and other users on the same network may access or alter electronic files stored on network computers. In this area too opinion of an expert in computer or electronic operation generally may be expedient to corroborate the evidence.

3. Public Records or Reports
In this paradigm an electronic or computer generated public document may be authenticated by evidence that a writing authorized by law to be recorded or filed and in fact recorded or filed in a public office, or a purported public record, report, statement, or data compilation, in any form, is from the public office where items of this nature are kept. The party relying on such public evidence need only show that the office from which the records were taken is the legal custodians of the records; which may be corroborated vide the testimony of an officer who is authorized to attest to custodianship or through a certificate of authenticity from the public office authorized to maintain the records. The explanation is contained in the Evidence Act which provides:

Every public officer having the custody of a public document which an) person has" right to inspect shall give that person on demand a copy of it on payment of the legal fees prescribed in that respect together with a certificate written at the foot of such copy that it is a true copy of such document or part of it as the case may be.

The certificate mentioned in subsection (1) of this section shall be dated and subscribed by such officer with his name and his official title and shall

---

[70] Section 153(1)

[71] Ibid. sub-section (2)

be sealed, whenever such officer is authorized by law to make use of a seal and such copies so certified shall be called certified copies.

An officer who by the ordinary course of official duty, is authorized to deliver such copies, shall be deemed to have the custody of such documents within the meaning of this section.[72]

Arguably, the position of the law is that, documents are said to be in proper custody within the meaning of sections 148 to 155 of this Act if they are in the place in which and under the care of the person with whom they would naturally be, but no custody is improper ifit is proved tt) have had a legitimate origin or if the circumstances of the particular case are such as to render such an origin probable.[73] Notwithstanding, the concern about the accuracy of such evidence merely goes to the weight to be attached to that evidence and not its admissibility.

4. Ancient Documents (Presumption of Document of 20 years old)

The theory behind ancient method of authenticating document particularly as it relates to electronic or computer generated document is that, because of the age of the document, its author or creator is likely unavailable to testify regarding its authenticity; thus, courts may presume the genuineness of such document or must consider circumstantial evidence to guarantee the genuineness of the document. For instance the Evidence Act provides that:

Where any document purporting or proved to be 20 years old or more is produced from any custody which the court in the particular case considers proper, the court may presume that the signature and every other part of such document which purports to be in the handwriting of any particular person is in that person's handwriting, and in the case of a document executed or attested, that it was duly executed and attested by the persons by whom it purports to be executed and attested.[74]

The reason accounting for this exception is founded upon the fact that the document was created long before the controversy arose and it is less likely that the document was fabricated or altered for purposes of the present litigation. Thus, in this circumstance electronic or computer generated document will be presumed to be genuine if:

---

[72] Section 104(1) – (3) See also Rule 1005 US Federal Rule of Evidence

[73] Section 156 Evidence Act (Nigeria)

[74] Ibid.; Section 155

1. Is in such condition as to create no suspicion concerning its authenticity,
2. Was in a place where it, if authentic, would likely be, and
3. Has been in existence 20 years or more at the time it is offered.

This mechanism of authentication is significant in that it can qualify a document under a corresponding hearsay exception, so that the document may then be admitted for the truth of its contents. In view of this courts may find that once a computer or electronically generated document is authenticated under section 83(1)(a) & (b), 83(2) and 83(3), it automatically becomes relevant and admissible.

5. Processes or System of producing electronic or computer evidence
Electronic or computer evidence may be authenticated by evidence describing a process or system used to produce a result and showing that the process or system produces an accurate result. This method is often used to authenticate evidence generated by, or stored on, a computer. Therefore according to the Act

    a. Information shall be taken to be supplied to a computer if it is supplied to it in any appropriate form and whether it is supplied directly or (with or without human intervention) by means of any appropriate equipment:

    b. Where, in the course or activities carried on by any individual or body, information is supplied with a view to its being stored or processed for the purposes of those activities by a computer operated otherwise than in the course of those activities, that information, if duly supplied to that computer, shall be taken to be supplied to it in the course of those activities;

    c. a document shall be taken to have been produced by a computer whether it was produced by it directly or (with or without human intervention) by means of any appropriate equipment.[75]

6. Computer-Generated Records
The authenticity of computer-generated records may be generally established in a similar manner traditional documentary evidence will be prove through the testimony of a witness who has the knowledge of how the such documents are recorded, stored and maintained. According to the provision of the Evidence Act:

---

[75] Section 84(5)

84(1): In a proceeding where direct oral evidence of a fact would be admissible. an) Statement made by a person in a document which seems to establish that fact shall, on production of the original document, be admissible as evidence of that fact if the following conditions are satisfied:
(a) if the maker of the statement either (i) had personal knowledge of the matters dealt with by the statement, or (ii) where the document in question is or forms part of a record purporting to be a continuous record made the statement (in so far as the matters dealt with by it are not within his personal knowledge) in the performance of a duty to record information supplied to him by a person who had, or might reasonably be supposed to have personal knowledge of those matters.

6. Self-Authenticating Documents

The Nigerian Evidence Act also identifies categories of evidence that may be authenticated without extrinsic evidence. Each of these categories provides an efficient method for authenticating evidence, but courts have identified three that are particularly relevant in the electronic evidence context.[76]

7. Official Publications

Here official publications purporting to be issued by public authority are self-authenticating under sections 104, 105 and 106 of the Evidence Act. However, to be self-authenticating the record must be: accompanied by a written declaration of its custodian or other qualified person certifying that the record was made at or near the time of the occurrence of the matters set forth by a person with knowledge of those matters, was kept in the course of the regularly conducted official activity; and was made as a regular practice.[77]

Admissibility of E-mails and Text Messages

In modern litigation, especially with proliferation of the use of Mobil phone in Nigeria since 1999, it is rare when a dispute will not involve some communication by e-mail or text messages. In investigating and establishing an individual criminal conduct, evidence may be retrieved or be detected from mobile phone. Such a communication is easily authenticated if the proponent of the communication can secure the admission of the author or sender of the communication that he drafted or

---

[76] See for instance, Rule 902 United States Federal Rules of Evidence (Cornell University Law School, Information Institute, 2015)
[77] Ibid., Rule 902(2) & (3) Evidence (US)

sent the communication.[78] Additionally, a recipient, or non-recipient with knowledge that the communication was sent, may authenticate an e-mail or text message. Also, a witness with knowledge of how the responsible Internet service providers or wireless telephone carriers sent and received an e-mail or text message, and how such messages are stored and retrieved, may authenticate such messages.[79] The threshold determination for authentication will often vary with the piece of evidence and the court the evidence is before. Comparing an e-mail or a text message with other e-mails or text messages already authenticated may serve to authenticate the e-mail or text message at issue. Inference to justify this proposition can also be drawn from Nigerian Evidence Act position which provides thus:

> The court may presume that a message forwarded from a telegraph office to the person to whom such message purports to be addressed corresponds with a message delivered for transmission at the office from which the message purports to be sent: but the court shall not make any presumption as to the person by whom such message was delivered for transmission.
>
> The court may presume that an electronic message forwarded by the originator through an electronic mail server to the addressee to whom the message purports to be addressed corresponds with the message as fed into his computer for transmission: but the court shall not make any presumption as to the person to whom such message was sent.[80]

Now that the nature of digital evidence is significantly different from the early days of mainframe or stand-alone computers, traditional foundations for computer records may no longer be adequate to address the complexities. Mobile transformation is upon us. Arguably, in order to demonstrate that the an e-mail message is what the proponent claims it to be, the foundation must take into account not only the legal requirements of procedure and evidence, but must also include an evaluation of each of the key components of the information system from which the evidence was generated. The rigor with which an evidentiary foundation must be established depends on the purpose for which the e-mail information is being offered in evidence, whether there is any reason to believe the

---

[78] Sections 25 and 123 Evidence Act (Nigeria)

[79] Ibid.; Section 68 Expert opinion

[80] Ibid.; Section 153(1) & (2)

evidence is or is not authentic, and the extent to which the data and information can be corroborated.

Proof of due Execution: Authentication of Electronic Signature

The terms "electronic authentication" and "electronic signature" are used to refer to various techniques currently available on the market or still under development for the purpose of replicating an electronic environment some or all of the functions identify as characteristic of handwritten signatures or other traditional authentication methods.[81] However, the UNICTRAL Model on Electronic Commerce did not define electronic signature, rather it provides: "Where the law requires a signature of a person, that requirement is met in relation to a data message if: *(a)* a method is used to identify that person and to indicate that person's approval of the information contained in the data message; and *(b)* that method is as reliable as was appropriate for the purpose for which the data message was generated or communicated, in the light of all the circumstances, including any relevant agreement. Paragraph (1) applies whether the requirement therein is in the form of an obligation or whether the law simply provides consequences for the absence of a signature.[82]

The UNCITRAL Model Law on Electronic Signatures defines electronic signature as data in electronic form, affixed to or logically associated with, a data message, which may be used to "identify the signatory" in relation to the data message and to "indicate the signatory's approval of the information contained in the data message."[83] Though the most widely used definition of an electronic signature is: "An electronic sound, symbol, or process attached to or logically associated with a document and executed or adopted by a person with the intent to sign the document."[84]

Importantly, the purpose of signature is to establish due execution of document, the signatory's identity, his or her intent to sign and his or her adoption of the contents. Traditional functions include validating official action and protecting the consumers and down-stream users who rely on

---

[81] See Article 2 UNICITRAL Model on Electronic Signatures 2001

[82] Article 7; UNICITRAL Model on Electronic Commerce 1998 (United Nations Publication, New York, 1999), see also section 8, Botswana Electronic Record (Evidence) Act, 2014

[83] Article 2 sub-paragraph (a) UNCITRAL Model of Electronic Signature 2014

[84] Uniform Electronic Transactions Act (1999), National Conference of Commissioners on Uniform State Laws, http:// www.law.upenn.edu/bll/archives/ulc/ecom/ueta_final.pdf

the signature and signed documents. There is also a fairly significant cultural aspect which includes providing the solemnity and ceremony of signing. In addition, people have an expectation of seeing an actual signature.

In electronic signature for instance an "X" can be a legally binding signature. In this perspective the legal definition of a signature thus means, "Anything that the signatory intends to have act as binding himself or herself to the contents."[85] At Common Law, a signature requires no particular form. The only requirement is that, it must be whatever it is intended by the signer to be the signer's signature.[86] Although signing with an "X" is legally acceptable, there are many good reasons not to accept the "X", even if it is legally sufficient. The reasons have to do with *proof, identity* and *trustworthiness*, not legal prohibition.[87] John D. Gregory, co-chair of the ABA Business Law Section Global E-commerce Policy Subcommittee, says: *"It is arguable that an electronic signature qualifies as a signature without any legislative assistance."*[88]

It is pertinent to note that almost all jurisdictions around the world have enacted legislation on E-signature. The main rationale is to create certainty of admissibility and acceptance e-signature and because of the symbolic importance of signatures[89]. Arguably there are no instances of statutory or case law that preclude the use of electronic signatures. Notwithstanding the Nigerian Evidence Act provides for mode of proving execution of content of an electronic/computer document and on this the Act provides:

> If a document is alleged to be signed or to have been written wholly or in part by an) person the signature or the handwriting of so much of the document as is alleged to be in that person's handwriting must be proved to be in his handwriting.[90]

---

[85] Jefferey, N. B. Legal Consideration of E-Signature

[86] Reed, C., "What is a Signature?", [2000 (3)] Journal of Information, Law and Technology (JILT), online at: http://elj.warwick.ac.uk/jilt/00-3/reed.html also see generally, Jeffery N. B., Legal Consideration of E-Signature,

[87] Ibid.

[88] John D. Gregory, Canadian and American Legislation on Electronic Signatures with reflections on the European Union Directive, (November, 2001), online at: http://pages.ca.inter.net/~euclid1/esiglaws.html

[89] Jonathan D. Friede & Leigh M. Murray, the Admissibility of Electronic Evidence Under the Federal Rules of Evidence (2011) XVII(2), *Richmond Journal of Law and Technology.*

[90] Section 93(1) Evidence Act (Nigeria)

Where a rule of evidence requires a signature or provides for certain consequences if" document is not signed an electronic signature satisfies that rule of law or avoids those consequences.[91]

All electronic signatures may be proved in any manner, including by showing that a procedure existed by which it is necessary for a person, in order to proceed further with a transaction. to have executed a symbol or security procedure for the purpose of verifying that an electronic record is that of the person.[92]

Equally it may not be out of pace for a court to further adopt the traditional methods of authenticating due execution in construing authenticity of electronic signature. Thus the following sections of the Evidence Act may be applicable:

Evidence that a person exists having the same name, address, business or occupation as the maker of a document purports to have. is admissible to show that such document was written or signed by that person. Evidence that a document exists to which the document the making of which is in issue purports to be a reply together with evidence of the making and delivery to a person of such earlier document. is admissible to show the identity of the maker of the disputed document with the person to whom the earlier document was delivered.[93]

Evidence that a person signed a document containing a declaration that a seal was his seal is admissible to prove that he sealed it. Evidence that the grantor on executing any document requiring delivery expressed an intention that it should operate at once is admissible to prove delivery.[94] In order to ascertain whether a signature, writing, seal or finger impression is that of the person by whom it purports to have been written or made, any signature, writing seal or finger impression admitted or proved to the satisfaction of the court to have been written or made by that person may be compared with the one which is to be proved although that signature, writing, seal or finger impression has not been produced or proved for any other purpose.[95]

The court may direct any person present in court to write word or figure or to make finger impressions for the purpose of enabling the court to

---

[91] Ibid. sub-section (2) of Section 93

[92] Ibid.; Sub-section (3) of section 93

[93] Section 94(1) – (2) Evidence Act (Nigeria)

[94] Ibid.; Section 95(1) – (2)

[95] Ibid.; Section 101 (1) – (3)

compare: the words, figures or finger impressions so written with any word, figure or finger impression alleged to have been written or made by such person: Provided that where a defendant does not give evidence, he may not be so directed to 'write such words or figures or to make finger impressions.[96]

After the final termination of the proceeding in which the court required a person to make his finger impressions, such impressions shall be destroyed.[97]

It is instructive to note that due to fact that e-signature is now been adopted in transactions, a number of different electronic signature techniques have been developed over the years. Each technique aims at satisfying different needs and providing different levels of security, and entails different technical requirements. Electronic authentication and signature methods may be classified in three categories:

1. Those based on the knowledge of the user or the recipient (e.g. passwords, personal identification numbers (PINs)),
2. Those based on the physical features of the user (e.g. biometrics) and
3. Those based on the possession of an object by the user (e.g. codes or other information stored on a magnetic card).
4. A fourth category might include various types of authentication and signature methods that, without falling under any of the above categories, might also be used to indicate the originator of an electronic communication (such as a facsimile of a handwritten signature, or a name typed at the bottom of an electronic message).

Instructively and because there are more concern with evidential procedure to proof electronic signature, it may not be overemphasized to mention the technologies currently developed and in use include digital signatures and this may include:

i)   Public key infrastructure (PKI),
ii)   Biometric devices,
iii)   PINs,
iv)   User-defined or assigned passwords,
v)   Scanned handwritten signatures,
vi)   Signature by means of a digital pen, and
vii)   Clickable; "OK" or "I accept" boxes.

---

[96] Ibid.
[97] Ibid.

Essentially and in some cases, the expression "electronic authentication or signature" is used to refer to techniques, depending on the context in which they are used and may involve various elements, such as:

i.   Identification of individuals,
ii. Confirmation of a person's authority (typically to act on behalf of another person or entity) or prerogatives (for example, membership in an institution or subscription to a service) or
iii. Assurance as to the integrity of information and
iv. In some cases, the focus is on identity only, but sometimes it extends to authority, or a combination of any or all of those elements.

The Model Law on Electronic Commerce uses instead the notion of "original form" to provide the criteria for the functional equivalence of "authentic" electronic information. According to article 8 of the UNICITRAL Model Law, where the law requires information to be presented or retained in its original form, that requirement is met by a data message if:

(a) There exists "a reliable assurance as to the integrity of the information from the time when it was first generated in its final form, as a data message or otherwise;" and

(b) Where it is required that information be presented, that information "is capable of being displayed to the person to whom it is to be presented."

In keeping with the distinction made in most legal systems between signature (or seals, where they are used instead) as a means of "authentication", on the one hand, and "authenticity" as the quality of a document or record on the other, both model laws complement the notion of "originality" with the notion of "signature."[98] For instance Botswana Electronic Record (Evidence) Act provides:

> Section where a rule of law requires a signature, or provides for certain consequences if the record is not signed, an electronic signature shall satisfy that requirement or shall operate to avoid those consequences subject to electronic communication and transaction Act, an electronic signature may be proved in any manner, including by showing that a

---

[98] Electronic Signature in Global and National Commerce Act, 2000, available at www.fca.gov/.../public%20law%20106

method existed by which it is necessary for a person in order to proceed further with a transaction, to have executed a symbol or security procedure for the purpose of verifying that an electronic record is that of the person.[99] Where the signature of a person is required by law and such law does not specify the type of signature, that requirement, in relation to data is met if an electronic signature is used.[100]

For the purpose of determining under any rule of law, whether or not an electronic record is admissible in respect of any standard, procedure, usage or practice concerning the matter in which the electronic record or stored having regard to the type of business, enterprise or endeavour that used, recorded or stored the electronic record and the nature and purpose of the electronic record.[101]

The matter referred to in section 7(2), 9 and 10 may be established by Affidavit.[102]

It is now not in contention that the National Assembly must enact law on due execution or electronic signature, it is clearly stated in the amended Act just as contained in UNICTRAL Model Law of Electronic Signature though people may seem to feel the need to seek explicit legislative permission before adoption. Essentially the most nations have adopted either the Model Laws or their functional equivalents. For example, the European Union has adopted the European Union Directive on Advanced Electronic Signatures.[103] Canada has enacted its Uniform Electronic Commerce Act,[104] the Personal Information Protection and Electronic Documents Act [105] and Secure Electronic Signature Regulations.[106] It is argued that technological advancement has globalized the use of electronic or digital information in transaction it thus not out of place the use of electronic signature technology in courts be legal, safe and proven. It is undisputable that the financial, legal and security benefits

---

[99] Section 8(1) –(2) Electronic Record (Evidence) Act, 2014

[100] Ibid.; Sub-Section (3)

[101] Ibid.; Section 10

[102] Ibid.; Section 11

103 EU Directive on Electronic Signatures, Directive 1999/93/EC, 1999, http://eur-lex.europa.eu/LexUriServ/LexUriServ.do?uri=CELEX:31999L0093:en:HTML

[104] Uniform Electronic Commerce Act (Canada), http://www.ulcc.ca/en/us/index.cfm?sec=1&sub=1u1&print=1

[105] 14 Personal Information and Electronic Documents Act (Canada), 2000, http://laws.justice.gc.ca/PDF/Statute/P/P-8.6.pdf

[106] (SOR/2005-30) (Enabling Statute: Canada Evidence Act (R.S., 1985, c. C-5), see generally, United States Uniform Electronic Transaction Act and E-Sign (1999) available at www.njleg.state.nj.us/2000/.../116

offered by completing the transformation to a fully paper-on-demand court through implementation of e-signature technology are compelling.

Part III
Affidavit Evidence

Definition of an Affidavit

An affidavit is a statement usually of facts made in writing, singed, by a person and declared by him on oath to be true of the facts in the affidavit and duly sworn to before an appropriate authority.[107]

Use of an Affidavit

The court may direct a party and or parties to a civil proceeding by making an order at any stage of such proceeding to the effect that specified facts be proved by affidavit, with or without the attendance of the deponent in court for cross examination.[108] A party who wishes to file an affidavit in court must file the original of the affidavit or an office copy of the affidavit that will be recognized for any purpose.[109]

An affidavit must be sworn to before a Commissioner for Oath, Magistrate or Registrar of a Court or a Notary Public. Provided that a person swears an affidavit before an official duly authorized to take oath, a court may permit it to be used even though it is defective in form.[110]

An affidavit sworn to before a person, which in legal parlance is considered to be an interested person in the case or a person on whose behalf the affidavit is offered or before whom the affidavit is to be used, will not be admitted in court[111]. In *Ekpetor v. Wanogh*,[112] the appellants' counsel in the matter filed two separate motions on behalf of their client but each of the counsel swore the affidavit, The Supreme Court *per Kutigi* JSC said:

> This is a very undesirable practice since it means that, counsel is giving evidence in the case in which he is appearing. Also if there is conflict in affidavit and evidence is called to clarify or resolve such conflict the counsel who swore the affidavit must give evidence. This is undesirable and must be avoided.

---

[107] Bryan A.G., *Black's Law Dictionary, op. cit.*, page 62

[108] Section 107 Evidence Act (Nigeria)

[109] Ibid.; Section 108

[110] Ibid.; Sections 110 and 112

[111] Ibid.

[112] *Ekpetor v. Wanogh* (2004) 20 NSCQR 333 at 350

Content of an Affidavit

Every affidavit used in court should contain only a statement of facts or circumstances to which the witness deposes. This position was emphasized by the Supreme Court in *Bamayi* v. *The State*[113] that:

> In any affidavit used in court, it is required that it shall contain only a statement of the deponent or from information, which he believes to be true. This is provided in sections 86 and 87 of the evidence Act. The test for knowing facts and circumstances is to examine each of the paragraphs deposed to in the affidavit. If it is such that a witness may be entitled to adduce them in his testimony on oath and are legally admissible as evidence to prove or disprove a fact in issue or dispute, then they qualify as statements of fact or of circumstances....

Every affidavit used in court should contain only statement of facts and circumstances within the deponent personal knowledge. Where it is not, he must state the source of his information, which he believes to be true.[114] The deponent must state with particularly, the name of his informant, the time, place and the circumstances of this information.

Every affidavit used in court must not contain extraneous matters or by way of objection or prayer, or legal argument or conclusion.[115] In *G.A.S LTD* v. *Thahat*,[116] the Supreme Court said:

> ...This means that affidavit evidence, like oral evidence, must as a general rule deal with facts and avoids matters of inference or conclusion which falls within the province of the court, or objection, prayer or legal argument; which must be left to counsel. If therefore, affidavit evidence is in the form of conclusion, inference legal argument, prayer or objection, it raises no fact, which need to be controverts, but is simply regarded as extraneous to the determination of factual disputes.

Note that where an affidavit offends the provision of Section 87 of the Act, it will be in competent and ought to be struck out or in the alternative; the court should not attach any weight to it.

Finally, the content of every affidavit, which is to be used in any cause or matter, must contain the following:

---

[113] *Bamaiyi* v. *the State* (2001) 6 NSCQR (PT 1) 18

[114] Section 115(1) Evidence Act (Nigeria)

[115] Ibid., Section 115(2), see *Bamayi* v. *State* (2001)

[116] *G.A.S LTD* v. *Thahat* (2004) 4 SC (pt i) 109 at 120,

i)   Headed in the court or cause or matter in which its to be used. The deponent must state his full name, trade or profession address and nationality;

ii) The statement of fact must be written in first person and divided into paragraphs numbered consecutively;

iii) The Commissioner for Oath or any competent designated officer shall attest to every interlineations, alteration or cancellation made before the affidavit is sworn;

iv) Every affidavit which is illegible or difficult to read or in the judgment of the person before whom the oath is taken, is so written as to facilities fraud, he may refused to be swear by the deponent;

v)   The affidavit must be singed by the deponent or marked if he cannot sign;

vi) The affidavit must contain a Jurat.[117]

Proof of Fact by Affidavit

Generally there is no rule regulating cases in, which the court may order a fact to be proof by affidavit. However, it is more usually used in application for prerogative orders like, Mandamus, Prohibition, and Certiorari and *Quo warranto*. The Court in any civil proceeding may, however order that a substantive matter be proof by affidavit and decides on it.[118] This position is captured in the decision of the Supreme Court in *Population Commission* v. *Chairman Ikere Local Government*[119] where Ayoola JSC observes thus:

> Whether proceeding may be heard entirely on affidavit evidence or not is not to be determined by the form of the proceedings but by the nature of the issues and the parties' reaction to the facts in the proceedings. Where there are no contentious issues of facts in the proceedings, no reasonable objection can be taken to a hearing on the affidavit. It is when there is serious dispute as to facts to be resolved that the trial on affidavits is inappropriate.

Contradiction in Affidavit Evidence

Where a court is faced with affidavits, which are contradictory on the facts deposed to, the judge may allow oral evidence from the deponent or such other witnesses as the parties may be advice to call at hearing to resolve

---

[117] Section 117 Evidence Act (Nigeria)

[118] Ibid.; Section 107

[119] *Population Commission* v. *Chairman Ikere Local Government* (2001) 7 NSCQR 255 AT 267-268

the conflicts. The court however, may not allowed oral evidence at hearing to resolve the conflict if, the conflict is not material as to affect the out come of the case. This is explained in the case of *A.G Anambra State* v. *A.G Federation*[120] where the Supreme Court held that:

> Where the conflict in affidavit evidence are not material to a case or where the facts there in are inadmissible in evidence, the court should not be saddled with the responsibility of calling oral evidence to resolve the conflict. The need to call oral evidence would not arise if the conflicts are so narrow and are not significant.

Filing a Counter Affidavit to Contradict an Affidavit

Where a court order that a matter be decided on affidavit evidence or an affidavit is filed for any purpose relating to the matter a party or parties who intend to challenge the facts stated there in must file a counter affidavit. Note however that, where a party failed to file a counter affidavit the facts in the affidavit would be deemed to have being admitted and no oral evidence will be allowed to contradict these facts.[121] However, he may be allowed to argue against the affidavit only, on point of law.

In any application (motion) before the court, which in law ought to be supported by affidavit evidence, oral submission of a counsel, however brilliant and ingenious in moving the application is not evidence in support of such application; the evidence is the deposition in support there to.[122] Onu JSC in *Adejubgbe* v. *Ologunja*[123] said,

> A denial can be express or by necessary implication. Once facts are deposed to, in order to negate the general drift of the depositions in the supporting affidavit, and then such are deemed denied.

Where in a counter affidavit, a respondent makes some feeble and shallow averments in denial of specific facts; such averments are mere general denial which is ineffectual as a challenge to serious averments made against him.[124]

---

[120] *A.G. Anambra State* v. *A.G Federation* (2005) NSCQR 429 and 452

[121] *The Honda Place Ltd* v. *Globe Motors Ltd* (2005) 7 SC (pat ii) 182 at 180, 190 and 202.

[122] *Magnosson* v. *Koiki* (1993) 12 SCN 114; *Nwagboso* v. *Ejlogu* (1997) NWLR (pt 527) 173 and *Ajomole* v. *Yardaut No 2* (1991) 5 NWLR (pt191) 266

[123] *Adejubgbe* v. *Ologunja* (2004) 2 SC (pt ii) 44 at 65

[124] *Ekiti State Governor* v. *Ojo* (2006) All FWLR (pt 331) 1298 at 1328.

Chapter 15

Wrongful Admission and Rejection of Evidence

The Supreme Court in the case of *Shittu* v. *Fashewa*[1] on the issue of wrongful admission and rejection of evidence said:

> A court is expected in all proceedings before it to admit and act only on evidence, which is admissible in law... and so if a court inadvertently admits inadmissible evidence it has a duty not to act on it.

This rule is very strict, thus, where a court wrongfully admits inadmissible evidence it ought as a duty to disregard the evidence in consideration of the judgment in the matter as contained in Section 251 (1) (2) and (3) of the Evidence Act that provides.

Grounds for Exclusion of Evidence

The grounds for exclusion of evidence according to the Evidence Act[2] include the following:

> i) A court may exclude evidence which though relevant or declared to be relevant if it appears to it to be too remote to be material in the circumstance of the case; and
> ii) This section shall not enable any person to give evidence of a fact, which is disentitled to prove by any provision of the law for the time being enforced.

From the spirit and letter of above quoted section, the following evidence if wrongfully admitted by court, the appellate court has jurisdiction to expunge it:

---

[1] *Shittu* v. *Fashewa* (2005) 7 SC (pt i) 107 at 117 to 118
[2] Section 1 (a) & (b) Evidence Act 2011

1) Hearsay evidence

Hearsay evidence no matter how relevant is inadmissible except, its purpose is to enhance the probability of the truth of the case in dispute. When hearsay evidence is wrongfully admitted, the court ought to exclude it and decide the matter only on admissible evidence.

2) Opinion Evidence

Generally, witnesses are not permitted to inform the court of the inferences they draw from the fact perceived by them but, they should confine their evidence to the fact within their personal knowledge. The evidence if wrongly admitted is liable to be expunged from the record and it cannot form part or influence the court decision on the matter.

3) Character Evidence

Evidence of act or acts to establish that an accused is of a particular character or reputation among his neighbour and as a man likely to have committed an offence charged, is usually inadmissible. The evidence will be excluded by appellate court if wrongly admitted.

4) Conduct

Evidence may generally not be given of a party's conduct in other occasion, if its purpose is to show that he is a person likely to have conducted himself in a manner alleged by the adverse party on the occasion in question. If admitted ought to be expunged by appellate court.

1) The wrongful admission of evidence shall not itself be a ground for the reversal of any decision in any case. That is, where it appear to the court on appeal that the evidence so admitted cannot reasonably be held to have affected the decision and that such decision would have been the same if such evidence had been admitted.[3]

2) The wrongful exclusion of evidence shall not itself be a ground for the reversal of any decision in any case if it shall appear to the court on appeal that had the evidence so excluded been admitted it may reasonably be held that the decision would have been the same.[4]

Note that where such evidence had been wrongfully admitted and acted upon and whether or not the opposing party objects or not, an appellate court has the duty to exclude the evidence and decide the case

---

[3] Section 251(1); *Buhari* v. *Obasanjo* (2005) 23 NSCQR 442 at 558

[4] Section 251(2); Evidence Act 2011 see also *Ojoh* v. *Kamilu* (2005) 24 NSCQR 256 at 286

only, on the legally admissible evidence. Note further that there are two categories of inadmissible evidence they are:

i) Evidence which is absolutely inadmissible is not within the competence of the parties to admit by consent or otherwise. It is evidence, which is by law inadmissible.[5] In *Onochie* v. *Odogwu*[6] on inadmissible evidence, Ogbuegu JSC said:

> It is settled that where inadmissible evidence has been admitted, it is the duty of the court, not to act upon it. It is immaterial that its admission was as a result of consent of the opposite party or that party's default in failing to make objection at the proper time. The...court has the power to reject such evidence and decide the case on legal evidence.

ii) Evidence which is admissible in law but upon fulfilling some conditions parties may by consent admit it notwithstanding the conditions not being fulfilled, example the admission of unstamped instrument that required to be stamped.[7]

Note that a wrongful rejection of admissible evidence if it may affect the just decision of a case the appeal court may reverse such decision.

---

[5] Section 1(a) Evidence Act 2011

[6] *Onochie* v. *Odogwu* (2006) 25 NSCQR 387 at 402

[7] *Etim* v. *Ekpe* (1983) NSCQR 86

Bibliography

Adrian Keane, *The Modern Law of Evidence* (3rd edition, Butterworth's London, 1994)

Alan Taylor, *Principle of Evidence,* (2nd edition, Cavendish Publishing London, 2000)

Chaundhry; *An Outline of the Nigerian Law of Evidence.*

Constitution of Federal Republic of Nigeria 1999

Cross & Tapper (1994) on *Evidence* 8th edition,; Butterworth London

Curson, Lesile Basil, *Law of Evidence.* (2nd ed. Pitman London, 1986)

Dennis I. H., *The Law of Evidence,* (Sweet and Maxwell London, 2002)

Evidence Act Cap E14 Laws of Federal Republic of Nigeria 2004

Evidence Act Cap E14 Laws of Federal Republic of Nigeria, (as amended) 2011

Fidelis Nwadialor; *Modern Nigerian Law of Evidence,* (Ethiopia Publishing Co. Benin City, 1981)

Heydon J.D., *Evidence cases & Materials* (Butterworth's London, 1991)

Okes; (4th ed): *An Introduction to Evidence.*

Okay Achike, (1971) *"The Doctrine of Res Gestae: The Nigerian Situation",* (1971), iv, Nigerian Bar Journal

Osinbajo Yemi, *Cases & Materials on Nigeria Law of Evidence* (Nigeria Macmillan Ibadan, 1992)

Phipson, *Law of Evidence.* (11th Edition Sweet & Maxwell London, 2000)

Petter Murphy, *A Practical Approach to Evidence,* (2nd Edition Blackstone Press Ltd, London, 1985)

Steve Uglow, *Evidence Text and Materials,* (Sweet & Maxwell London, 1997)

Aguda T. A., *The Nigerian Law of Evidence in Nigeria,* (Sweet & Maxwell London, 1974)

Index

Malthouse Law Books

Abdulrazaq, M T, *Revenue Law and Practice in Nigeria*
Asuzu, C., *Fair Hearing in Nigeria*
Bambale, Y Y, *Crimes and Punishments under Islamic Law*
Bambale, Y. Y., *An Outline of Islamic Jurisprudence*
Bambale, Y. Y., *Islamic Law Relating to Property and Commercial Transactions*
Beredugo, A.J., *Nigerian legal system: an introductory text*
Emiri, F, & Deinduomo, G., *Law, Oil and Development Challenges in Nigeria*
Emiri, F. & Deinduomo, G., *Law and Petroleum Industry in Nigeria*
Emiri, F., *The Law of Restitution in Nigeria*
Emiri, F., *Law and Medical Ethics in Nigeria*
Fogam, P, *Law of Contract*
Emiri, F., *Equity and Trusts Law in Nigeria*
Goldface-Irokalibe, I.J., *The Law of Banking in Nigeria*
Igweike, K, *Nigerian Commercial Law: Agency*
Igweike, K, *Nigerian Commercial Law: Contract*
Igweike, K, *Nigerian Commercial Law: Hire Purchase*
Ikoni, U.D., *An Introduction to Nigerian Environmental Law*
Ladan, M.T., *Introduction to Jurisprudence: classical and Islamic*
Maidoh, D.C., Oho, F. *et al., Judicial Administration and Other Legal Issues in Nigeria*
Okoh, Sheriff E. E. *Succession under Islamic Law*
Olong, Adefi *M., Administrative Law in Nigeria: an introduction*
Olong, Adefi M., *The Nigerian Legal System: an introduction*
Omorogbe, Yinka, *Oil and Gas Law in Nigeria*
Omotesho, Aboaba, *The Law of Tort in Nigeria: Selected Themes*
Sagay, I, *Law of Succession and Inheritance*
Sagay, I, *Nigerian Family Law: Principles, Cases, Statutes and Commentaries*
Usman, Adamu Kyuka, *Environmental Protection Law and Practice*
Utuama, A A, *Nigerian Law of Real Property*
Utuama, A A, *The Law of Trusts and their Uses in Nigeria*
Utuama, A. A., *Planning Law in Nigeria*
Uvieghara E E, *Labour Law in Nigeria*
Uvieghara E E, *Sale of Goods (& Hire Purchase) Law in Nigeria*
Yalaju, J.G., *Media law in Nigeria*

Printed in February 2023
by Rotomail Italia S.p.A., Vignate (MI) - Italy